Matisse and Picasso

BY FRANÇOISE GILOT

Life with Picasso (with Carlton Lake)
Paloma Sphynx (poems)
The Fugitive Eye (poems)
Interface: The Painter and the Mask
An Artist's Journey
Matisse and Picasso: A Friendship in Art

Françoise Gilot

matisse

and

Picasso

A Friendship in Art

NAN A. TALESE

DOUBLEDAY

NEW YORK   LONDON   TORONTO   SYDNEY   AUCKLAND

PUBLISHED BY DOUBLEDAY

a division of Bantam Doubleday Dell Publishing Group, Inc.
666 Fifth Avenue, New York, New York 10103

DOUBLEDAY and the portrayal of an anchor with a dolphin are
trademarks of Doubleday, a division of Bantam Doubleday Dell
Publishing Group, Inc.

Book Design by Marysarah Quinn

Library of Congress Cataloging-in-Publication Data
Gilot, Françoise, 1921–
Matisse and Picasso : a friendship in art / Françoise Gilot.—
1st ed.
p.   cm.
1. Matisse, Henri, 1869–1954—Friends and associates.   2. Picasso,
Pablo, 1881–1973—Friends and associates.   I. Title.
N6853.M33G45   1990
709′.2′244—dc20
[B]   90-34869
CIP

ISBN 0-385-26044-X

Printed in the United States of America

October 1990

FIRST EDITION

Acknowledgments

Special thanks to Gloria Loomis for encouraging me to write this book, to Nan A. Talese for her consistently constructive suggestions, to Sergei Boissier for his careful attention to the text and to Gail Buchicchio for her assistance, to Marysarah Quinn for her handsome design and to Sabra Moore for her picture research; also to Lydia Delectorskaya for helping to select photographic documents by Madame Adan, to Claude Duthuit for allowing the reproduction of Matisse's works, to Ami Koide and Barbara Robinson for typing the manuscript, and to my friends Lisa Alther and Priya Mookerjee for taking the trouble to read and comment on the early versions of the manuscript.

Contents

CONTENTS

The only kind of art worth talking about is the art one happens to like.

—T. S. ELIOT
letter to Ezra Pound, February 2, 1915

Introduction

Who can utter the name Matisse without visualizing a flamboyant array of colors? Who can think about Picasso without evoking a revolution in form? The artist from French Picardy and the Andalusian painter stand like the North and South poles of a surge toward modernity in the plastic arts, at the onset of the twentieth century. Their discoveries and achievements will leave an indelible mark on this period and beyond. Not only did they know each other, but they struck and maintained a friendship full of light and shadows that I was privileged to witness between 1946 and 1954.

This book relates the meanders of a relationship whose foundation and *"raison d'être,"* sprang on both sides from a relentless passion for art, and endured because of Matisse's and Picasso's mutual curiosity about the unique way each managed to transcend aesthetic taboos, and to bypass the boundaries of accepted good taste.

I don't remember which author wrote that friendship is an honorable form of love. Someone else said that friendship is the reward of unselfish love, and when Montaigne was asked to explain his enduring affinity for La Boétie he simply answered, "Because it was him and because it was myself."

It is my wish to make portraits with words as well as with paint, and also to describe here the philosophy of art and the revolutionary qualities developed by both painters and their friends in the areas of composition, movement, rhythm, heightened contrast, and negation of perspective.

When they have not met their subject in person, biographers usually rely on already written material or on other people's memory; therefore they may repeat the errors made by others. Even in science, there is no such thing as objectivity. I want to evoke rather than describe, to draw arabesques rather than straight lines, to daydream rather than give cold hard facts alone. I will rely on my own memory, which is subject to my thoughts and feelings. In this I comply with Cézanne's admonition: "Painting is nature as seen through a temperament." By concentrating on the whole, I hope to come closer to the truth, including unknown or less divulged observations based on my own experience.

I even focus on seemingly unimportant events, which, because I have remembered them, have the significance of unconscious notation, and thus may lead to the revelation of the less obvious.

In this double portrait, as in a Byzantine icon, I see Matisse and Picasso surrounded by other figures; in action, at work, at rest, or involved with friends and foes. The dialogues are not verbatim; the visits to Matisse are not quite in chronological order, and at times several meetings are contracted in one. Painters have recurring preoccupations, their thoughts are cyclical rather than linear, and they are likely to come back again and again to certain topics, to problems they must solve in their own works. I narrate the visits as if one main theme was explored in each conversation, when in fact there was more randomness and repetition.

As regards Matisse, I try to be both detached and involved so as to depict the human being both within and outside his *oeuvre* since, in the twentieth century, an artist is a demiurge, present in his own creations. I shall say less about Picasso because I already wrote about him.

I dedicate this effort to the memory of Marguerite Duthuit who always encouraged me and to the memory of Pierre Matisse who played such an important role in furthering modern and contemporary art in the United States.

Matisse and Picasso

Henri Matisse. *The Young Sailor I*
(Jeune Marin à la Casquette), 1906.

Looking Back

Of course I came across the work of Henri Matisse long before I ever met him.

Adolescence always has been a season of ardent enthusiasm. In my generation, my schoolmates and I used to battle for certain thoughts, being for or against this writer and that artist. As far as writing was concerned, my closest models were Colette, Rimbaud, D. H. Lawrence, Virginia Woolf. In painting I loved Degas's boldness of themes, the exacerbation of color and rhythmical qualities in van Gogh's work, and the symbolism and flat decorative aestheticism of the Nabis.*

In reaction to my father's intellectualism, I wanted to get rid of past traditions; I was determined to celebrate the moment. Dedicated to sensualism, I believed in expressing the thrust of immediate experience as directly as possible. There was, of course, a huge gap between my

---

*The word *nabi* means prophet in Hebrew. The group included Aristide Maillol, Pierre Bonnard, Édouard Vuillard, Maurice Denis, Paul Ranson, Paul Sérusier, Félix Vallotton, Ker-Xavier Roussel, and Jan Verkade. Their common denominator was their admiration for Gauguin, Japanese prints, and popular images.

conviction and my ability to give it form, but I was already quite determined as to the direction I would follow.

I must have been fifteen when I first set eyes on some of Matisse's paintings, shown in Paris at the International Fair of 1937 in a pavilion dedicated to French art. Then I came upon a book about his work at a friend's home. As I eagerly leafed through it, I was immediately struck by some color reproductions. Two paintings of a young sailor, made in 1906 at Collioure, especially captivated me. The first one was a spontaneous study, but the second one, which was more decisive, revealed the concentrated, crouched pose of the sitter, his toughness and his bold looks, the ambiguous intensity of his gaze, the sensuous appeal of his mouth. Above all, the extreme simplicity of the pictorial vocabulary created a beguiling image, with a power as hypnotic as that of a panther at rest. (I did not know that the model was not an actual fisherman but Matisse's son, Pierre, made to look older than he was. His sideways glance and his pout probably reflected utter boredom rather than an eagerness for mischief.)

These two images brought back the memory of a playmate I had met earlier in the south of France, while vacationing. We had climbed rock cliffs and tall trees until one afternoon after racing each other we fell to the ground, out of breath and laughing, in a field of narcissis. The sandy soil was loose, and as we became entangled in a mock fight, the peppery odor of the boy's red hair and the nauseatingly sweet smell of crushed narcissis flowers made me want to faint from an as yet unknown delight. We remained motionless, probing deep into each other's eyes and with the fathomless, all-knowing smile that comes to adolescents when they tread inadvertently on the unmapped territory of adult emotions. In *The Young Sailor* Matisse expresses well this *fureur de vivre*, this primal drive that pushes adolescents toward the land of desire.

While reading the preface of the book, I realized how much this wild Fauvist work must have scared the collectors of well-rounded niceties at the beginning of the twentieth century. Weary of the ruling classes' self-indulgent conformity, the Fauves had wanted to consider the world anew, regardless of academic convention. To the naughty eroticism of Adolphe Bouguereau, these artists had opposed the freshness and simplicity of pagan desire.* According to Vincent van Gogh, color was to be incandescent, more vivid than nature's own harmony.

A year later I began to paint with oils. While exploring this new medium, I was bent on discovering how to relate such heightened tones to each other. I would start the same still life over and over again, choosing a dominant color and tuning in the other colors accordingly. The next day I would decide that a red tomato could become bright blue, but everything else had to change accordingly to achieve a valid interplay. Matisse, I soon realized, gave a sense of third dimension on a flat surface by the simultaneous tension of different sets of complementary colors and created animation with the arabesque. Free and arbitrary, the transposition of the dominant color would not be logically orchestrated or be followed through and through; there was always room for invention, spontaneity. Matisse broke his own rules any time it enhanced the marvelous sensuousness of the work, the feeling of wholeness, or even a certain quality of childlike innocence. Nature was not to be described; it was to be recreated over and over until the viewer could smell, feel, touch, be at one with the artist's vision and feelings.

This exaltation of the senses evoked the hedonism of Colette, his contemporary, whose writings I also greatly admired. I mused about the seeming lack of anxiety, the superb faculty of well-being, that distinguished so many people of that generation. My grandmother was the same; the strength of moral fiber in her fragile body always amazed me. I did not yet realize that it was a conquest as well as a natural gift, in the same way that happiness is a figment of the imagination more than an objective experience in reality. Still, I already knew that the Arabic poets had spoken their words of pomegranate and honey from the brazen mouth of the most torrid deserts.

I toiled and studied and tried to see Matisse's paintings whenever I could. His art spoke of joy and happiness almost beyond human reach; it carried the dream of an ever-present golden age and a promise of beauty for tomorrow.

---

*The Fauves, most active between 1905 and 1909, included Georges Braque, Charles Camoin, André Derain, Raoul Dufy, Othon Friesz, Henri Manguin, Albert Marquet, Henri Matisse, Jean Puy, Kees Van Dongen, and Maurice de Vlaminck.

Meanwhile, the march of history could not have been in greater contrast with my personal aspirations. Dark clouds gathered over Europe until in September 1939, after the invasion of Poland by Hitler's armed forces, it was no longer possible for Western democracies to adopt conciliatory measures; a tragic storm was unleashed, engulfing countries and their peoples in the suicidal tragedy of World War II. In 1940, the collapse of the French army led France to an armistice that looked especially shameful to young people of my generation. After the student demonstrations on November 11 of that year, I was included on a list of hostages, until my father somehow succeeded in having my name erased from the list. It was stated that I was no longer a law student but a designer for *haute couture*. My new profession enabled me to develop my interest in art more thoroughly and even allowed me to go officially to the free zone of France to purchase fabrics—a convenient escape if my life was again threatened.

During this time of gloom, I developed a friendship with Endre Rozsda, a young Hungarian painter, and I often went to draw at his studio. Among the models we used was a very beautiful Hungarian gypsy in her early thirties, who had often sat for Henri Matisse between 1935 and 1940 and of whom he had made a remarkable series of drawings in 1939. Her name was Vilma; full of vitality, lithe as a dancer, she moved with utmost grace and always found poses that revealed interesting combinations of forms. She had a sallow but luminous complexion, small breasts, round hips, dark hair and eyes, a very straight nose, and a sensuous red mouth, and she was very bright. She admired Matisse, both as an artist and as a person. She said he was always most attentive to her needs during the sittings, interested in her well-being, her moods, her thoughts.

The picture she drew of him when she chatted with us after the sittings reflected her sincere enthusiasm. To make the discussion livelier, Rozsda contradicted her by saying that in 1938 and 1939 he had many times observed Matisse at the Dôme, a coffeehouse at the corner of boulevard Montparnasse and the rue Delambre. To Rozsda, the master had looked more like a *grand bourgeois* or a famous surgeon than an artist. He had found him most forbidding.

At that time, when Matisse was not in Nice, he stayed and worked at his studio-apartment on the boulevard Montparnasse. He had formed the habit of coming regularly to the Dôme between 5:00 and 6:00 P.M. for exactly an hour. He was always dapper, well groomed, and composed, wearing gloves and carrying a cane with a gold pommel. When he arrived, he would make his way to his usual small round table and sit alone with a cup of tea or a glass of mineral water. No members of his family, no friends or models, ever accompanied him or joined him there. His back was very straight, he would look blankly in front of him, apparently lost in thought—stern, aloof, a perfect sphinx. So formidable was his mien, so evident his desire for isolation, that no one dared disturb him or say hello. Other artists, such as Picasso, Braque, and Giacometti, also went to the Dôme to meet one another and have informal discussions, but no one ever intruded or even signaled from a distance, so obvious was Matisse's wish to be left alone.

Rozsda's description of the Fauvist master contradicted the Hungarian model's. Was Matisse the affable, sensitive artist Vilma described or the stern loner and egotist Rozsda believed him to be? Perhaps he went to the Dôme to get away from his canvas for a while, to avoid compulsive overwork, so that he could start anew upon his return. Far from being haughty, he probably did not engage in conversation simply because he did not want to lose concentration, or because he was concerned about the anxieties of the time.

Throughout 1941 and 1942, as oppression increased and everyday life became more difficult, many of my friends joined an underground network. Some even succeeded in reaching England and joining General de Gaulle. More than ever I put my hope in upholding cultural freedom, and my art started to express the spiritual values I believed in, through simple symbols. In addition to Matisse, I greatly admired the recent works of Georges Braque, including his large meditative still lifes with skulls that I wanted to emulate in my own compositions. Geneviève, a friend of mine from our school years, had also decided to become a painter. Living in the Languedoc, she had taken some lessons from Aristide Maillol. I visited her twice and in 1943 succeeded in bringing her back to Paris, with enough work for us to have a joint exhibition in May.

Our show was well received, and we made new friends among the painters. We even encountered Alain Cuny, an actor who was then quite famous. He invited us to meet at the Café de Flore, the usual haunt of the anti-Nazi intelligentsia. Later we went to dinner at a restaurant called the Catalonian on the rue des Grands Augustins. By chance, Pablo Picasso, Dora Maar (the well-known photographer and painter who was Picasso's companion at the time), and some of their friends were sitting at a nearby table. For dessert, they got a bowl of cherries at their table, and Picasso could not resist getting up to offer us some and to ask Cuny, whom he knew, not to be selfish in keeping his beautiful friends to himself. So we were duly introduced.

Picasso was sturdy and much shorter than I had imagined. The gaze of his basilic eyes was hard to meet. His face radiated intelligence and mischief, while his blasé grin indicated a measure of boredom. Learning that we were young painters having a joint exhibition, he asked for the address of the gallery and said that he would come to our show and that we should visit his studio. We were not present when he came, but he was apparently satisfied with what he saw, since he left a message reiterating that we were welcome to visit his studio.

We decided to go there on the following Monday. Jaime Sabartés, Picasso's secretary, opened the door, looking at us suspiciously, but we affirmed that we had an appointment so he let us in.* After crossing a small foyer, we went through a long room full of knickknacks and waiting people, then entered a huge studio space replete with sculptures, large and small, mostly bronzes except for *L'Homme au Mouton*, which was still in plaster. Black blinders were drawn over most of the windows, and it was relatively dark, rather like the den of a wizard, but I was dazzled by the *Still Life with Oranges* by Matisse which was prominently displayed. I was struck by the fact that the main part of the painting, the basket of fruit itself, with strong colors and dark outline, seemed still to belong to nature. What set it in the realm of intangible poetry was the boldness of the pink, magenta, and ultramarine tablecloth. The competition between the

---

*Jaime Sabartés, a Catalonian from Barcelona, had started as a sculptor and later became a writer. Since his youth he had revered Picasso, and after an unhappy sojourn in Guatemala, he returned to Paris in 1936 and became Picasso's secretary, a position he held for the rest of his life.

green, the cadmiums, the diverse fuchsias, the strong darker red and intense blue created on ascending scale, an exultation.

Sabartés was not pleased that I dared to express my admiration for Matisse within Picasso's studio, but dutifully he escorted us upstairs, where Picasso stood surrounded by a few friends. Mindless of the cultist attitude prevalent around the Spanish master, I reiterated words of admiration for the *Still Life with Oranges* that I had just seen. Picasso was very amused, I think, by this outburst, which for once was not intended for himself, but he was gratified when I added that only an artist of his caliber could afford to place such a masterpiece among his own works, in the center of his atelier.

This visit was to be the first of a series of similar visits during which Picasso showed himself to be very flirtatious, extremely witty, at times profound—all in all, quite a charmer.

My friend Geneviève went back to the Languedoc, and I soon followed her. We spent the summer working on drawings and then traveled capriciously on our bicycles all the way to Arles and Les Baux, some two hundred miles away. Upon my return to Paris, after bitter arguments with my father, who did not want me to abandon my studies at law school completely, I went to live at my grandmother's, to devote myself exclusively to painting. After a while I resumed my visits to Picasso's studio, and after a few months of misgivings and tentative advances and fast retreats on both sides, we embarked on a romance, supposedly with great lucidity but most certainly with the same desire for secrecy.

These shared moments were precious in themselves but also because they affirmed life in the face of sorrow. The man who had painted *Guernica* was a hero for me because he had said no to oppression. On my side, I brought him the image of youth and hope. War raged everywhere; it was vital to steal some joy to better overcome the hardships of the time. Since no one knew how long the war would last and who would be alive to see its end, it seemed almost natural to resort to extremes and to challenge fate. Probably in peacetime Picasso and I would have passed each other in equanimity, but in the presence of doom, passions usually repressed became inflamed. One had to leave a mark, to achieve the impossible before the end.

Just after the liberation of Paris in August 1944, and during the final victory of the Allied forces, a progressive return to normalcy took place. There was now some happiness to look forward to, and the intensity of feeling that had been a powerful magnet for Picasso and myself during the time of tragedy had to be transformed. He seemed to want less secrecy and was bent on finding a way to make room for me in his life. I, however, began to have some misgivings, and tended not to visit him as often. He started to come to see me at my grandmother's house or to look for me in the Bois de Boulogne, where I used to ride in the morning, and to follow my movements from his car, since he supposedly intended to make an equestrian portrait of me in sculpture.

But nothing was rigid, I had not made up my mind one way or the other about the continuation of my relationship with Pablo Picasso, so early in 1945 I went one morning to the rue des Grands Augustins to join the usual throng of visitors and was rewarded for my positive attitude, because Dina Vierny, Aristide Maillol's model, came in soon thereafter. I will always vividly remember the impact of her presence. Her head was small and compact, as precisely delineated and well chiseled as a bronze, and her dark hair was drawn severely back and tied in a bun at the nape of her neck. As she emerged from a thick fur coat, her torso thrust forward like the prow of a ship, needing no adornments. She was wearing a simple black jersey dress with a tight-fitting bodice, a leather belt, and a short flared skirt that followed the motions of her shapely hips and danced around her knees, revealing fine legs in silk stockings and tiny impatient feet in high-heeled sandals.

She was the very image of victory, the perfect Nike of the ancient Greeks. Perfectly poised and intelligent, she was in the full bloom of youth, perhaps just twenty-six at the time. Her bearing was regal; she was more than a muse, she was a priestess of art. She was the exact symbol of life, a rock of affirmation and certainty. Picasso already knew her, and far from being ironic or sarcastic, as he often was with other guests, he was quite pleasant and even subdued, perhaps because it was her first visit to his studio since Maillol's death in 1944. I did not share much in the conversation, I was too amused observing him. Because of his tribulations with his ex-wife, Olga, Pablo was always in awe but also wary of Russian women. Nevertheless, he fussed around Dina. He was deferential and attentive—a most unusual attitude indeed—as if beguiled by her charm and mastery. If he had not been afraid of being pursued by Maillol's ghost, he might have expressed his admiration more openly. As it was, instead of being flirtatious, he treated Dina like a queen, perhaps thinking that not only Maillol but Ambroise Vollard, Maillol's great friend and dealer, or even Phidias himself, would rise from the grave to protect their goddess from his sacrilegious thoughts.

I would have loved to befriend Dina, but her triumphant femininity made me shy. I felt that with my intellectual and spiritual preoccupations, my androgynous persona was much less accomplished than her womanly one, so I did not try.

I deeply admired her mentor, the Catalonian Maillol, for his Mediterranean spirit, his spontaneous classicism, which did not hinder the modernity of his creation, and his sense of symbol. He had been a part of the Nabi movement in the 1890s. In 1900 he met Henri Matisse and began a lifelong friendship with him. Together with their families they spent many summers at Collioure, in the company of André Derain and other artists.

Since Picasso knew that for my friend Geneviève, Aristide Maillol was the master above all others, and since I had already openly declared my allegiance to Matisse, I thought that he might misinterpret too much eagerness toward Dina Vierny, so I chose to keep a low profile that morning.

Later in the spring of that year, in a part of the Museum of Modern Art on the quai de Tokyo, a very important exhibition was held. I don't remember if it was in the Salon des Tuileries or the Salon des Indépendants, but it was a regal display of all the major trends in modern art. I went to the opening on my own, but later accompanied Picasso to the exhibit. We looked at some of his works, in particular a stunning still life with a coffeepot in a very thick white impasto, and at a group of Georges Braque's meditative still lifes, then we wandered around. Occupying the central panel of another large hall were several recent works by Matisse. In one of them, *Girl Reading*, painted in March 1944, it seemed that the model could have been myself. Picasso was startled. Jokingly, he said, "Can my old friend have such a far-reaching vision that it enables him to paint a face that only exists in my dreams as yet? He already has an answer, while I am simply brooding about what should be done with your features."

To humor him, I answered that in the famous limited edition, the SUITE of 103 etchings that Ambroise Vollard had published in the thirties, many of the girls he had sketched from imagination were true premonitions of me, created at a time when not only had Picasso not met me but when I was only a child. We also know that nature follows art and not the opposite. He smiled.

"What a good diplomat you would make."

Then we began to discuss Matisse's *Red Still Life with Magnolia* of 1941. Picasso found it too decorative. Furthermore, the open composition, with the copper caldron partly out of the picture and the objects barely touching each other, not isolated or intersecting frankly, was anathema to the master of Cubism. It set his teeth on edge. Not so

Henri Matisse. *Annélies, Tulips and Anemones*
(*Annélies, Tulipes et Anémones*), 1944.

Henri Matisse. *Red Still Life with Magnolia*
(*Nature Morte Rouge au Magnolia*), 1941.

with me. I found the unexpected juxtaposition of elements rather intriguing, inasmuch as it did not deter the whole from achieving unity. It was true that there was a total disregard for classical composition, at least as far as the rules of Western art were concerned. There was a complete lack of rhetoric in the exposition of the theme. The relationship of one object to another was neither logical nor contrived—it just happened. It was mysterious, irrational; I could see why the Surrealist poet Louis Aragon had always revered Matisse. I wondered how such balance was achieved. It obviously had nothing to do with a conceptual geometry of space. I guessed that the bold interplay of colors, the exquisite balance of qualities and quantities, and the linear design had enough architectonic strength to make any rational connection appear unnecessary and obsolete.

I glanced back at the red still life; it was radiant, full of bliss and yet elusive. It was impossible to analyze why it worked. It continued outside the boundaries of the canvas; it completed itself in the mind of the beholder like an intuition of joy. It had some of the aspects of a mandala, the mystic diagram of the East, a map for the journey of the soul. The positive shapes and the negative space coexisted. Nothing came forward or receded, nothing was given precedence. The seashell alone stood on its own, separated from the other objects by a narrow channel of pure vermilion while all the others were linked. They related in the same way as the figures forming a garland in *The Dance* of 1910, which create a powerful concatenation of joyous capers but for two hands that do not quite reach one another. Like the index fingers of God and Adam in Michelangelo's *Creation* in the Sistine Chapel, they almost meet but do not touch, thus creating tension and suspense.

I must have looked absorbed and thoughtful, because as we came out of the museum, Pablo concluded the visit by saying, "So you think it works, this juxtaposition of objects without cause-effect relationship? Matisse is a magician, his use of color is uncanny. This makes me hungry all of a sudden. Let's go and have some tea and toast at Martin's, place de l'Alma."

Joyfully, I agreed. After all the ersatz during the war, it seemed that there existed no problem, however complex, that could not be solved with a cup of real tea or coffee, and we began to chat about Picasso's retrospective. I especially loved his ferociously humorous painting *Woman in a Rocking Chair* and the ominous *Cat with a Bird*. I gossiped.

"Do you know that people call you Ivan le Terrible? [*Il vend le terrible;* 'he sells the terrible.'] They enjoy being *scared* by what you do."

"That's good. Since they can't love me, I am glad to know that they are afraid of me."

"But you can be mild, lyrical, and poetic when you want, as in many of your paintings between 1927 and 1935."

"Someone loved me then!"

After that little bit of *pro bono* propaganda, we parted in good cheer.

In 1945 my work had become mostly nonmimetic, not based on the limitation or interpretation of natural forms, yet I went on being intrigued by Matisse's work; I thought that such greatness deserved attention and careful study. Most of the young painters who were then my friends disagreed with me, not because they were not appreciative of his work but because they believed that all links to past generations had to be severed in order for us to create a movement of our own. Their attitude toward figurative art was puritanical, and what's more, they made a point of never going to a museum for fear of being contaminated by the masters of the past, any reference to art history being considered obscene.

In Paris at that time, following a tradition inherited from the nineteenth century, when the artists and the members of the intelligentsia had flocked together to strengthen themselves against the oppressive hostility of the philistines, writers, painters, critics, enlightened art dealers, and patrons formed groups and belonged to coteries, relating to one another on very egalitarian terms. Age and success were not relevant. Once accepted by one of the ''in'' groups, you were a full-fledged member of the creative community, free to uphold your opinion against anyone else, free to associate with whomever you pleased, and welcome in all the coffeehouses, restaurants, and homes where other intellectuals and artists of the same persuasion met.

As I said, a negative attitude about figurative art prevailed in the group I frequented. I thought that such a position was untenable and that if implemented, it would boomerang later. Nevertheless, I agreed to exhibit with this group at the Salon des Surindépendants in 1945, after which I received good reviews and was asked to participate in the formation of a larger group. This included very well-known European artists of different generations, such as Alberto Magnelli, Jean Deyrolle, Jean Atlan, Sonia Delaunay, Gérard Schneider, Jean Dewasne, and especially Nicolas de Staël, who acted as one of the leaders. Together they initiated a movement called ''the New Realities.'' Soon thereafter I had a confrontation with de Staël apropos the purity of what he called my ''artistic platform'' in regard to figurative art. He also wanted to convince me not to go on visiting Picasso at his studio.

I flared! Altogether renouncing figurative art was for me as pointless as renouncing Satan the trickster. Purity cannot be achieved by surgery; I believed in developing naturally, without constraint. As to the visits to Picasso's studio, I could not promise anything. I mentioned the fact that in the art world de Staël himself was considered to be

Braque's spiritual heir, since they entertained an ongoing aesthetic dialogue, and de Staël was known to visit his elder almost each morning. I was as stubborn as de Staël was opinionated, and since he was very short-tempered, he got extremely angry and even shouted at me. The meeting ended by my being excommunicated from the group and his breaking a chair at Deyrolle's studio, where we had all met to discuss theoretical points and conflicting concepts.

I felt sad, of course, because I had enjoyed being an integral member of a group that was considered the most radical, the most avant-garde at the time. But if I had to be a loner, so be it. I was not about to be subjugated by anyone, even if, as in the case of Nicolas de Staël, I liked his work and his passionate dedication to art. At that time de Staël worked mostly in sedate camayeus and earthy tones, building up impasto and pouring lyrical and powerful nonfigurative rhythms onto the canvas until some lines contradicted others and entered a fierce battle, reflecting his own inner conflicts. He strove for excellence and he excelled; he had that touch of madness that makes for greatness in an artist.

The public does not always realize that most painters entertain love-hate relationships with their elders, or that they spend time comparing themselves to the famous artists of the past. Even if they seldom admit it, they are more interested in what Raphael, Rembrandt, or van Gogh would have to say than in the appreciation of their contemporaries. The desire to emulate and surpass the old masters is a strong motivation. Art arises from art as much as from nature, and it is often very revealing to trace an artist's chosen ancestry.

At that time it was important for me to entertain imaginary dialogues with Uccello, Piero della Francesca, Jean Fouquet, Georges de la Tour, Paul Gauguin, and Vincent van Gogh, even though my work was not visibly altered by these conversations with the dead. I spent most of 1945 interested in texture, using only black, white, gray, and a strong yellow to establish and achieve simple compositions.

After so much concern for balance, in late November I fell down a marble staircase while holding a puppy in my arms. I broke my left elbow in an effort to protect the little dog. I had to have surgery, and after the operation my arm remained in a cast. I felt idle and despondent, in fact very depressed. Trying to lift my spirits, Picasso came to see me quite a few times at my grandmother's house, where I had my studio. He even sent or brought flowers, which was very uncharacteristic of him. His most memorable present was a huge pot of azaleas adorned with shocking pink and angry blue ribbons, a monumental oddity that he thought would make me smile. And I did smile, because this kitsch offering was intended to placate the jealous gods that had allowed my accident. This tribute to bad taste coming from him was meant to screen our happiness and to protect me from further mishaps.

In January 1946 Picasso was at his sweetest, most thoughtful, even most tender. He was so convincing that I no longer doubted his feelings. I was too young to see that his need for me was in direct proportion to my independence. He was afraid that I would escape from him.

The previous summer he had rented a small apartment overlooking the harbor of Golfe-Juan near Cannes, hoping that I might want to use it, but I had gone to Douarnenez in Brittany instead. Now he reiterated the offer. Ambitiously called Villa Pour Toi (Villa For You), the house belonged to old Monsieur Louis Fort, a retired master-printer who had worked for Ambroise Vollard. Picasso insisted that I could go there, no strings attached, and make some etchings. It would be a welcome change of scene from the mushy and drab winter in Paris. He also described the decoration of the small apartment as crazy and comical. Finally I made up my mind, took the night train, and arrived in Golfe-Juan on my own in early February 1946, with enough drawing paper in a portfolio to last me a month.

Villa Le Rêve, Vence.

The Door Opened

AFTER LEAVING the station I had an easy time finding the Villa Pour Toi, which faced the fishermen's harbor. I rang the bell, holding my letter of introduction from Picasso. A little old man with a beret came to open the door. To the right of the landing was a room filled with huge etching presses. I wanted to have a peek but had to follow my guide to the third floor, since Monsieur Fort was eager to show me my lodgings, which he had hand-painted himself. The walls were navy blue spangled with stars; the plinths, tables, chairs, and closets were red strewn with more white stars; and a huge bay window opened on the ultramarine expanse of the Mediterranean Sea and the glare of a cloudless sky. On the fourth floor, also a part of my allotted dwelling, the walls were devoted to horse chestnut foliage in relief. The taste was abominable but the effect hilarious.

In my mind it was quite improbable that Picasso might think of joining me there, so I wrote asking my friend Geneviève to come from the Languedoc and spend some time with me. I also knew that Pauline Denis, a friend who attended the School of Fine Arts with me and was Maurice Denis's younger daughter, meant to come from Paris to visit

Pierre Bonnard in Le Cannet and would stay a while in the vicinity.*
With all this to look forward to, I was elated and straightaway started
to draw in the hills nearby; I even walked to Vallauris and to Antibes
to sketch. Eagerly Monsieur Fort handed me some zinc plates, and I
began to work in drypoint, just with lines. After a week he was already
pulling a few trial proofs in his workshop.

Feeling happy and relaxed, I wrote Picasso a letter to thank him
for giving me the opportunity to make some etchings and to ask him
not to take the trouble to visit me, since I was doing fine. That was
certainly a psychological faux pas. How dared I be happy so far away
from him? To top it all, Geneviève arrived just then, much later than
she had promised. We were enchanted to see each other; we had not
met since the end of 1944. That evening we went to an excellent fish
restaurant, and the next day we started to draw the harbor from the
window, entirely oblivious of the world at large, aware only of the joy
of working together. The day went by peacefully until 6:00 P.M., when,
unexpectedly, Picasso arrived by car with his chauffeur, Marcel. That
provoked quite a lot of commotion in the house, as well as some
unwelcome scenes, and changed the game altogether. All hell broke
loose. Pablo burned my right cheek with a cigarette to "brand" me and
then behaved outrageously to Geneviève, thus provoking her departure.
If not for his entreaties, I would have left with her, but he appeared so
repentant that I agreed to stay.

When the uproar and the fury abated, we began to work a little,
went sightseeing, and started to discuss the relative merits of such and
such a painter. A week later Pauline Denis came from Paris. From
Cannes she telephoned me to come along and visit Bonnard with her,
but this was not to Picasso's taste, so after a heated argument I had to
decline the invitation. When he prevented me from doing what I wanted,

---

*Maurice Denis (1870–1943), a disciple of Cézanne and Gauguin, was the theoretician of
the Nabi group. He believed in the necessity of symbolism. Later he oriented himself more
toward classicism and a revival of sacred art. He was a close friend of Pierre Bonnard's and
owned many of his works. In October 1943 he was accidentally killed by a German truck. I
met Pauline a month later at the Julian Art Academy.

he often tried to make up for it in other ways, which he called "trading." He knew that I was likely to get into a very sour mood if he frustrated me one more time and that I might very well opt for open revolt. Mostly he resented my ability to do interesting things on my own or with my friends, without being indebted to him in any way.

So the next morning, as we were watching the sailboats from the windows of Monsieur Fort's quaint dwelling, he said; "Let's go and visit Matisse in Vence. You ought to wear your blouse of mauve silk and your almond-green slacks. He will like such colors together."

Henri Matisse! The name rang in my ears like the tinkling of joyous bells; Matisse was indeed my favorite among the moderns. For fear that Picasso might change his mind, I did not show any special eagerness and merely asked where Matisse lived.

Picasso answered, "In a house called Le Rêve ["The Dream"], route de St. Jeannet in Vence. I'll telephone Lydia Delectorskaya,* his secretary, and tell her that I want to bring along a young painter who admires him a lot. If the answer is yes, we shall leave right away."

Being favorably inclined toward Picasso, Lydia agreed, and Marcel, the chauffeur, was summoned. Soon we got into the Peugeot and drove at full speed, following the coast to Antibes and afterward meandering into the hills. The view completely evoked a thirteenth-century Siennese painting, with its olive trees, its elongated cypresses silhouetted against the sky, the pink villages towering above the valleys.

Picasso was obviously in a good mood, anticipating a pleasurable reunion with his friend, whom he had not seen for quite some time. Matisse had been very ill in 1941. In Lyon he had undergone a drastic operation for cancer of the colon and another one for subsequent complications. Afterward he had convalesced and then remained in the South of France, where he was once more producing marvelous work.

Picasso remembered that when they had first met, Matisse, his senior by twelve years, had disapproved of his rebellious attire and extravagant behavior. Nevertheless, Pablo had soon been invited to spend

---

*Matisse's long-time companion and model.

21

a day at the older artist's suburban home in Clamart, and once there had been offered a horseback ride. Thoroughly terrified of horses, Picasso, who had previously thought that Matisse was a bit of a bourgeois, had had to cling to the saddle to keep from falling. This had had a very sobering effect, since he did not know that Matisse himself felt far from comfortable on horseback.

At the beginning of their relationship, Picasso and Matisse experienced more than a touch of rivalry over mutual friends such as Gertrude Stein, her brothers Leo and Michael Stein, Georges Braque, André Derain, and Juan Gris. To be sure, they felt a sense of competition as artists, and they often found ways to test each other. But as years went by a mutual respect developed, a deep understanding and a sincere appreciation of each other's greatness. Both having reached the status of demigods, they provided one another with a unique challenge. They had often exchanged paintings, including those I had seen prominently displayed in Picasso's studio in Paris.

Soon we crossed the little city of Vence and reached the route de St. Jeannet. Uphill to the left, a yellow-ocher villa with a red-tiled roof hid behind a screen of shrubbery and trees. Together we walked briskly across the garden on the narrow path leading to the villa.

The door opened to reveal a hollow hall gaping in utter darkness. It reminded me of a Matisse of 1914, *The Door;* it had the same starkness, but this time it was brightened by Lydia's wlecoming yet enigmatic smile. Her presence emanated peace and radiance. Her almond-shaped eyes were as blue as mountain lakes in the snowscape of her face—what contrast! We entered one room and then another silently. All shutters were closed; everything stood still in obscurity. As our eyes accommodated to the darkness, the objects gradually emerged from the shadows. A blue china pot with white polka dots looked almost alive on the table and even more so in some oil paintings hanging on the wall. A pineapple sat on a wrought iron garden seat, echoing other fruits in some recent Matisse canvases. In a spacious cage, exotic birds flew from one perch to another. Doves cooed and hopped at random about the room. A date tree swinging its palms in the garden outside was framed by the window's colorful Tahitian curtains and was repeated, larger than life, on the wall, as if the strength of the painting allowed reality to become a mere reflection, the mirror of the artist in a world where truth was a more elaborate form of fiction.

When the last door opened, there was no darkness. Matisse was sitting in bed in full daylight, very upright, playing gently with a cat. Despite the fullness of his features, he communicated energy. There was no heaviness, no cumbersome mass, just the opposite—an élan, a sense of weightlessness. We met the youth of his light blue gaze through his glasses.

His handknit sweater matched my almond-green slacks. Obviously pleased to have us visit, he had a most benign smile. His lucidity, and an acute sense of humor, added a touch of whimsy to his good-natured-ness. He at once stated that he might very well make a portrait of me, in which my hair would be olive green, my complexion light blue, and in which of course he would not forget the angle of my eyebrows in relation to my nose. He closed his eyes for an instant and went on. "The pose could stem from the rich design of a pale madder and alizarin Persian rug, while the upper part of the figure would match the intensity of the ambiant light." Then, addressing Pablo directly: "I see it very well, do you? You could bring her back for some sittings, couldn't you?"

Pablo wiggled in his chair, mumbling something unintelligible or cursing under his breath, but he finally managed a half-hearted assent, with no intention of complying.

I was astonished. I had not expected Matisse to be so direct and straightforward. Was he paying an indirect compliment to his friend for his good taste in women? More probably he was abandoning himself to the joy of an inspired moment, regardless of any possessiveness Pablo might feel. Our relationship still being secret, Pablo had just introduced me as a young painter eager to meet the French master for whom I had such admiration, and Matisse may well have believed that it would be a pleasurable opportunity for me. It is also possible that he was being mischievous and wanted to test his friend's reactions and degree of playfulness.

Matisse's voice also surprised me: well-timbered, urbane, mellow, and temperate; the clarity of his diction was such that one could hear each word even when he confided and came close to a whisper. As his face never lost composure, so his voice did not hasten or falter. He took his time to say what was on his mind, and as he went, he seemed to select what to omit, which made his speech rather elliptical. Often he stopped after a few sentences, as if engulfed in a daydream of his own, out of which a new proposition came forth, followed by a pause for reflection, after which he ventured a few more sentences. Superficially his voice had the calm of a lazy river; it rounded the obstacles rather than overcame them. Yet behind this nonchalance Matisse was willful and never lost his purpose. If something displeased him, a single incisive phrase uttered in a slightly sharper tone dealt adequately with the interference in the film of his inner vision.

Even at close range his voice seemed to come from afar; it was meant to bridge the distance from his own world to his listener's ears and to penetrate. It was deep without being low, polished without any hint of the northern, Picardy accent. Because of his stature and the sheer bulk of his sturdy frame, his voice was rich in echos and harmonies—like an opera singer's, it was melodious, well-toned, unpretentious, and yet more than attractive: seductive. Who could refuse Matisse anything, if he only cared to ask? Unaware of his natural magnetism, he remained entirely unaffected, making no manipulative use of the charm of his voice. Or did he, at least toward Picasso?

After each pause the conversation continued most amiably. Matisse was serene, full of self-confidence. He was even disarming, when he expressed the hope of some improvement in his recent work. Then there was a discussion about the extent to which shapes should depart from the naturalistic and become more arbitrary when colors were transposed. Picasso, who longed to get the upper hand, tried unsuccessfully to persuade his friend that a blue nude, where the sensuous curves of a female body were still quite recognizable, could not be pictorially acceptable as long as the shapes belonged to the descriptive rather than to the purely conceptual realm.

Matisse stood his ground. "Don't you see that it corresponds to my sensation? What I am looking for is an interplay of color that carries my emotion. I don't want to be theoretical, and in the end I just want the interaction to culminate in a unity that radiates light."

While this was going on, I managed to have a peek at the series of line drawings piled high in a corner. They displayed a unity of feeling despite the diversity of expression and the numerous variations. Matisse's lines were so spontaneous and so dynamic, their impetus had such vitality, that it always seemed as if they were about to collide with one another. Instead the masterful strokes stopped suddenly before any fatal encounters, allowing the passage of light, giving ample breathing space. His hand obviously knew exactly when to lift away from the paper; the lines were drawn going at full speed toward each other, so that they almost touched but did not meet.

Finally it was time for us to leave, and we promised to return whenever possible. On the way out I again noticed the majestic palm tree and several silver-leafed olive trees swaying in the wind. I was astonished to find the garden unkept; it was obvious that no one had tended it for quite some time. Though large, it had no design and was not at all my idea of the way a garden should look to delight an artist. There were no rare plants or interestingly varied flowers and no landscaping of any sort. As the daughter of an agronomist, I was used to more elaborate arrangements.

As Marcel drove us back to Golfe-Juan, Picasso, who as yet had not made any paintings of me except two small black, white, and gray studies, exclaimed, "Did you hear that! Matisse said that he might make a portrait of you. What would he say if I proposed to make a portrait of Lydia?"

Very matter-of-factly, I remarked that it was not at all the same, since Lydia had appeared in several of Matisse's important works for over a decade, that no one had any inkling about a privileged relationship between Pablo and me yet, and that neither my face nor my features had entered his inner world to become transformed into elements of his style, except in a series of original lithographs.

He brooded a bit, then laughed. "We shall see about that."

Matisse's appreciation of me acted like a visa on my passport to the realm of art. Pablo began clinging to me; he was now adamant that I should share his life. All the while I was very reticent, so he continued campaigning during the rest of the month in Golfe-Juan and during the trip back to Paris, but to no avail. I went back to my grandmother's home. By then Pablo was in dead earnest, and there was nothing he would not do to get his wish fulfilled. He stirred my love, my admiration, and even my pity for his unhappiness. He so persuaded himself that he also persuaded me of the necessity to come live with him at his studio at 7 rue des Grands Augustins.

Against my better judgment, I finally agreed in early May 1946. I was extremely shaken and sad about the pain I was inflicting on my grandmother, since I left without explanation and only sent a letter, not even telling her where I was. I knew she would not find my present situation acceptable. I begged her not to look for me, since further conflict would only make matters worse. While I was experiencing this almost unbearable anxiety, Pablo seemed enchanted, as if I had become for him the very symbol of the joy of life.

So the visit to Henri Matisse brought expected and unexpected results. A few days later, Picasso began *The Woman-Flower*. First a fairly realistic figure appeared on the canvas, sitting on a curvilinear African stool. The thinness of my waist and the fullness of my breasts were emphasized. My legs were schematic and already a light blue tone: "Because you are a bluestocking!"

He worked with alacrity while I read a book at the other end of the studio, keeping an eye on what was happening. The work went on for several days. The African stool was the first object to disappear. Soon thereafter the pink tile floor was reduced to a horizontal band at the base of the picture. By contrast the figure began to grow, to free itself from anatomical or naturalistic references. The two legs became one; they fused with the torso; they became stemlike. The figure stood upright, taking on volume and invading the upper portion of the canvas.

Until then the head and hair had been realistic; now they no longer matched the more inventive emerging forms. "Matisse isn't the only one who can paint you with green hair!" Pablo said, and he tentatively painted that area leaf-green, changing the balance of quantities several times and adding volume to the breasts as he did so. Still imitative, the face had now become alien to the whole. Pablo decided it should be more in keeping with the rest—ethereal and dreamlike, "a little blue moon." He proceeded to cut five forms out of paper he had painted sky blue, four round ones and an ellipse. Eyes, nose, and mouth were sketchily drawn on these in charcoal. He tried the first four one by one, pinning them onto the canvas so he could look at the effect from a distance and move each to the left or right, up or down; none suited him. Then he tried the last one, the horizontal ellipse, pinning it with determination in a specific spot. A miracle! It fit perfectly and was fully convincing. "Now it's your portrait," he said, taking off the paper and painting, slowly and carefully, exactly what was on it.

Then the uneven forms meant to be the arms no longer satisfied him. One appeared to be hanging from a green mass of hair and was no longer attached to anything else, since the delineation of the shoulders had disappeared. It was holding a globe—half earth, half water—and the form seemed to drag the rest of the composition down. By making the arm a horizontal triangle supporting one breast and projecting the globe laterally, Picasso restored balance. Then the shape of the other leaflike arm looked too broad, and he reduced it.

"You're like a growing plant," he said. "I'd been wondering how I could get across the idea that you belong to the vegetable kingdom rather than the animal. I've never felt impelled to portray anyone else this way. It's strange, isn't it? I think it's just right, though. It represents *you.*"

That was how I saw *La Femme-Fleur*, the woman-flower, develop. At the time I didn't wonder about the title, I just felt that it described the picture adequately. Later, while reading Celtic legends, I learned of Blodeuwedd, the girl-flower, a mythical being created out of flower pollen by a god to be given in marriage to a hero who had been cursed and could not marry a mortal woman. After the wedding, Blodeuwedd had dramatic adventures and misadventures; in the end, for all that she did or instigated, she was changed into an owl and flew away into the night.

Toward the end of May, Pablo started a series of attractive curvilinear pencil drawings, all of them my portrait. Such leaning toward the arabesque was unusual in his graphic work. It was fascinating to see that Matisse's flowing lines became somewhat less flowing but more incisive and sharper under Pablo's hand.

I felt stimulated to compete and contribute in relation or in contrast to what Matisse and Picasso had said and done. I produced a great many drawings, linear expressions of my own face, large and small, broad and narrow, guided mostly by the desire to depict mood. Through this difficult period of adaptation to a new life, I held on to drawing as to a lifebuoy. As a matter of survival I had to assert myself fearlessly; I had severed the last link to my family and could no longer retrace my steps. Whatever inner trepidation I felt, I had to appear secure and composed in my new life. Had I not reached an essential challenge, now that I was facing the Minotaur all alone?

But perhaps I was not entirely alone with Pablo at the studio, since several paintings by Matisse were displayed. Absent or present, he was a part of our everyday life. To please me, Pablo went to his large safe at the bank and brought back a 1906 Fauvist portrait of Marguerite Matisse as an adolescent, dressed in a green dress with a high black velvet ribbon around her neck; he placed it in the bedroom upstairs, where she followed us with her gaze like a guardian angel. Matisse had painted the name of his daughter in large letters on the picture and had given it to Pablo soon after its completion. In the adjacent room I was also comforted by an early still life, a gray pewter chocolate pot, in which the free interplay of colors in the background and an acute pink already announced some of Matisse's best-known harmonies.

Downstairs in the large sculpture studio the famous still life of 1912, the basket of oranges contrasting with the hot pink and ultramarine tablecloth, occupied a central position. It was the canvas I had so admired when I had entered Picasso's studio for the first time in 1943. During the first visit to Vence I had mustered the courage to inquire directly of the master how he had succeeded in expressing so much *joie de vivre* in a work of art. Matisse had answered that the explosion of joy in the painting sprang from his notion that a work of art should be an intensification of all the sensations able to enrich the inner life of the viewer. It had nothing to do with his personal feelings at the time; on the contrary, when he had created it he had been entirely penniless in Tangiers and had been seriously contemplating suicide. Transcending personal doom, his masterpiece might in fact have been his swan song.

I found this anecdote very telling, because art lovers have a definite tendency to equate the exaltation they receive from looking at a painting with the psychological state they imagine the painter to be in when he conveys such splendor in an especially appealing work of art. Stendhal was right when he stated that one must write when cool about the feelings experienced in the heat of passion.

It is this ice-in-fire or fire-in-ice act of supreme control that is a trademark of French art, though the ability to dissociate the moment at which an emotion is felt from the time when it is brought to the higher fire of artistic expression can also be found in ancient Chinese and Greek art. In this alchemical process the painter must be able to fuse his inner drive and his human experience, remaining open to the spark of creativity or the specific sensation that makes a moment unique. Artistic fire feeds on the wood of human nature and personal experience; it consumes all.

Apart from the paintings by Matisse that stood scattered in Picasso's sculpture studio, one could admire a woman in a brown dress by Modigliani, a poetic landscape by the *douanier* Rousseau,* a very intimate Vuillard of the Nabi period, and a medieval sculpture of Christ from Catalonia, all contributing to a glorious disorder. As Picasso was rather proud of the works by other artists that he had collected, it was not difficult to convince him to show a number of Seurat drawings and other marvels that were piled up here and there. In the afternoons he often came down from the painting studio for a respite and meditated for a few minutes in front of one of his favorites. When looking at Matisse's rather small *Woman Sitting in an Armchair*, he wondered if he would be able to match such a mauve with such a green. Actually he had painted a masterpiece in 1942, of a goat's skull in front of a window, in which violet and green appear simultaneously. Since they were separated by masses of black and white, he was still dubious about his ability to use such colors directly next to each other.

His most recent acquisition was a still life by Matisse—a vase full of pink tulips on a red-ocher table ornamented with oysters and lemons, the whole assemblage offset by a black background crisscrossed with thin diagonal scratches that designed large lozenges. Pablo's rationalization for acquiring that piece was that its *raison d'être* escaped

---

*Henri Rousseau (1844–1910), nicknamed "the customs officer," was a self-taught painter of genius. His naive creations enchanted Picasso, Apollinaire, and their friends.

Henri Matisse. *Young Woman Sitting*
(*Jeune Femme Assise*), 1942.

him completely. He got attached to it all the more because he could
not find why he liked it so.

One afternoon in June 1946, while we were contemplating it, he
become possessed by a strange idea. He addressed me: "Since you
admire Matisse so much, why don't you make a copy of this work in
your own style?"

I found the idea ludicrous and told him so.

"Then find the diagrams for the composition—that's the least you
can do. I have seen you sketch in that manner at the Louvre, you can't
refuse."

I retorted, "What can easily be done from a painting by Poussin won't be easy to achieve with a painting by Matisse, because there are no such diagrams in his work, as you know very well."

Pablo said, "Don't argue, find *some* diagrams. It will be a good exercise."

"All right, if I have to, I'll do it in pencil or india ink, and I won't spend too much time on the assignment, and you will not make any comment until the end."

"Agreed," said he, with a slightly sarcastic grin.

That's when I knew that I had to pay for admiring Matisse as much as I did.

Each element in that painting was playful and not at all regulated or contrived. Playfulness in a work where the artist has removed the traces of his own effort has nothing to do with randomness. There were no concessions to perspective. Flat areas of strong colors interacted, creating an unbroken ornamental surface, as in an Indian miniature. The elements were not a collection of unrelated objects, the number and orientation of which could be augmented or diminished at will. The result was playful, but the original organization was not something to tamper with.

The first day I had plenty of time to study how the tulips radiated from the vase and how they were echoed on the table by the appetizing oysters on a plate and by the lemons, as far as quantities went, but not in color or form. The second day I decided that it would be better not to stay too close to Matisse's recognizable patterns, because Pablo could certainly see them as well as or better than I could and thus would find that I lacked discernment. The third day I was still brooding. I wanted to avoid imitating the inimitable and was concerned about not betraying Matisse's intentions in any shape or form. I began small tentative sketches that I tore up as soon as I finished them. On the fifth day I produced a black-and-white india ink abstraction. The vase with the tulips had become a series of concentric circles with spikes; everything had undergone a metamorphosis. It was a diagram all right, but it no longer had anything to do with the spontaneity and freshness of the original Matisse. Faithful to his word, Pablo had not yet looked at what I was scheming and had worked upstairs.

Françoise Gilot. *The Target and the Arrows*, 1946.

Since it seemed silly to leave the experiment at that stage, I used the diagram to pursue a goal of my own, and the exercise ended up as a gouache, mostly white, yellow, and brown, of a target accompanied by arrows in a quiver and a boomerang (what was left of the plate on the table). As if guided by a sixth sense, Pablo came in toward the end of the afternoon, as soon as I was through.

"Is that what you produced?" he inquired.

"Yes, I learned a lot by looking carefully at that painting, but in the end a work of art must keep its own secret and I had to use whatever analysis I had done to my own ends."

"But that's excellent," said Pablo, to my surprise. "You did not retain any of the color interactions that are in the painting, and in trying to use a part of the underlying composition you discovered arrows and a target as well as a boomerang. That says a great deal about your relationship to Matisse's work. He is your ideal, your target, and you are trying to reach it both with arrows and with a boomerang. Ideally you are tracing with the arrow a linear trajectory to the center of the concentric circles, and by adding the curvilinear motion of the boomerang, you are hoping that some of what you have thrown around Matisse will come back to your hand."

I gave a lot of thought to this interpretation. I certainly learned much from the experience and even more from Pablo's sophisticated attitude. He probably wanted to show me that artists' trajectories are on parallel courses and meet only in the infinite.

In June another incident gave me food for thought about Pablo's complex behavior, which could be exercised negatively as well as positively. Jean Cocteau came to the studio rather early one morning with a request. He asked permission to take me along to visit Colette, the famous writer. He added that it would not take long, but that she had heard about me from various friends and was eager to see me.

"Am I supposed to come too?" inquired Pablo.

"Well, she knows that you are always so busy! Of course she would be delighted. Being an invalid now, she has but few distractions. It would please her, you know, to satisfy her curiosity and find out what mettle Françoise is made of. As far as you are concerned, she will understand that you owe yourself to the many visitors who expect to see you here."

"This is all well and good, but why should I send Françoise to meet the sphinx of the rue de Beaujolais? Does Colette send me any of the interesting young people who come to see her? I bet that she does not even appreciate me. She does not care for my work, preferring Dunoyer de Segonzac or Luc Albert Moreau, and now all of a sudden she is curious about someone close to me! Look at Françoise, she is beaming. Under her apparent detachment, I know, she is only too eager to go. She is obsessed by Colette's writing, by her cult of nature. She even compares her style to that of Matisse. For sure, once she meets her, she will care only for her, no longer for me."

Cocteau smiled. I remained silent; I knew that any insistence on my part would be interpreted as total betrayal and would later give rise to endless recriminations. Pablo could be very dictatorial as far as my actions were concerned. I never revealed myself too clearly, since I did not intend to change my opinions. I never met Colette, but it did not matter; I continued to be inspired by her writings.

Since I had avoided that trap, Pablo soon found another way to test me. At the beginning of July I fell very ill with a bizarre abscess on the forehead. After spending a week in a clinic, during which time Pablo busily drew different aspects of my swollen face, I recovered from what could have led to general septicemia, thanks to the intervention of the surgeon and huge amounts of penicillin. Pablo then decided that it was time to leave for the French Riviera. Soon after Avignon, however, the chauffeur turned left, and we ended up at Ménerbes in the Vaucluse, where Pablo's former mistress, the painter Dora Maar, owned a house (given to her by Picasso). She was not there, but Pablo had a key and said she had agreed to his staying there.

I was not to be persuaded that Dora could willingly have accepted my presence, and, personally, I found the situation demeaning for both of us and therefore intolerable. After two or three weeks, unable to make Pablo change his mind, I just decided to leave, happen what may. I could go join some relations in Toulon and then go to Tunisia, where I had friends and the possibility of a job recording local arts and crafts. I left the house unnoticed and was already some distance away, hoping to hitch a ride on a truck, when Pablo and Marcel caught up with me and unceremoniously threw me into the car, both protesting that I must have lost my mind or misconstrued all of Pablo's good intentions on my behalf.

Fortunately, at the end of the same day our friend Marie Cuttoli, a famous patron of the arts, arrived. Married to Senator Paul Cuttoli, president of the French National Assembly, Marie was an important collector, an Egeria for art and politics who had initiated a renaissance of tapestry in France. Elegant, intelligent, and aristocratic, she had a dashing personality. I told her how I felt about the stay at Dora Maar's house and she understood, all the more so because she knew how unhappy Dora was.

Marie was a good advocate. Pablo was soon persuaded that we should follow her to the Riviera, and the next day we all ended up at Shaddy Rock, her villa at Cap d'Antibes. We stayed at her home for a week, under her spell. Then we went to Golfe-Juan, again residing in the tacky apartment we rented from Monsieur Fort. Because of a lack of space, we just drew most of the time. Pablo started a series of jousts between bizarre centaurs and fauns and also some more idyllic mythological scenes. Luckily, Monsieur Dor de la Souchère, director of the museum at the Chateau Grimaldi in Antibes, invited us to come and work in a very large room upstairs. It was during these months of intense activity that Picasso continued the idyllic series and other studies that culminated in *The Joy of Life*, a panel painted on Masonite that carried a title that Matisse had made famous in 1908. The two works were stylistically as well as temporally far apart, yet thematically they were closely related.

My own emulation of Matisse went on during all of 1946. It was not an obsession but a leitmotif in my work and thus a frequent feature in my conversations with Pablo. Matisse's health was not good, and therefore we did not see him often during that period. Nevertheless, this was for him also a moment of renewed activity. Three books with his illustrations were published: Marianna Alcaforado's *Letters of a Portuguese Nun*, Tristan Tzara's *Le Signe de Vie*, and Pierre Reverdy's *Visages*.

Emmanuel Tériade, the publisher of *Verve*, often liked to relax in his villa at St. Jean-Cap Ferrat, not far from Vence, where Matisse was residing. He went to visit and was enthused by what he saw. Since it was difficult at that time to find good typefaces and since the artist's handwriting was legible and handsome, it was an inspired idea to produce a book of cutouts accompanied by Matisse's thoughts of the moment in his own beautiful handwriting. After many meetings and much work, a splendid book was born. It was entitled *Jazz* and published in 1947.

Besides Matisse, Tériade had certain artists in mind for similar works, but first he wanted to pay tribute to his friend Pierre Reverdy. Since Matisse's book was already well underway and quite satisfactory and since Reverdy's handwriting was also calligraphic, Tériade decided that Reverdy should write his poignant and somber poem *The Time of the Dead* in longhand on pages that could be transposed to copper plates, and that Picasso should introduce illustrations as he saw fit.

Given the tragic theme and the degree of abstraction of the poem, it was not easy for Pablo to decide what to do, and since he did not know whether the poem referred to the war deaths or more pointedly to deportation camps, he asked me for advice. All of a sudden I remembered some Arabic manuscripts of the eighth century from Spain that I had seen once by special permission at the library of the School of Medicine in Montpellier, and I mentioned them to him. Audaciously simple, without any figurative illumination, the text in black ink on parchment was ornate with capitals and abstract designs in vermilion. Intrigued, Pablo asked Lucien Schoeller, a dealer of medieval illuminated manuscripts and incunabula—books printed before 1500, generally illustrated with woodcut engravings—whether he had such a rare piece in his collections. He did not own anything as astonishing as what I had seen, but he was able to produce an eleventh century folio with the red-and-black combination. Pablo liked it and purchased it. He studied it, and it served as a springboard to his imagination. He then proceeded to paint bold abstractions directly on the copper plates to accompany the text, in the sugar-lift technique. This aquatint technique allows the painter to draw the image directly on the plate with a water-soluble solution, usually containing sugar. The plate is then covered with a ground or vanish and submerged in a bath of water and nitric acid, which dissolves the sugar solution, thus lifting the ground and exposing the image areas so the plate can be etched.

Because of all the time that Pierre Reverdy had needed to do the calligraphy of his poem and then the time that Picasso had needed to do his illustrations, the book came out in 1948. It was stunning, but not as successful as Matisse's *Jazz* in 1947. *Jazz* was a joyful explosion of colors, whereas *Le Temps des Morts*, stern in concept and execution, came into its own only much later. Bold straight or curved lines branched out and ramified in the margins of the calligraphic manuscript, always ending in full circles looking almost like wax seals. Picasso went on to use such linear configurations in lithography, and later they appeared in many of his paintings, mostly in portraits of me and in two abstract kitchen compositions, the first of which can now be seen at the Museum of Modern Art in New York and the second one at the Picasso Museum in Paris.

Matisse's *Jazz* was not realized in etchings or with the lithographic process but through an elaborate stencilling technique, which enabled the craftsmen to print with the same tempera colors that enlivened the painted sheets of paper Matisse used for his cutouts. Many pages reproduced his fleeting thoughts in his bold flowing handwriting. According to the master himself, "The images presented by these lively and violent prints came from crystallizations of memories of the circus, of popular tales, or of travel."

Color-forms at their brightest degree of intensity directly met each other without any halftones or shading. I believe that the joyous din, the syncopated encounter of forms and the wild clash of colors, playing on their complementary contrast in order to outdo one another, gave Matisse an idea. Knowledgeable as he was about music, the similarity between American jazz and his cutouts must have struck him, thus giving him the title for the book.

One should not believe that such images are simplistic. They are synthetic and simplified, which is not the same thing at all. Discarding unnecessary details that are simply descriptive and aiming at the essential requires the problem-solving process of a very complex mind. *Jazz* was the primal outburst of Matisse's last heroic creative phase, which was to include some of his most monumental works.

Henri Matisse at Le Rêve in 1946.

Friends and Foes

EARLY in 1945 I had read *Picasso and His Friends*, the memoirs of Fernande Olivier; also Gertrude Stein's *The Autobiography of Alice B. Toklas* (1933) and *Picasso* (1938), where I found accounts of Pablo's early encounters with Matisse. That same year Pablo decided it was time for me to meet Gertrude Stein. As soon as we arrived she began to shoot questions at me as if wanting to assess my IQ and she interviewed me thoroughly as if I had to show my capacities as a potential writer. In the end she was apparently satisfied, and so was Pablo, who took my performance as a credit to his flair for discovering young talent, but Alice Toklas was averse to being seduced and all the while tried to stuff me with her cakes and cookies, hoping that I would choke.

Afterward I did not try to visit Gertrude again at her apartment in the rue Christine. Knowing that Alice, who had shown such spontaneous antipathy to me during the first visit, would not let me in if I went alone, I decided I had to find another way to meet Gertrude. Since I found her quite unique, a literary phenomenon and a philosopher, I wanted to know more about her ideas and also to learn about her entourage and her salon, especially between 1905 and 1910. Fortunately, as I often crossed the rue de Buci on my way to Picasso's studio, I soon noticed that Gertrude, dressed in a monklike brown garment and wearing sandals, walked her dog, Basket, and did some shopping in the area around 11:00 A.M. So I came along as if by chance and chatted with her whenever I could.

I did not believe that spontaneous empathy had marked the first encounters of Henri Matisse and Pablo Picasso at the Steins' in the fall of 1905. Matisse, already a mature artist, was in the process of becoming the acknowledged leader of the Fauvist group. He was well read and naturally eloquent. Perhaps his training as a law student helped him to expound his theories in a logical, clear, and meaningful fashion. In contrast, the youthful Picasso was withdrawn and taciturn, his French being far from fluent. Nevertheless, he had the romantic aura of the foreigner, which turned his irrationalities and erratic pronouncements into enticing enigmas, even if the sentimental and picturesque appeal of the blue period and the charm of the rose period were not altogether convincing to the serious-minded Matisse.

In addition to his artistic accomplishments, Matisse led a well-balanced life. His wife had poise; she was intelligent and supportive;* they had children. Pablo's mistress, Fernande, for all her wit, beauty, and bohemian flair, was not one of those solid characters destined to be the cornerstone of a painter's career. From the start, each artist must have felt threatened by the other's potential assets and actual achievements. Under a polite veneer, a battle of wills was smoldering. Yet as intelligent as they were, they must have recognized the necessity of a peaceable coexistence that protected their pride, since they had to share the same friends, the same collectors, and even some of the same dealers. Understandably, there were tensions, but both played it cool, especially at the Steins', where the situation was often explosive because Leo and his sister, the witty Gertrude, played the part of *agents provocateurs*.

Initially there were more Matisses than Picassos on the walls of the apartment in the rue de Fleurus and at their brother Michael's and

---

*Amélie Matisse modeled for her husband, encouraged him, and earned some money by making fashionable hats.

his wife Sarah's place in the rue Madame, but soon all the Steins acquired some important Picasso paintings. Michael commissioned a portrait of himself and another of his son Allan. In 1906 the turning point in the complex network of interactions was reached, with Picasso's famous portrait of Gertrude. The sittings started in 1905 and went on for almost a year. He set aside the canvas for a while, and in the end completed it, in the fall of 1906, without the model. It was a powerful composition, all in earthy tones. The forms were sculptural, sturdy, and simplified, quite architectonic in the ancient Iberian mode, yet the treatment of the hands—the foreshortening of one hand and the sensitive modeling of the other—bespoke a skill inherited from the Renaissance. All in all, it was as a striking piece indeed. At first Gertrude liked it as a painting, but she did not think it resembled her. Picasso reassured her that even if it didn't look like her, she in time would come to look like it. Whether or not she was convinced, she declared herself satisfied.

The numerous sittings enabled them to talk and to try their ideas out on each other. Even if each did not listen attentively to the other's arguments, they did establish mutual notions of their as yet unrecognized greatness. Both agreed that they were the only geniuses around and that they were willing alternately to use and to hold the ladder that led to recognition. This platonic and neophilosophical friendship did not meet with everybody's approval. Georges Braque always disliked Gertrude and believed that she was just a big bag of wind unable to think—a narcissistic egomaniac putting words together like a crazed automaton and having the worst influence on Picasso. Gertrude's brother Leo, though very fond of her, thought along the same lines; for him she was no thinker, and he judged all her literary attempts to be plain gibberish.

Even if there was not an actual meeting of minds between Gertrude Stein and Picasso, these equally bombastic introverts shared a lust for power and knew they had to reinforce each other to achieve their goals. This was the beginning of an offensive and defensive alliance that would shake well-established notions of what art and literature were all about, but this understanding did not become manifest right away. The evenings at the rue de Fleurus went on undisturbed for a while.

Always eloquent and composed, Matisse was a welcome guest whom the Steins were proud to introduce to their American friends. But

Picasso's presence had to be reckoned with and also commanded un-divided attention. Soon the Stein family became polarized. Michael and Sarah, who had collected Matisse's work since 1902, upheld their al-legiance to him. With the assistance of Hans Purrmann, Sarah even helped run his Académie (first at the former Convent des Oiseaux, then at the former Convent of the Sacred Heart). Moreover, Leo and Ger-trude partitioned the collection they had purchased together, Leo taking all the Matisses except one and Gertrude all the Picassos except one.

Nevertheless, the two painters maintained amiable relations with each other. Picasso was impressed by Matisse's solidity of character and single-mindedness, while Matisse could not help being mesmerized by Picasso's imagination and radicalism. With Matisse, each day added something to the quality of his knowledge; with Picasso it was the opposite—each day he would rid himself of some skill he no longer found necessary. Matisse wanted to express an affirmative vision of the world, but Picasso dared to question everything, looking not for what to add but for what to delete from any previous accomplishments. With Matisse, the doer, things were augmented by accretion. Like King Philip II of Spain, Picasso could have adopted the emblem of the well with the motto "The more one removes, the larger it becomes." Matisse was generous, but Picasso led the way toward a total conceptual asceticism. He certainly stimulated Matisse to shed the comfort of any preconceived sense of order. Picasso had a flair for the new, the unexpected. In order to liberate instinctual forces, Matisse intensified color interplay, while Picasso's revolt was aimed at structure and form. Their polarity was mutually invigorating. In that sense, they needed each other as a per-manent challenge.

Apart from the Steins and their coterie, there was Sergei Shchukin, a wealthy Russian merchant of oriental rugs who owned an impressive number of well-chosen Impressionists and Postimpressionists, such as Gauguins and Bonnards. He had also collected Matisses from early on and was the artist's most dedicated supporter (by 1914, he owned thirty-nine major works by Matisse). When he returned to Paris to augment his collection and include younger talents, the leader of the Fauves introduced him to Picasso, a feat of generosity bordering on heroism, since Shchukin bought about fifty paintings from the Spaniard during the following six years. The pattern repeated itself when Ivan Morosov, another wealthy Russian collector, came along. In view of the pettiness that often mars artists' relationships, Matisse's open-mindedness was even more exemplary, since at that time he and Picasso were not yet friends, just colleagues. Only a real sense of greatness on both sides allowed these men to share the laurels without acrimony.

It may have been even more difficult for them to deal with their relative influence on their fellow artists. Matisse was a born leader, but Picasso had the charismatic personality. The most gifted of their contemporaries were very much evolving on their own, yet as they had no following to speak of in the public at large, they all needed to reinforce one another, to argue, to encourage one another, and to exhibit together. Many people think of Fauvism as a movement, but it was nothing of the sort. The name "Wild Beasts," as applied to artists who exhibited in the same hall at the Salon d'Automne of 1905, was coined by the art critic Louis Vauxcelles on account of the bold color schemes most of them used. The name stuck to them, and it is only after the fact that they looked for some conceptual cohesion as spiritual heirs of Gauguin and van Gogh. All went well for two years, until Cézanne's apples became a source of discord.

All the painters of that generation looked up to the master of Aix. It was not a new phenomenon; previously Cézanne's vision had marked Gauguin and van Gogh, and soon after it had enlightened the Nabis (Bonnard, Vuillard, Maurice Denis, Roussel, and others). But in the aftermath of a Cézanne retrospective at Ambroise Vollard's art gallery, the Fauves (who had mildly acknowledged Cézanne before) started to consider his oeuvre as seminal for a revolution in the very structure of a picture. This concern provided a springboard for a complete revision of priorities: a new asceticism replaced sensorial perceptions, intellectual preoccupations overrode passionate feelings. Each artist understood Cézanne's message differently. For Vlaminck and Derain, the two friends from Chatou, this influence proved catastrophic, especially for Vlaminck, who was unable to construct abstractly and who lived the rest of his life in the pseudodrama of artificially stormy landscapes. He lost his fire because his temperamental boldness was of no help in solving theoretical problems. The ideas of Cézanne also had a disastrous effect on Derain,

Paul Cézanne. *Still Life*, around 1900.

whose London landscapes had achieved true greatness and magnificence. In comparison, his subsequent "Romanesque" period looked arid, as if he were trying too hard to conform in a way that did not fit his robust nature.

In his Fauve canvases, Georges Braque had worked in comparatively sedate harmonies, using the complementarity of light purple and yellow as the dominant contrast and muting the other tones in saturation and intensity. The touch was rectangular, sometimes elongated to the extreme, animating large patches of white or unpainted canvas. When Braque came back from his second trip to L'Estaque, a small harbor close to Marseilles on the Mediterranean shore, with landscapes worked out mostly in volumes that were termed Cubist, Matisse must have experienced a sense of loss, since the quiet but very talented young artist was one of the stars in his group. For a man of Matisse's sensitivity, it must had been sad to see the group explode so soon after it was formed, and stranger still to witness the way in which Cézanne's lesson was being interpreted, especially since it had been an ongoing interest of his since 1899. But his natural curiosity kept him alert, he did not take things personally, and above all he possessed a sense of self that allowed him to keep his equanimity with the swings of the pendulum in aesthetic trends.

By the end of 1907 it had become obvious that André Derain and Georges Braque had joined the Picasso gang, *la Bande à Picasso*, along with Max Jacob, Guillaume Apollinaire, Marie Laurencin, André Salmon, Manolo (a Spanish sculptor), and some other Spaniards of lesser note. Except for Apollinaire, who continued to write articles in favor of Matisse's art, and the laconic Braque, who enjoyed boxing with Derain or just playing the accordion when he was not at work, and Marie Laurencin, who did not indulge in such foolishness, these artists carried on, verbally abusing the Fauvist master, who, they said, was finished, a nonentity. They went as far as to throw cigarettes, matchboxes, and matches at Matisse's *Portrait of Marguerite* (1906), which hung in Picasso's studio. On these occasions Picasso exhibited his characteristic weakness in front of his sycophants. Since he appreciated the painting, which had been given to him by Matisse himself, he could easily have stopped the silly demonstrations, but he did nothing of the sort; he remained passive or paralyzed, unable to stand up for his beliefs.

A year later Matisse went to a café in Montparnasse for a drink and was ignored and snubbed by all the members of the Picasso gang, who sat at the next table. Years later he confided once to his friend Brother Rayssiguier, a Dominican priest, "All my life I have been put in quarantine." Being proud, he armed himself against the hurt by isolating himself and becoming sphinxlike, always composed, inscrutable. Yet if he felt most betrayed by the artists who were closest to him in their pictorial style, he was far from isolated emotionally, with loyal friends like Albert Marquet, Charles Camoin, and Henri Manguin among the Fauves and Aristide Maillol, Pierre Bonnard, Édouard Vuillard, and Maurice Denis among the Nabis. Georges Rouault, whom he had met at the School of Fine Arts, also had a great regard for him.

The attention Matisse received in Germany among the Expressionists was also reinforcing. Their research echoed in his own preoccupations with a necessary return to primeval sources, with the exaltation of color, and with the unveiling of the innermost recesses of the human psyche. Robert Delaunay, a younger painter, wrote manifestos on his behalf and helped foster joint shows and international exhibitions of modern trends in Germany.

If Gertrude Stein exchanged all her Matisses but one with Leo to get all his Picassos but one, it was not because of a waning regard for Matisse's art. She felt that her special relationship to Picasso's art made her idiosyncratic style as a writer the exact equivalent of a Cubist painting. Owning more Picassos increased her credentials. The Michael Steins not only remained steadfast patrons, friends, and disciples but in 1914 acquired all the Matisses from Leo Stein's important collection, some of which they later sold to their friends Dr. Claribel Cone and her sister Etta, the well-known collectors from Baltimore.

Sergei Shchukin was also a competent supporter. Occasionally he shied away from a piece that he had commissioned, but after a while he would make up his mind to acquire it anyway, as was the case with *Music*, a major picture that was designed as a companion piece for *The Dance*. Considering the stuff that was being exhibited and purchased at that time, such as work by Bouguereau, Boldini, and Carolus Duran, it took almost as much boldness to own and display a Matisse in Moscow as it had taken Matisse to dare such a radical treatment of color and form.

Whether Matisse was readily understood or not, he was not inclined toward bitterness, he was not keen on retaliation, and he was interested in neither fending off opposition nor competing for the affection of wayward friends. His only competition was with himself; each year he wanted to transcend what he had been able to achieve the previous year. His goal was always to surpass himself while remaining consistent in his approach. Yet he was not blind to the currents around him, and he was quite able to assimilate concepts that were foreign to his temperament if they enlarged his vision of the world and augmented his expressive power.

As early as 1906 his inquisitive mind had led him to take an interest in African masks, which had been brought to his attention by Hans Purrmann, a young German painter who was his assistant at the academy. Matisse had spoken to Derain about them, and Derain became enthused and took Picasso to the Ethnographic Museum at the Trocadero, or so the story went. The magic intent and the abstract geometry of these idols must have awakened early childhood memories in Picasso, since in Málaga he must have watched many sailors disembark carrying African masks and sculptures as souvenirs of the strange places where they had landed. Later, in Barcelona, similar scenes probably were a familiar sight.

In the studies leading to *Les Demoiselles d'Avignon*, Picasso included a medical student holding a skull, and also a sailor, whom he not only sketched but painted several times on separate canvases. Both disappeared in the final state of the painting, but while three of the prostitutes at the Barcelona brothel remained Iberian in style, the two figures to the right hid their faces behind oversized African-style structures. Limbs and draperies were swept into the same lyrical rhythms, transformed into dynamic abstract diamond shapes. Thanks to Matisse's interest and Derain's intervention, the tribal masks in the Ethnographic Museum called forth blurred memories and were directly responsible for this metamorphosis in Picasso's style. He wanted magic to replace aesthetics. (Georges Braque's Cubism, in contrast, was undoubtedly indebted to Cézanne; he told Picasso that *Les Demoiselles d'Avignon* was painted with ignited gasoline, and he at first shied away from it.) African fetishes were at the core of Picasso's inner revolution and subsequent breakthrough in 1907, even though Daniel-Henry Kahnweiler, the art dealer, maintained the opposite. For Picasso the impact of Cézanne's lesson did not come as an instant revelation but was slowly assimilated over time, mostly between 1910 and 1914.

In 1906 José González, a young man from Madrid, came to Paris to reside near Pablo Picasso, who was the only young Spanish painter he had heard of as being a leader in the vanguard. In Montmartre there was a decrepit wooden building ironically called *le Bateau-Lavoir*, the wash-house barge, by its tenants. Picasso lived there with Fernande Olivier; Max Jacob rented a tiny abode on the lower floor. José González was able to rent the studio-apartment on the ground floor to the left of the entrance, with a window opening on the place Ravignan. Other artists, such as Braque, Modigliani, and the poet Pierre Reverdy, lived in the vicinity.

While making a living with satirical drawings for weekly papers such as *L'Assiette au Beurre*, the young González started to paint. By 1910 feeling self-assured, he abandoned his work as a cartoonist and adopted the pseudonym Juan Gris to sign his pictures. He decided to dedicate himself entirely to art and was determined to develop his own conception of Cubism. Noticed by Kahnweiler, who gave him a contract, he was able to support himself until World War I broke out in 1914. Just then he happened to be spending the summer with his wife, Josette, in the small city of Céret, near Perpignan. They were stranded with no news from Kahnweiler, who had become, as a German national, an enemy alien and had left Paris for Rome.

Fortunately, Matisse arrived in Céret in September and did his best to help Gris out of his financial straits. He gave Gris money himself and also wrote to several collectors to ask them to send Gris a monthly allowance according to their means. Even if Matisse was not altogether successful (Gertrude Stein, for example, promised to do something but then thought better of it), between one thing and another the help Gris received allowed him to wait until Kahnweiler was able to resume his allowances. More important, the mature artist and the young one struck up a friendship that became very significant to both of them. Their conversations and their renewed interaction the following summer created the strongest personal link that Matisse ever had with a Cubist painter, and enabled Gris to increase the saturation of his color schemes and the serenity of his compositions, which set him apart from the essential pair, Picasso and Braque, often referred to at the time as the Wright Brothers.

So for Matisse, the years from 1908 to 1918, which coincided with the development of Cubism, were a challenge toward a truly heroic style. Confronted with the abstract idealism of Cubism, his own structures became less spontaneous, perhaps, but more essential. He maintained only the dynamic aspect of the arabesque, not the ornamental one. His work gained power and often extended to monumental size. Secure in his boldness, he further simplified both shape and color. His only concern was for the whole; any unnecessary detail was discarded. Nevertheless, thematically his own work evolved in sequence according to an inner logic. The garland of dancers that animated a middle-ground plane of *The Joy of Life* was magnified and amplified to become the central theme of *Dance I* and *Dance II* and parts of the group were also used in some other canvases to bring the activity of the human figure into some still lifes. Some of his sculptures appeared within other pictorial compositions, as did his ceramics, while significant parts of other paintings, like *Le Luxe* and *The Young Sailor*, found their way into *The Artist's Studio* (1911) and *The Red Studio* (1911). Members of Matisse's family often permeated this parallel universe. Willingly or not, they became transfixed, and each acquired an archetypal persona. The painter's own work, environment, familiar objects, landscapes, and memories of travels were again and again put to the question; they had to enter the dance. Stable architectonic statements pulsated with life through vivid color interaction. At other times the dynamism came from the intensity of movement. In *The Dance*, for example, the idea of motion was accentuated by the emphasis on the limbs, the joints, and the garland effect of swinging arms and hands clasping each other, except in the front plane, where they reached out but did not touch.

Matisse's inner world was strong, disciplined, and stable. Bold and daring, it embraced, and yet no circle was ever complete, no subject was ever enclosed within the confines of the canvas. No limits were set, and the theme could develop without bounds in the imagination of the viewer. This being at one with oneself and with the world was the exact opposite of a Cubist composition, which built a totality of its own, entirely complete within its own limits.

With World War I many painters were mobilized. On the German side, August Macke and Franz Marc, two leading Expressionists, were killed—the first in 1914, the second in 1916. On the French side, Braque suffered a head wound and had to be trepanned, and his lungs were hurt by gas inhalation, so that he had emphysema for the rest of his life. Derain was also enrolled in the armed forces; for some time nobody knew his whereabouts. Matisse tried to enlist but was rejected; he was already forty-four. Being Spanish, Picasso could go on working as usual. But for all of them, the arguments, the companionship, the rivalries, the sense of humor, and the hope and enthusiasm of the avant-garde were over. From then on each painter had to fend for himself. What was more, some were not as successful as others and younger generations were coming along; a unity of spirit was no longer possible.

After a first visit to Nice in the winter of 1916–17, Matisse went back regularly each winter to work. There the combined quality of the light and repeated visits to Auguste Renoir and to Pierre Bonnard subtly softened his mood. He felt like embarking on a more intimate and painterly approach; the roar of the tiger was for a while replaced by the purring of the cat who went his way alone.

In the meantime, Picasso had met Sergei Diaghilev, the choreographer. He started to work on sets and costumes, and in 1917, while in Rome with Léonide Massine and Jean Cocteau, he was impressed by an excursion to Pompeii and the Museum of Antiquities in Naples, which subsequently led him toward a neoclassic style. At the beginning of the twenties, when Matisse accepted work for a ballet called *Le Chant du Rossignol*, choreographed by Massine with a musical score by Stravinsky, it seemed that a sense of competition was not altogether absent. But as the years went by, it became clear that the two colleagues had outdistanced all their contenders and that they would have to share power on Mount Olympus just as they shared the laurels they had previously reaped on Montparnasse. Matisse's sensual orientalism and addiction to Delacroix's lyricism did not go unnoticed by Picasso. When the temptation became irresistible, he *symbolically* killed two birds with one stone—his own wife, Olga, and the master who had passed into Delacroix's camp—by painting a mock odalisque whose pink macaroni limbs were grotesquely spread on an armchair. This burst of aggression was soon followed by a complete, simultaneous surrender to love and to the arabesque, a synthesis of Picasso's new grand passion Marie-Thérèse Walter's features and Matisse's elaborate rhythmical curves.

Most probably the real friendship between Picasso and Matisse began around 1930, after Picasso's conversion to flat decorative surfaces enflamed by a lyrical system of curves. When Picasso exhibited these paintings at the Galerie Georges Petit, Kahnweiler was furious and Braque was outraged. For them this change of heart was anathema. Picasso began to say that he was no longer fond of his old friends.

Matisse must have smiled at that, but undaunted, he welcomed the rebel, who like his patron saint, Paul, had been struck by revelation on his way to Damascus. Even Picasso's sculptures of the 1930s looked like blown-up, radicalized replicas of Matisse's own work from 1911 to 1913.

Matisse had been mindful of Cubism in the war decade, and now Picasso paid tribute to his sustained Fauvism and subsequent evolution. Their pictorial conquests overlapped. Clearly a covert tug of war would have been a waste of energy. Both were beyond that stage in their relationship, and on both sides an intense curiosity opened the door to friendship. Each of them wanted to know the why and the how of their mutual creative power. The sense of rivalry had all but disappeared, but its impetus added spice to their encounters and acted as a stimulant the rest of the time.

Picasso and Matisse enjoyed each other's evolution, creativity, and interest in different masters of the past, in particular Delacroix and Ingres, Manet and van Gogh. Again they exchanged some paintings. They softened to each other, and a deep emotional bond was sealed. After all, no one could understand them as they did each other.

The political developments of the 1930s became a threat to them both and to other recognized leaders of contemporary art. Economic crisis and political conflicts led to the rise of Nazism in Germany and to the rise of Facism in Italy, and later to Franco's subversion in Spain. Hitler, a would-be painter, and Goebbels, his chief of propaganda, branded modern trends as degenerate Marxist Jewish decadence. Many artists from the Bauhaus, such as Paul Klee, left Germany; others were to suffer worse tragedies and death. Matisse and Picasso must have been deeply disturbed by such developments. Both had found early recognition, friendship with colleagues and disciples, and the support of faithful collectors such as Count Kessler and Tannhauser in Germany. The German intelligentsia were renowned as the most enlightened in Europe, but now books were forbidden or burned publicly, and artists were vilified while their works, often extorted from their rightful owners, were secretly sold through Switzerland to make money for armaments or found their way to Goering's collection. He apparently had a taste for the decadent.

The exaggerated musculature of warriors and athletes by Arno

Brecker, the middlebrow descriptive art extolling the virtues of young SS athletes and of fair-haired women producing babies for the nation, triumphed in Germany, as did the flaccid Fascist statuary or the new Mussolini forum in Rome. But far stranger things were happening at the other end of the ideological spectrum. Since Stalin's rise to power, in the USSR the only possible form of art had become social realism, which was just as uninspired. In the land of Shchukin and Morosov, the important collections had been nationalized and were no longer shown to the public. Matisse's and Picasso's work was now frowned on because of their "decadent formalism." Shchukin, who had escaped to the French Riviera, was now like a broken puppet, unable to make a new start as a trendsetter. Of course, Matisse and Picasso were mostly concerned for the fate of their friends and fellow artists, and for the fate of democracy in Europe, but as artists and human beings they must have been vexed by the waning of their influence.

As years went by, matters only got worse. Franco's uprising, the bombing of Guernica, and Picasso's reaction, the painting *Guernica*— are well-known events needing no further elaboration. After the French collapse in 1940, Picasso, who usually would not go out of his way for anyone, took the trouble to protect Matisse's artworks that were kept in storage in Paris in a huge room-sized safe at the same bank as Picasso's own pictures, while his friend was seriously ill in the South of France. In each bank all safes had to be opened. The Nazi bureaucrats were taking an inventory of all the works of art and valuables, which at any time could be arbitrarily confiscated and sent to Germany or sold for the war effort, or even destroyed. When owners or their representatives were present, the Nazis had to provide a copy of the inventory, which was a proof of the vault's contents. It could also be that both artists influenced each other to reach the decision to stay in France during the tragic years of the occupation, though their art was reputedly decadent and was banned from public display in museums and in all art galleries in Paris during that period, and though they were personally at risk.

Soon after I met Picasso in 1943, I often heard him say with a sigh, "I wonder what Matisse is doing these days!" Perhaps they wrote to each other, but more probably they did not, even though Matisse corresponded with French friends such as the painter Charles Camoin, the poet André Rouveyre, and others. Nevertheless, the artists managed an exchange of paintings in 1942 and obtained news from each other by telephone and through mutual friends. Of course, they were unable to see much of each other's work during the war period. They shared the fate of being attacked and often denounced in collaborationist newspapers, and this was one more reason why they were so eager to communicate as artists as soon as the nightmare ended. It was fortunate for me that I was present when, from 1946 to 1954, these artists entered a positive phase in their relationship, bringing a difficult and rare friendship to its apogee.

The Wild Beasts

MATISSE was a cultured man, both artistically and intellectually. From the start he did not neglect the ancient masters but dutifully made copies of their work at the Louvre. Well aware of oriental art and thought, he also cultivated the lessons of Cézanne, and under Paul Signac's guidance he even got involved in pointillism for a while.* These inquiries gave him a firm foundation for his ideas and a methodical approach to the art of painting. All this theoretical and experimental training was necessary but not sufficient; Matisse still had to make the great leap forward.

The crucial breakthrough, the revelation, came in 1905. In the late spring and summer he went to Collioure with his wife, in the company of André Derain, who was just returning from military service. Disgruntled with little colored brushstrokes, the confetti of pointillism, he

---

*Paul Signac (1863–1935) was a Postimpressionist painter who developed the theory of pointillism with Georges Seurat and Henri-Edmond Cross. The pointillists painted simplified forms in light with very small dots of pure color.

undertook a series of small landscapes and studies of his wife, Amélie, in a Japanese kimono, all in a joyous and playful mood. He was elated and stimulated to be working outdoors in the company of his friend, who eagerly toiled next to him. For northerners like them, the Mediterranean environment held a strong appeal, perhaps especially so in French Catalonia, a segment of the Languedoc where the early cultures could be traced all the way back to the ancient Greeks, the Phoenicians, and even more primeval ancestors.

Amélie Matisse personified the spirit of daring and steadfastness so characteristic of the region of her origins. She was born in Toulouse, but her forebears came from Catalonia. Matisse's friend Aristide Maillol, also a French Catalonian, lived and worked nearby, in Banyuls. Not only did the two men rekindle the relationship that they had initiated in 1901, but they freely discussed new topics of mutual artistic concern.

Matisse had seen some Gauguins at Ambroise Vollard's and had even exchanged one of his paintings for a Gauguin in 1899, but because of his interest in Cézanne, the full impact of Gauguin's importance had not yet dawned on him.

Nine years older than Matisse, Maillol had occasionally met Paul Gauguin in Paris. Maillol said that while he had no particular personal empathy with Gauguin, on account of his cantankerous disposition, he admired him deeply as an artist. He felt that Gauguin's quest for a return to innocence was the key to a valid future in art. What the reprobate artist had sought in the savage cultures of the Pacific Islands was the dream of a lost paradise that lay dormant within himself. Maybe he had needed to go so far away to summon the courage to become himself and to reveal himself to the fullest in unforgettable images.

According to Gauguin, Western culture had always honored knowledge and in general emphasized intellectual concepts, valuing mathematically organized compositions based on systematized descriptive observation and symbolically favoring a cult of science, which led people's aspirations further and further away from the tree of life. As a result, Western art had been weakened and bastardized. It was a spiritual fall into banality. To ascend again, it was necessary to free the instinct—

in other words, to reopen the gates of the unconscious—and create in a renewed state of innocence.

Gauguin had said: "I am not a painter from nature. . . . Now more than ever, everything takes place in my wild imagination. My artistic center is my brain. I am strong because I do what is within me." He opposed both the descriptive and the literary style and proposed *suggestion* through an arrangement of colors, shapes, and design that would resonate mysteriously in the viewer's psyche. To create compelling images, the artist had to release the unconscious material in himself from the censorship of reason; he had to awaken mnemonic visions and combine them with a recognition of similar arrangements provided by willful perception. In a notebook he wrote: "An image must fuse unconscious pulsions and conscious ideas, it must fuse emotion and intellect, it should reach the depths of savagery where genius remains unfettered and where dreams and perceptions are meshed with the fabric of nature. . . . One should work freely and madly." And he added in a letter to the painter Émile Schuffenecker (whose family was the subject of one of his paintings), "Above all don't sweat over a painting, a great sentiment can be rendered immediately. Look for the simplest form in which you can express it. . . . *Color, what a deep and mysterious language, the language of dreams*" (italics mine). He believed, like Baudelaire, that modern art consists of an evocative magic that simultaneously contains object and subject, the world outside the artist and the artist himself. If he was not the only artist in his time to look toward origins in an effort to rejuvenate Western art, he was the first to say: "My art goes way back, further back than the horses on the Parthenon—all the way back to the dear old hobby horse of my childhood."

In order to release the barbarian within himself, Gauguin had looked even beyond the exotic primitivism of traditional cultures in the islands of the Pacific; he had gone deeper, realizing that the real savage to be accepted as a trustworthy guide was to be found within himself; it surfaced at times in his dreams and in the memories of his childhood. This was the golden key that would enable artists to be regenerated, by becoming true to themselves and therefore to the world.

Maillol, who was one of Gauguin's faithful friends to the end and who clearly saw the importance of his ill-fated quest* for "the golden age," did more than reminisce about him; he took Matisse to visit Daniel de Monfreid, who still held in trust, until the settlement of the estate, most of Gauguin's Tahitian pictures. Two other friends of Maillol's, Maurice Fabre from Narbonne and Gustave Fayet from Béziers, also owned remarkable Gauguins that the young painter was able to see. Both spiritually and creatively, Gauguin's work was the touchstone Matisse needed to set his own brain on fire.

Discovery is supposed to favor the prepared mind, and for Matisse this was the right information at the right time. He had reached the point where he was ready to free his intellect and release his emotions. He understood how Gauguin, who knew Chevreul's theories, not only worked with the contrast of different sets of complementary colors but orchestrated each color with all its derivatives and used ternary accompaniments as well, thus succeeding in being both strong and subtle in his harmonies while allowing clashing contasts to culminate and increase the iconic vitality of the whole. (Michel Eugène Chevreul, a physicist, wrote "The Principle of Harmony and Contrast of Colors and Their Applications to the Arts" published in 1834.)

At a time when so many artists took pride in being decadent, when the theme of most novels could have been labeled "The Loss of Innocence," this hope for a return to innocence was both heroic and prophetic. The insight that was to be found in the innermost recesses of the unconscious, in memories and dreams, appealed to Matisse's imagination. He had already been attentive to the natural freedom and spontaneity of his children's paintings. With no more hesitations, he began to express himself as clearly and boldly as possible, throwing overboard any concern not directly related to the pure thrust of his vision.

In addition to the impact of Gauguin's revelation, and in addition to the Mediterranean mastery of Maillol, the cheerful avant-garde approach of his young friend Derain and the flair of his wife for new ideas prodded Matisse forward. It was not by chance that the resolution of

---

*Ill-fated not because it was not a valid and worthwhile pursuit, but because of specific shortcomings in Paul Gauguin's personality: his bad temper and aggressiveness.

years of inner turmoil occurred at Collioure in French Catalonia where the Albigensianism heresy had flourished centuries before.* Time and again ideas had been thrown into a boiling caldron in that area—metaphysical questions about the nature of reality and illusion, and libertarian theories about the necessity of political freedom and freedom of expression. So the Mediterranean light, the natural and human environment, the proximity of his peers and the impact of Gauguin's genius—coincided to release Matisse's inhibitions and launched him on an entirely new course of action. He worked, worked, and worked, going from discovery to discovery.

Upon his return to Paris in 1905, he went about organizing Room VII at the Salon d'Automne, where his most recent canvases were hung together with those of Camoin, Derain, Dufy, Manguin, Marquet, Puy, Vlaminck, and others. In the center of that hall, on a pedestal, stood a fairly mild bust of a child by a sculptor called Marque. In the next issue of *Gil Blas* magazine, the critic Louis Vauxcelles sarcastically commented: "The candor of this bust comes as a surprise amid the orgy of pure tones; it is Donatello among the wild beasts [*fauves*]." Matisse and his friends were also labeled the Incoherents and the Invertebrates by less important journalists.

Of course everybody dashed to the salon to guffaw at the apostles of this new heresy. Though meant to be pejorative, the first nickname stuck to the painters exhibiting in Room VII. Once singled out, their best defense was to coalesce and to form a unified group. Considered the leader, Matisse was the most criticized and the most abused, but the nickname was apt, it was lucky. It created a strong image. The Wild Beasts had made a dent in the fabric of the establishment; the boldness of their vivid color schemes was there to stay. Apart from all the disparaging comments of conventional amateurs, the group as such received the attention it deserved, even if for the wrong reasons.

---

*Albigensianism, also called Catharism, was practiced by a rigorously ascetic Christian sect in the Languedoc. Its followers maintained a dualistic theology and believed in the necessity of leading a very pure life in order to achieve "perfection." Deriving from the theories of Arius and Bogomile, this mode of thought became prevalent in the Languedoc during the eleventh century. Its adepts were mercilessly exterminated during the thirteenth century by Simon de Monfort and the Inquisition.

Matisse himself was singled out by intelligent foreigners: Sergei Shchukin and Leo, Michael, and Gertrude Stein. After two visits to the salon, Leo and Gertrude decided to meet the artist. They acquired *La Femme au Chapeau*, a recent portrait of Matisse's wife, a glowing symphony of pure colors laid in large lyrical brushstrokes. Michael and his wife, Sarah Stein, acquired *The Green Line*, soon followed by *The Joy of Life*, *The Gypsy*, *The Young Sailor*, *Self-Portrait*, *Blue Still Life*, *Women with a Branch of Ivy*. Sergei Shchukin had been collecting Matisses since 1902. The dealer Berthe Weill was also supportive. Relieved from immediate material worries, Matisse was free to explore, following in the footsteps of two pioneers.

Van Gogh had known that color is not bound to be true to life but in his own words "should be tuned higher than nature's own harmonies, to evoke the terrible human passions." Gauguin, through simplification and synthesis, had used flat tones in an arbitrary fashion, both for the harmony of the picture and as a symbol for the mind. These two artists had been the first to recognize the importance of pure color as a direct means of expression and not only as an ornament of form. Both had suffered, both had been destroyed; they had come too early in a world too old to receive them. Far from being a naive enthusiast, Matisse was well aware that he was initiating a dangerous quest.

For the red-haired painter, the experience of Fauvism was something real.* By liberating color at its highest degree of intensity, Matisse knew that he was freeing the instinctive impulses of the unconscious, literally releasing the wild beasts within himself. He did not want to tame the forces he was unleashing; that would have been an emasculation of the power he sought. Like Orpheus, he had to enchant the wild beasts of his unconscious, to rein them in without inhibiting their intensity. Contiguous colors had to be apposed and opposed; each one had to allow itself to be progressively contaminated and modified by the adjacent tones as they appeared. The effect of the optic modification of one by the proximity of another is called delayed contrast. "A certain blue entered the soul, a certain red had an effect on blood pressure, it was

---

*The word *fauve* means a large wild animal but also describes the glowing, fiery tone of a lion's mane; hence the reference to Matisse's red hair!

the concentration of timbres that allowed forms to be modified according to the reactions of neighboring colors," as Matisse put it.

Each tone had its own natural power of expansion, which was larger for warm tones than for cold ones. That power varied according to size as well as to the degree of compatibility or the strong contrast with the neighboring tones. Matisse saw how he could use the arabesque to prevent neighboring colors from swallowing each other. The arabesque was the charmer; it was natural, it moved, it was musical. It had its own sonority. It had already been used in the outline of certain cave drawings. It was the impassioned impulse that swelled these drawings, gave them life and movement. The arabesque was not a definition of form but music allowing the rhythmical circulation of forces.

Each painting became an adventure, a process of discovery. Matisse's mind was incandescent, almost bursting with enthusiasm. Arising from emotions, color knew no bounds. How difficult it must have been to face the wild beasts from within before unleashing their untamed energy onto the canvas, to uncover this savage self heretofore hidden under the veneer of reason and civilization. But Matisse was intelligent and resourceful.

There are three primary colors in the light spectrum: yellow, red, and blue. Each primary color is opposed and complemented by a secondary color that is a mix of the other two primaries. In the light spectrum, blue, for example, if complemented by orange (a mixture of red and yellow), recomposes white. The same would occur in painting, except that the mix would result in a black mess instead of white light because of the materiality of the pigments. Strong saturated tones can be opposed, but not at the expense of structure. Matisse discovered that color *was* structure. While remaining surface-oriented, colors define positions in space if they are used in complementary couples. Warm colors naturally proceed, while cold colors recede. A bright yellow appears to be located on the first plane, while a purple seems further away. Because of the added contrast of light and dark, this contrast is called an extreme contrast. The contrast between red and green, though obeying the same physical laws (the red proceeding and the green receding), is less extreme, because red is a relatively dark tone and green is a relatively light one, so it creates a mild contrast. Orange and blue create a medium contrast, and the contrast of black and white is called absolute.

Far from being a small separate brushstroke, as in pointillism, each color was thus expanded by Matisse to define an area or a plane. Each in turn could be accompanied by less saturated tones and halftones of the same family or orchestrated with ternary harmonies. Yellow could ally itself to red through orange, modifying that part of the chromatic wheel. The contrast of orange with blue in that case would be augmented in direct proportion to the size and intensity of the respective hues involved. All this was not theoretical, because it was based on the expressionistic impact of the painter's emotions.

The physical laws of color perception had been discovered by Chevreul, but Matisse knew (after his passage through pointillism) that these laws had to be used and abused arbitrarily, provided the transgressions contributed to the vitality of the whole. He made ingenious use of the mild contrast of red and green by accompanying his cadmium reds with light or saturated alizarin crimson, thus subtly inflecting the primary vermilions toward blue, then using emerald as a base for most of his greens, whether they were saturated or not; inflecting his green tones in the direction of blue, therefore operating a continuous transition, he allowed an affinity between red and green, while benefiting even more from their mild contrast. Emerald green was a royal color in the palette of a painter: pure, it was transparent, almost like a glaze, and resolutely on the side of blue; tempered with white and a touch of red, it could give beautiful grays that held their plane and didn't recede; mixed with some alizarin crimson, it was transformed into the most sensuous purple. Viridian was also compatible with yellow to produce leaf-green and warmer greens scintillating with light, as opposed to a green made of blue and yellow, which always remained coarse.

The portrait *La Femme au Chapeau* is a beautiful example of how colors can be yoked with each other in harmony without losing their intrinsic qualities. Without giving up their innate power, colors are coupled two by two but interact three by three, thus becoming attuned, the royal viridian being their common denominator and justifying Matisse's enigmatic sentence "Each color has its gray." Emerald is each color's gray, as well as being the invisible axis of the whole.

In the well-known *Portrait of Marguerite* (1906) that Matisse gave to Picasso, emerald green is the dominant color, but the overall impact of the painting lies in the childlike simplicity of the composition, which is treated in a few flat tones and includes the almost naive vertical inscription of the name Marguerite in the upper left of the canvas. Such spontaneity mesmerized Picasso. He admired the courage of the Fauvist master to show such candor. Many years later, he still regretted having allowed his friends to make fun of that painting, when he knew so well the important statement that it was making.

Fauvism as such was not a long-lived gathering of artists, as it lasted only from 1905 to 1909. Matisse alone turned the flame of that burning fire into a lifetime quest. During the years between 1910 and 1920, Matisse's architectonic preoccupations came to the fore, and his compositions acquired heroic qualities and dimensions. Yet for him such constructive concerns went hand in hand with the radical use of daring color schemes. Those years were also marked by the addition of the major contrast of black and white, a contrast understood in terms of color and not as an opposition of light and darkness. Black was a force; Matisse depended on it to simplify design. White was solid; it allowed the other colors to breathe, to expand. It played the part of silence in music. Matisse's more painterly approach of the twenties was geared toward a renewal of Fauvist spontaneity and imaginative complementary contrasts, with added textural effects and a new virtuosity of treatment. Through the 1930s his remarkable quest on the path of color continued. Exalted, essential colors now met one to one as configurative signs. They became the language of sensuous encounters on the canvas and of idealized synthetic abstractions in the mind.

The Magician

MY SON, Claude Picasso, was born on May 15, 1947. By the end of June, Picasso and I were ready to leave Paris with the baby to reside once more at Monsieur Fort's place in Golfe-Juan. Soon we were settled and happily at work, both of us drawing and painting.

We saw Matisse a few times during that summer. The encounters always had to be preceded by an exchange of telephone calls. Because Matisse was older and his state of health was unreliable, Lydia was usually the one to initiate the process and propose a propitious date; she would call our chauffeur or Madame Ramié, the director of the Madoura pottery, since Pablo had prohibited the installation of a telephone at home because he did not want to be disturbed. Unless we had the most pressing engagements, the wishes of our benevolent patriarch were a command to be obeyed. We would not have missed such an opportunity for anything in the world. All other concerns were dropped or postponed—the ceramics remained unfinished, my gouaches dried unattended, and Claude had his nurse. Though Pablo hated phone calls, he would call back himself to agree on the time, and we would get busy with the projected visit, admonishing Marcel not to be late and anticipating the pleasures of the visit. I would try to dress in a color combination that would appeal to our friend. Pablo would look feverish and joyous, but on the way to Vence he would try to decide whether Lydia's tone of voice had been cheerful, warm, cool, or cold. If he thought that the latter was true, his anticipation would become tainted with anxiety. Was Matisse ill, or worse, was he in a bad mood? He would go on conjecturing all the way, by turns hopeful or pessimistic. My role then would be to comfort him and to affirm that all was well in the best of all possible worlds.

At other times, if the interval between one visit and the next seemed to lengthen, Pablo would ask Madame Ramié or me to telephone Lydia. If he really became impatient, he would dial directly, being then the initiator of a possible meeting. If the answer was negative, it meant one of two things: either his friend was unwell and unable to see us, or he did not wish to have visitors. Both eventualities were awful for Pablo, who would start to brood and subsequently become quite depressed. Since he felt a genuine affection for Matisse, he hated to be denied the precious moments that they could share. Therefore, though he did not call too often for fear of a refusal, he preferred to expose himself to a certain amount of anxiety, knowing that if he made no effort, Matisse in turn would feel frustrated or unloved. Whatever has been said or written to the contrary, this was the one relationship in which Pablo was extremely careful not to be negative in any way.

It was rather touching to see how patient and flexible he could be in order not to challenge or hurt his friend's feelings. I wondered if he did not bring into that relationship the sentiments he had entertained for his father: the tenderness, the admiration, the wish to please, the fear of rejection, as well as the not-so-paradoxical need to rebel or to criticize. All that was included in his form of love. While in France Matisse was the acknowledged patriarch of modern art, for Picasso he was also a benevolent father figure, someone who could perhaps be satisfied more easily than Pablo had satisfied his own father, a more traditional artist. This did not mean that Pablo would not eventually betray Matisse with a kiss, with equal zeal. Physically, Matisse, in his youth a redhead with a short beard, was not entirely without resemblance to Don José Ruiz Blasco, Pablo's father, except that he was sturdier and stockier.

What was the source of the affection on Matisse's side? Under his patrician poise and nonchalance lay not only an unquenchable curiosity about what was different and therefore unknown to him in human nature, but also a genuine need for affection, a feeling that was all-encompassing, especially for that which was most foreign to his own temperament and therefore more attractive to him. Picasso's radicalism appealed to him. Unknown even perhaps to himself, he wanted to fix and conquer the unconquered, to move and transform the moody, mercurial nature of the Spaniard. He indulged Pablo's whims and capers with as much pleasure as he had previously experienced when he had painted *The Young Sailor* in Collioure, relishing the sensuousness and provocative attitude of that urchin. Matisse, with all his northern seriousness and sense of decorum, enjoyed in his friend all the fire, gusto, and panache that he did not want to cultivate personally, even though deep down he was possessed by the same anticonformist spirit.

They were in fact as complementary as red and green, as opposed as white and black. They were two sides of the same coin. Matisse's high-tension electricity corresponded to Pablo's magnetism, and their presence in the same room created an extraordinary field of force.

Be that as it may, one morning in August Lydia telephoned to say that Matisse wanted to spend a few days in Juan-les-Pins (perhaps to see his doctor or to alleviate the monotony of his routine). We learned that he was not feeling very well but wished to arrange a meeting for the following afternoon, provided we did not linger too long.

Pablo got all excited. "What can we do? We should bring him a present. Not a cake, he does not eat such things; not flowers, he would think that we are visiting him in a clinic. What then? What would he like, do you think?"

Previously we had met Monsieur Reszvani, a famous Iranian magician who was staying with some friends of ours. We had seen him perform astonishing tricks, with his wife's assistance, and I suggested that it would be both unusual and fun to bring him along. Everybody agreed, and we made the necessary arrangements. We had to bring more guests than we cared to, because Monsieur and Madame René Batigne, the Reszvanis' hosts, could not be dissuaded from coming, and Manuel Angeles Ortiz, a not-so-gifted Latin American painter who was one of Pablo's devotees, followed suit.

We all arrived at the appointed time. Lydia opened the door and was a little put out by the number of people. Matisse was in bed, regal as usual, all in white in a sand-colored room. We jammed the hotel suite.

Monsieur Reszvani invented tricks and taught them, but he did not perform commercially. He explained that through a method similar to yoga, he could activate at will the motions of most muscles in his body while at the same time attracting our attention in other directions, which allowed him to conjure things away. We settled in a wide circle around Matisse, the magician and his wife standing on one side close to the bed and Lydia also standing, but on the other side. Reszvani's movements could not escape being noticed at least by some of us. Nevertheless, objects began to disappear and reappear mysteriously. Watches left their owners' wrists and found their way to some unknown destination before being extracted from our ears or noses. Cards passed from one box to another. Cages were flattened while Bengali birds reappeared within an empty hat. When the magician admonished us to follow his movements more carefully, we were unable to catch him red-handed, much less to reproduce any of the tricks he demonstrated or even explained.

Matisse was as happy as a child enjoying conjuring tricks for the first time. Everyone's eyes began to bulge out of their sockets. We were beguiled. It was eerie. Then the magician, seeing that he had his audience well in hand, asked Matisse to concentrate and to think about one of the twenty-six letters of the alphabet, visualizing it as a capital, without uttering it, of course.

Everyone remained silent. The painter concentrated for a few minutes and finally signaled that he had chosen and was ready for the test. During the same span of time Reszvani inscribed a capital letter on a sheet of paper; he folded it and placed it in an envelope, which was then sealed by his wife, who handed it to Lydia across the bed. Then Reszvani asked Lydia to give the sealed envelope to Matisse, for him to open himself and check whether the capital letter was the one that he had chosen.

Matisse unsealed the envelope, unfolded the paper, and showed us a capital K. He was bewildered, because, he assured us all, it was the letter that he had indeed mentally selected. We were dumbfounded, since there was no rational explanation for the phenomenon. Was it a case of hypnotic suggestion or telepathy? Matisse said that he had emptied his mind to reflect and then a capital K had sprung out of nowhere and invaded his consciousness with such force that he had not wanted to alter his choice in any way. As for the magician, he just smiled and mumbled something about esoteric teachings in the Orient and the traditional transmission of special powers.

After that climax it was time to leave. We remained together through the evening and enjoyed listening to our friend Ortiz playing the guitar and singing flamenco; he was particularly good at allegrias, malaguenas, and soleares. While Manuel lost himself in the nostalgic accents of the "Cante Rondo," accompanied by Pablo's frequent clapping of hands and appreciative exclamations—"Olé, hombre," and such—I began to wonder if the probability of Matisse's selecting one specific letter out of the twenty-six could be narrowed down by someone who, like Reszvani, had a good intuitive knowledge of the human psyche.

It was unlikely that Matisse would have chosen any of the letters contained in his name, because he was not an egotist. As he worked with the arabesque, a system of curves, any curvilinear capital could also be eliminated as a possible choice, because its form was too obvious and too simplistic to approach the organic sensuousness of his flowing lines. Then structure came to mind, and the importance in Matisse's work of the interplay of a vertical vector accompanied by two diagonals, one ascending and the other descending. The letter K was in fact a good model of such fundamental directionality.*

---

*Matisse had written: "The ascending vertical is always on my mind. It helps me to be precise about the direction of lines, and in my rapid sketches I don't indicate a curve, for example, that of a branch in a landscape, without acknowledging its relationship to the vertical" (*Jazz*). "Possessing as I do a feeling for horizontality and verticality has enabled me to make the resulting diagonals more expressive, which is not easy" (letter to André Rouveyre, October 18, 1947).

Pablo Picasso. *Les Demoiselles d'Avignon*, 1907.

Pablo shook me out of my absorbing hypothesis by asking why I looked so deep in thought. I explained that I was trying to find an inner necessity in his friend's choice of the letter K and to see if it was consistent with the basic structure of many of his paintings.

Pablo scratched his head. "There is something in what you say.

Now, tell me what letter I would have chosen, according to your theories."

"This is a wild guess, but I believe that you might have chosen an X, a letter that in algebra symbolizes an unknown quantity. It is in keeping with your way of using crystalline and pyramidal forms, as in your Cubist period or in *Les Demoiselles d'Avignon*, for example."

"You have bizarre notions but interesting thoughts. Which letter would you have chosen yourself? And do you think Monsieur Reszvani would have guessed right?"

"For me, perhaps a Y, because I am a woman and because I like ternary shapes. As to Monsieur Reszvani, he may be able to feel and guess the signs that we are most likely to empathize with. Perhaps he uses semihypnotic suggestion. I don't know what to think about telepathy. It could be telepathy—after all, why not? Maybe the answer is even simpler, and he used a subterfuge of some kind. He may have been closer to Matisse than we realized when Matisse opened the envelope. Whatever really happened does not matter, as long as we all enjoyed the enigma. Some mysteries are better unsolved."

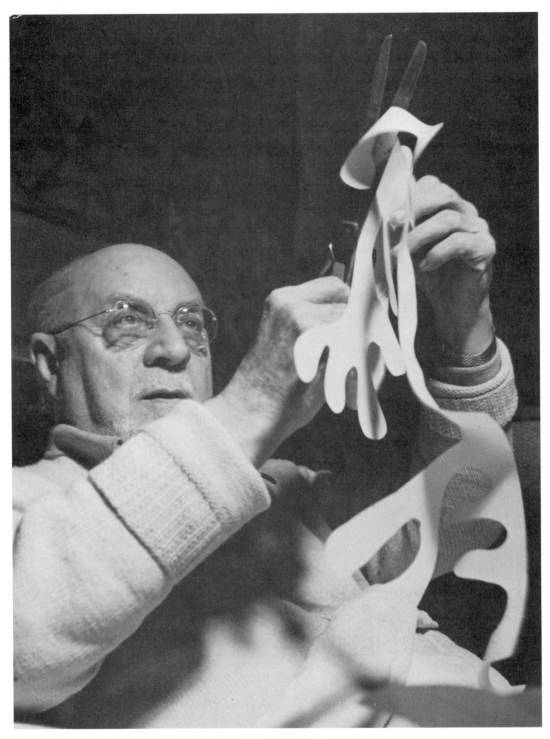

Henri Matisse at Vence.

Carving in Pure Color

THE AUTUMN of 1947 was very balmy, so we lingered in Golfe-Juan, thinking that the mild Mediterranean climate was good for Claude, who could stay outdoors almost all the time with his nurse. In December we were still around, since Picasso had become interested in ceramics and experimented with passion at the Madoura pottery, owned by Monsieur and Madame Ramié. One day Lydia called to say that Matisse was feeling better and it would be nice if we could make the trip to visit him.

When we arrived, we found Matisse armed with a huge pair of scissors, carving boldly into sheets of paper painted in all kinds of bright colors. Each one had been painted in a flat tone according to his instructions. Delicately holding the piece that suited his purpose in his left hand, he wound it and turned it while his right hand skillfully cut the most unpredictable shapes. Women, vegetation, birds, dancers, bathers, starfish, abstractions—a complete world emerged from his hands, full of strength and vitality.

It was fascinating to watch him at work, carving in pure color.

The leftovers were examined carefully; sometimes they provided un-expected elements of design, or he used them to manifest the void, to give life to a keyhole effect. On wild areas of colors pinned on the wall, these shapes were adjusted a little more to the left, a little more to the right, up or down, according to his indications, until finally the entire assemblage started to interact and bloom.

Next to his bed he had a revolving bookshelf, which he used mostly for his tools, his pills, and his handkerchiefs, which he called *at-chi* (supposedly the word "handkerchief" in Tahitian). Labels were written on each compartment. Painkillers he named happiness pills. At the top of the shelves stood an army of lead and graphite pencils of different degrees of softness, all impeccably sharpened.

"How lucky can you be," said Picasso, "to have someone who so deftly prepares everything for you? When I look for a pencil it is always broken, and if it is any good it belongs to Françoise. She is selfish; she works all the time and never proposes to help me."

Laughing, Matisse replied, "I do feel sorry for you!"

We went on chatting as the cutouts went on dropping joyously over the bedspread. Up to that point Matisse had been busy creating designs but had not assembled anything. All of a sudden he retrieved a tiny black shape that had fallen during the elaboration of a larger form. He looked at it. "It is a portrait in profile of Françoise with her long hair—a small figure kneeling. Now I see what I must do."

He got hold of a sheet of paper painted bright green and a piece of magenta paper, and considered the shocking clash of these two colors and the sobering effect that would be achieved by the addition of the black shape. He nodded approvingly at his choice and began to cut a strong, intricate pattern in the glaring magenta paper, much larger than the tiny kneeling figure. He then went back to chisel two black sea-weedlike patterns. Using a tray in front of him, he began to set the cutouts on the meadow-green rectangle. Soon the strong magenta form was established vertically in the center and the tiny figure was firmly positioned toward the lower left corner. Several times he arranged, displaced, and oriented the two seaweed pieces, one in the upper left corner and the other in the upper right, until he was finally satisfied.

In the same spirit he cut a black form for the lower right corner, but when it was placed the whole composition looked too even, a bit dull, the effect of symmetry too strongly affirmed. He removed that element immediately and with his gigantic scissors began to reduce it mercilessly, until it became quite small but sharp-edged. All prettiness had been eliminated, but in the process of miniaturization the energy had been maximized.

We were spellbound, in a state of suspended breathing, knowing that Matisse was about to locate the remaining part. But he did not hesitate at all; he seemed driven. Slowly but with determination his fingers brought down the chiseled, three-lobed form and applied it firmly to the lower right side of the apple-green surface. It was just perfect. It all closed in, achieving instantaneous unity, with enough balance but not too much, with enough tension and enough rest, enough feeling of danger and of elation, enough zest and respite—a complete satisfaction for the being, for the mind, for the senses. A fragile masterpiece was there in front of us, defying eternity.

In the impressive silence that followed, Lydia, armed with pins, managed to attach the five forms to the background without displacing them. We sat there like stones, slowly emerging from a trance. We had traveled with him all the way, in complete empathy with his every movement and decision. In the meantime a smiling and triumphant Matisse carefully chose one of his well-sharpened pencils, wrote a dedication, and presented the small marvel to me. It read:

To Françoise Gilot
Respectfully
   H. Matisse Dec. 47

I was very moved . . . and there it was in my hands.

Picasso looked a bit like a child who has been deprived of his favorite candy, but Matisse knew better than to leave him craving in vain. He went back to his scissors. "Now for you," he said.

As a background he chose a sheet of a rather sedate red, somewhat Phoenician in tone, and then he selected a dull, slatelike type of dark gray, almost a black, from which to cut out a powerful arabesque. Its repetitive rhythm surged, majestical, magnetic, self-contained. It was not

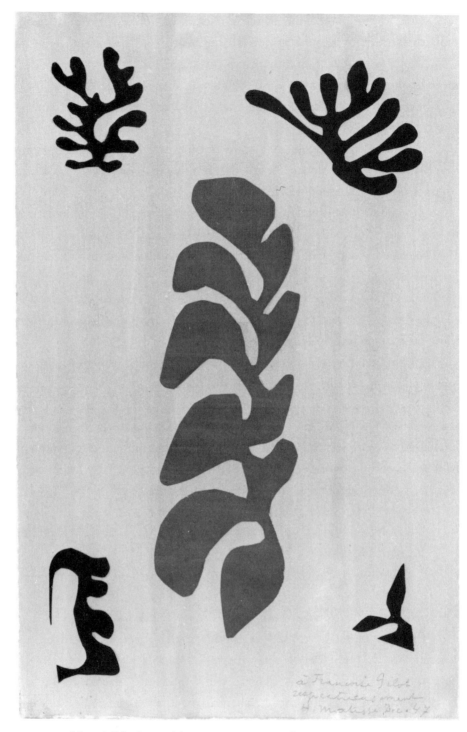

Henri Matisse. Abstract portrait of Françoise Gilot,
December 1947.

Photo of Françoise Gilot, 1948.

redundant but quite elaborate in its apparent simplicity. He dropped it on the red paper and began to play with it. After a few minutes of reflection, he decided to center it and to set it vertically; then Lydia pinned it in place, gave it back, and he took a pencil to sign it.

It was his gift to Pablo Picasso that day. We were both delighted—more than delighted: fulfilled, enchanted, and beguiled. In a way that escaped analysis, these cutouts were mysteriously in tune with each of us. They had the essentiality of a Chinese ideogram. They were synthetic portraits of what "Pablo" and "Françoise" were and would ever be, but they also had the charm of spontaneity and playfulness.

Again in December of 1947, we discussed the topic of portraits, how the elusive nature of a human being can eventually be communicated and captured. Picasso believed in chance occurrences, and one day with Matisse he related the story of an old Spanish painter he had known who used to say, "If it comes out with a blue coat, I know she must be the Virgin Mary; if it comes out with a beard, out of necessity it must be Saint Joseph; and if I try to paint a Venus and a splash of green comes out, I know I must paint a frog instead."

"By the way," Picasso said, "in the cutout that you gave Françoise, why did you say that the black shape pinned toward the lower left corner evoked Françoise, kneeling? In fact she is there twice. The whole thing is her, and yet she is also in it, in the same posture as a donor in a religious painting of the fifteenth century."

Matisse answered, "I don't know. The small black figure was for me a chance occurrence, then in an instant of recognition it became Françoise. I used the flash of awareness as a key, a module from which her whole universe would naturally spring forward and unfold, asking to be revealed, to be expressed with the simple means of color and proportion."

Picasso became thoughtful and then replied, "There is a point that is not clear. Why should the flash of recognition point out the tiny black silhouette as Françoise *kneeling*? There is an innuendo there. Do you associate her in your mind with a posture of devotion? Or with praying, perhaps? I can tell you she is just the opposite, quite a rebellious character, without consideration or respect—a nihilist! I can imagine her only standing erect or proudly riding a horse. That's the way I see her."

Matisse retorted, "Nevertheless, there is a reclining nude in the Museum of Antibes who seems to be taken from—"

Picasso interrupted. "No, no, that painting originated from an old habit of painting reclining nudes. The one I did in the spring of 1946 with Europa riding Zeus in the shape of a bull is much more to the point."

Matisse concluded, "In life there are many facets; opposite truths are not mutually exclusive. You might ask Françoise herself if she acknowledges any kinship with the kneeling posture and its meaning."

I ventured that I was perhaps a proud supplicant, and we had a good laugh.

I pursued the topic of self-portrait and self-characterization, examples of which could be found in the work of both painters at different times. I was intrigued by the fact that Matisse had repeatedly included his own presence in his canvases and in his drawings—mirror images that included himself at work or, even more bluntly, his own hand and the drawing in progress. Apart from straightforward self-depiction in the early years, such as the famous "suite" of one hundred etchings he had made for Ambroise Vollard in 1930, Picasso pictured himself in the guise of mythical figures or playing the part of Rembrandt making his self-portrait. He masked his own identity and used metaphors and paraphrases, but the allusions to himself were clear, either through physical resemblance or through the metaphor of an artist in the process of self-depiction.

"Well," Picasso said, "if I can appear only in disguise, that means that I am as modest as a violet, and more romantic than you French people are with your objectivity, your reason, your realism."

"That's right," I replied, "we are looking for the truth."

"Yes," said Matisse, "we observe reality and strive for the truth. For example, if I make a self-portrait, I won't conceal the cigarette I smoke, my glasses, the few hairs at the top of my head. My approach is not aesthetic. I want to characterize, eliminating what is not essential and what is therefore detrimental to the hypnotic power of the image. Integrating meaningful elements into a coherent whole is my unique goal."

Pablo was nonplussed that Matisse dared not to give a damn about aesthetics, so he interjected that the Fauvist master had better at least admit that he subordinated everything in a painting to the interplay of flat decorative surfaces and did not care about the personality of the sitter. But Matisse was not about to beat a retreat; he stood his ground, stating that in his canvases the interplay of flat areas of color was intended only to create surface tension, certainly not to please the eye. What's more, the colors were attuned to the particular mood of the model.

It was hard for Pablo to accept that remark, which he considered an invasion of his territory, since he did not strive for ideal beauty but for the full expression of the particular. Matisse saw his irritation and concluded: "But you go even further—you attempt to displease!" So peace was restored by agreeing that if Matisse did not care about the aesthetic, Picasso was fundamentally antiaesthetic, which was stretching the truth in both cases.

Two days later, as an afterthought, Matisse sent me a short letter, along with a photograph of himself looking at his cat and a photograph of a linear drawing—an unflattering, quite humorous self-depiction. I appreciated his quizzical gaze and the funny pout of the lower lip, firmly holding on to a cigarette. Both helped me to evoke his features in my mind. Though he was a bit austere at times when he remained silent, the penetrating look of his blue eyes behind gold-rimmed spectacles probed deep, and his face, with its well-trimmed beard, was shapely and firm, his complexion very pale; the general impression was one of stability and alertness. Everything about him was neat. Always stylish in his dress, he usually wore in public elegant homespun tweed jackets with matching flannel trousers, good leather shoes, and a felt hat in the winter, loose smocks with lighter slacks and a large-brimmed Panama hat in the summer. At home, while at work, he sometimes wore a hat tilted backward or covered his bald skull with a turban. During the day he smoked cigarettes and small cigars as an outlet for nervous tension. He had a fondness for impeccable light blue or white shirts, and he owned a complete collection of cashmere sweaters, handmade cardigans and pullovers in all colors. His cleanliness was a mark of his origin in northern France. He had the patrician looks of a British gentleman. People who did not know him could have mistaken him for a famous surgeon or a physician.

In his youth Matisse had enjoyed rowing, hiking, and even horseback riding, though he complained of his lack of proficiency in this sport. Later, in his seventies, when I knew him, he became quite stout,

Henri Matisse with his cat, December 1947.

Reverse side of photo showing Matisse's inscription to
Françoise Gilot.

Self-portrait drawing of Matisse, July 1947.

because he could no longer exercise. He always stood with his back very straight, his movements showed good coordination, and because he had great grace and dignity, he did not appear to be heavy. His regal bearing conveyed the same huge feeling as that of an opera singer, whose broad chest implies the projection of powerful resonances. Matisse's large chest enabled him to breathe out rhythms and color in a way that never cluttered his compositions.

While I kept looking at the photographs and daydreaming about the Fauvist master, Pablo's inarticulate grumblings brought me back to reality. He did not see why these tokens of affection should have been sent to me rather than to him, as an echo of our conversation about aesthetics or the lack of it, but he seemed to accept this proof of his friend's interest in my future development as an artist with good grace, as if it reinforced his own appreciation of me.

In addition to painting, Pablo had started working on a series of sugar-lift aquatints to illustrate a limited edition of sonnets by Góngora, a Spanish poet of the golden century (1561–1627), whose elaborate style he enjoyed. Góngora's elliptical refinements also delighted me; we had a wonderful time selecting which poems were most appropriate for the project. One written in praise of El Greco, this *strange* and *foreign* painter, was of course selected. Other sonnets that I remember less well were dedicated to beautiful ladies and allowed Picasso to express the women's typical stately Spanish grace with incredible skill and lyricism. For once he let himself go and did not allow his intellect to tamper with what had been a spontaneous response to deeply felt emotions. He was also pleased because I helped somewhat to improve the translation and was as passionate as he was about that project.

I always wondered what kind of art Picasso would have produced if he had remained in Spain all his life. Even returning once in a while would have brought him solace, but on account of Franco's regime, of course, he did not want to go. Residing in Golfe-Juan, so close to the Mediterranean Sea, was the next best thing, yet silently he longed for his arid land and its proud people.

In Provence there was always a moment of gloom toward the middle of December, when the sea became dark and angry and the southeast wind brought clouds from Italy that started to burst open over the Alps and brought torrential rain from Monte Carlo to Marseilles. That year a violent storm created havoc in the small harbor of Golfe-Juan, and many yachts at anchor broke their moorings and ran amok, sinking other yachts. The following morning the harbor was a shambles; from the windows of the Villa Pour Toi it looked as if large white birds had collapsed onto one another.

Since Pablo had finished etching the plates for the Góngora, we decided that it was time to go back to Paris for a while, to take the plates to the Lacourière engraving workshop, where they could be processed and printed before they oxidized. Sitting back with Claude on my lap while Marcel drove, I found it pleasant to watch the changing landscape. During these trips Pablo was always relaxed. He felt a reprieve, a temporary respite from impending doom; while he was on the road, nothing and no one could catch up with him. Coaxed by Marcel, we even savored a nice meal in Saulieu, drank some burgundy wine (an exceptional treat, a breach in our spartan diet), and arrived rather late at the studio in the rue des Grands Augustins.

The next morning we enjoyed the subtlety of the gray light, the pale northern sky, the harmony of blue slate and zinc roofs matching the honey tones of the ancient stone buildings. We were home. We resumed our normal lifestyle. Visitors came in the morning, and after a light lunch we invariably worked until late at night; then dinner and more work. We enjoyed the same routine day in and day out, but at the same time, creatively, things were in permanent motion; paintings kept changing, a process of genesis was unfolding. Apart from work and more work, Pablo's main preoccupation was the elaborate cultivation of artistic friendships and the reflections that followed such interactions.

Whenever Pablo cared about someone, he expected complete candor from that person. Out of possessiveness, he wished for the person concerned to become transparent to him. But once he learned what he wanted to know, he gossiped, became manipulative, or altogether lost interest, so his friends tended to be secretive if they wished the relationship to endure. Jealous of their privacy, his French friends especially resisted Pablo's direct or oblique lines of inquiry. They remained elusive with delight, probably enjoying Pablo's frustration. If he could not rely on facts, his imagination was at work, building up one seemly or unseemly hypothesis after another. He would try to interest me or his secretary, Jaime Sabartés, in his most recent flight of fancy. Both of us usually dismissed his incongruous fantasies with a shrug of the shoulders, especially when he thought he had gained some new knowledge about his friends' private lives or sexual behavior.

At times Pablo was in luck; he found out something that no one had told him. Events played into his hand, so to speak, and it was harder for people to keep cool and remain unconcerned.

One morning Fernand Mourlot of the Mourlot lithographic workshop came to visit and casually said that Matisse was in town for a few days. That called for an expedition. Pablo could hardly wait until the next day to call on his friend without warning. We went to the handsome apartment building where Matisse resided and worked on the two upper floors. Coming out of the elevator, we found the door slightly ajar. Probably Lydia had gone upstairs to bring back a painting. Dragging me behind him, Pablo did not hesitate to enter. First we went through the hallway, left as usual in complete darkness. As we proceeded silently toward the sitting room, Matisse popped out from behind a tapestry door-curtain, shouting, "Coo-coo, coo-coo!" Not expecting such a close encounter, we jumped backward.

Matisse, who had probably wanted to play a practical joke on Lydia, was as flabbergasted as we were to meet us face to face; he was embarrassed, knowing that Pablo would take advantage of the situation and probably gossip later on. And, in fact, Pablo looked as satisfied as a tomcat with a mouse under his paw. Innocently he said, "Well, my friend, I did not know you played hide-and-seek with Lydia."

Matisse smiled rather weakly. Fortunately for him, Lydia came back soon thereafter, carrying a beautiful painting and looking at us in a very no-nonsense and businesslike fashion.

After a few more ironic comments, Pablo, for once generous, decided it was time to leave. Once in the elevator, he started to laugh. "So the master was playing hide-and-seek with Lydia, at his age! I never dreamed I would catch him at a thing like that."

On the boulevard Montparnasse, which had witnessed so many of the pranks and eccentricities of his own youth, he sobered up and asked, "Well, in the light of this incident, what do you make of Matisse's relationship to Lydia?"

"Nothing, really. As far as friends are concerned, I don't probe. I am satisfied with the information they volunteer; I take things at face value."

Pablo snapped back, "You mean at face-to-face value! Where is your sense of humor? I find you very priggish today. As far as Matisse is concerned, you become as protective as if he were made of sugar. I am not attacking him, mind you—on the contrary, I am happy if he can enjoy a moment of playfulness, since I am so fond of him. But why is he always so formal with me, so composed? He could confide in me, trust me. Am I not his best friend?"

I replied that most certainly his feelings were reciprocated, but that he, Pablo, had to understand that his friend was not necessarily ready to live a fully transparent life, like a goldfish in a fishbowl, even though he painted goldfish often enough.

Pablo went on: "My curiosity is legitimate. If I did not care, I would not want to know about the emotions underlying a specific work by Matisse, like *Blue Eyes*, for example.* It is not like with any of his other models; there is a definite feeling, more than a casual aesthetic or sensuous interest. In any case, I can't understand how Matisse can manage not to lose his head in front of a model like that."

"Quite right—that's why you are better off working from memory. That way there are only creative conflicts, not existential ones. What's more, you have such good visual memory that the women in your life don't have to sit for you to find themselves glorified, caricatured, or even metamorphosed into monsters or giantesses, according to your mood of the moment. In fact, there is something uncanny about your visual memory. I have seen you leaf through an art book halfheartedly and come up with new ideas derived from some of the material that you stared at for a second."

Pablo interjected, "It means I have a well-trained eye, and after all, these images are just more vocabulary that I can incorporate into my own."

I followed suit. "Yes, but the way you capture the essence of so many of nature's creatures is truly amazing. I can't begin to enumerate them all: monkeys, bulls, horses, dogs, cats, roosters, lobsters, owls, fish, toads, even insects, whether abstract or realistic, seem willing to enter your oeuvre as if it were Noah's ark."

Pablo smiled. "Right, there are enough animals in my drawings, etchings, and paintings to fill a zoo, but, you see, it's very simple. I identify them with a few signs, just as you might evoke them with a word. It suffices; the belief in presence is created."

I agreed. "Yes, but there is a difference between an iconic image† and a descriptive painting. In fact, I believe that you rejoin Matisse there, though your methods are entirely different. He puts a model in front of him almost as a decoy, to pacify his rational mind, while at the same time the person, object, or landscape is only there as a mirror

---

*This is the title of a famous portrait of Lydia by Matisse, painted in 1935.

†*Iconic image* meaning a sacred picture in general, not simply a Byzantine, Greek, or Russian icon.

reflecting his own project, his imaginative self in the process of becoming. He looks through the model rather than at the model. Matisse questions nature to invent his art by condensing his most intense sensation, whereas you don't start with sensation and perception, you focus on subjective and objective *notions* that already exist in your mind and then project a synthesis through hieroglyphics or at times more readily identifiable signs. Nevertheless, I think you succeed, because during childhood you drew from nature and confided your observations to your excellent memory for future use and combination."

Pablo was really elated. "Well, after all, God was only an artist like us all, never being able to make up his mind once and for all, creating on the same day the kangaroo and the giraffe because he was already bored with the sensibility and appropriateness of form he had expressed with the lion and the tiger. Diversity, diversity, that's the point, and yet all mammals have the same number of vertebrae and other similarities, which avoids confusion and simplifies organization: disorder in order and order in disorder. What a mess—nothing to be proud of!"*

Since Pablo had now settled God's account and put nature back in its place, ignoring on purpose all he knew about evolution, he was in an excellent mood and felt the urge to go home and work. In his encounter with Matisse, he knew he had had the upper hand, at least that day. Therefore he was inclined toward leniency and generosity, as for once he was in empathy with another artist's need for childish practical jokes to relax from the incredible tension necessary to produce beguiling icons rather than simple works of art.

More than ever convinced of a parallelism or a convergence in his and Matisse's efforts, Pablo showed special regard for his friend. He later remained silent and did not indulge in any cynical gossip. I was impressed and pleased to see that when he really cared, he could exercise a measure of self-restraint.

---

*Picasso claimed that he did not believe in God, but he used God's name in speaking, and finding this metaphoric God at fault was one of his favorite exercises.

Henri Matisse in the garden at Le Rêve, Vence, around 1943.

Generation Gap and Time Perspective

HENRI MATISSE was born on December 31, 1869, in his maternal grandmother's house at Le Cateau-Cambrésis in Picardy. Pablo Ruiz Picasso was born in Málaga on October 25, 1881. And I was born in Paris on November 26, 1921. Matisse's mother had been artistic and so was my mother; as to Picasso, he was the son of a painter, a professor at the School of Fine Arts.

Between Matisse and Picasso there was a gap of twelve years, between Matisse and me a gap of fifty-two years, and between Picasso and me a gap of forty years. The differences in our life experience and background mattered a great deal, even though no one at the time seemed to recognize the difficulties they entailed. The twelve-year gap between Matisse and Picasso was easier to bridge than the gap between them and me, because Matisse had not started painting seriously until the age of twenty, and only after he had passed the exams called "capacity at law," and worked as a clerk in an attorney's office. In contrast, Pablo, the son of a painter, unable (or, more probably, unwilling) to study anything at school, had been tutored in painting by his father from early childhood and was a full-blown artist by the age of fourteen.

As to myself, even though I was tutored in art history and art by my mother and other teachers (mostly in drawing and watercolors), art was considered a secondary activity. Like Matisse, I had to go through the normal French curriculum of a B.A. in Philosophy (passed, fortunately, at age sixteen and a half), to which were added a year of English literature and two years of law school, before I had the courage to drop everything and dedicate myself just to painting.

So on one side were two full-fledged artists, two celebrated masters of the twentieth century, and on the other side was my meager person. On their side, the wealth of an already acclaimed body of work; on my side, a bright mind and a vivid imagination but most of the achievements still to come in the future.

Because I was intellectually quite mature for my age, they both adopted the fiction that they could converse with me on equal terms, and they indulged me because I was a woman and not unattractive. They also talked to me as if I were one of them, which I knew I was not. They assumed that, starting from the same premises, I would necessarily reach the same conclusions they did, which I often did not. They had a tendency to include me in their world, which I was glad to study with the greatest interest, yet my deeper feelings were telling me that I did not belong there, because I already had precise notions of what I wanted to achieve. Even though it was a rare privilege to be present and to participate in so many dialogues, it was also an uneasy and at times confusing situation.

I felt that many of the conversations were reiterations of the men's artistic convictions, spelled out in part for my benefit. Even though voices were kept at a pleasant pitch and the tone was conciliatory, there were undercurrents. Contradictory, unspoken statements stood there, towering like concrete walls in my mind's eye. Outwardly playful sentences were exchanged, but I could not overcome the ominous feeling of being witness to a covert battle rather than to a conversation. From the start Matisse had known that my aesthetic inclinations were on his side—Pablo himself had made that clear—so he counted me in his camp. At the same time, Pablo knew that I loved him and cared for his work, so he counted me in his camp.

Since all is fair in love and war, I played all kinds of useful parts:

arbiter, hostage, ambassador of good will, *agent provocateur*, and so on. With me around, both painters enjoyed their *guerre en dentelle* and their friendly debates twice as much.

On the positive side, both Matisse and Picasso probably saw my aptitudes more clearly than I did and were interested in developing my native gifts. It was as if they were inscribing things in my mind so that I would become their future witness. I believe they wanted me to collect evidence, to record their dialogues, to bear testimony to the true nature of their relationship, to its artistic necessity. They were talking to me in the present but also cogently making a statement for the future.

Afterward it took me a great many years to develop a vision of what things were really like underneath as well as on the surface, to extract a meaning from all the fragments of conversations I remembered, including some apparent contradictions. They certainly did not see eye to eye on many things. Matisse wanted to reach a nondualistic, global vision of the universe as permeated by love in the broad sense of the term. His primary goal was to unite. Pablo was possessed by the desire to know, to analyze, to discover, even if that meant in part to destroy or to divide. Matisse seemed to believe that the ultimate reality in the universe was an innate thrust toward coherence in all things, and he wanted to join in, while Pablo suspected an inherent malignancy in the general scheme of things. Basically Manichean, he felt that the die were loaded, that it was incumbent upon him to find out where and why. Positive in itself, this principle of cogent doubt was at times pursued to such extremes that he overshot the mark. Rational deductions could start from such illogical premises that they led eventually to absurd rationalizations.

Once in early 1948, Matisse was as usual in bed when we went to see him. He was in an exuberant mood, showing all the small gadgets that were readily available in the revolving bookshelf. Since he could have died in 1941 or 1942 from the numerous complications after his cancer operation in Lyon, Matisse now greeted each new day as a day of respite, and thus his work during the latter part of his life was a permanent miracle, going against all the odds that threatened his very existence.

Pablo was also in high spirits, and the conversation started with alacrity. The topic was drawing. Wasn't linear drawing the most demanding form of expression and also the purest, since each stroke had to define itself and the positive and negative space on each side as well? They concurred that day on the desirability of avoiding the angular intricacies of German Gothic style, preferring the openness and the flowing clarity of the Italian school, but above all they praised Ingres's pristine perfection and the utter conciseness of Cézanne.

In the revolving bookshelf, Matisse kept a sketchbook, among other paraphernalia. He showed it to us. It was full of rapid, signlike notations, an intimate document of his inquisitive mind at work. From it the conversation followed general considerations about what the two artists respectively tried to accomplish, and then Matisse came to the notion of trends and families of artists, in the sense of traditions handed down from generation to generation, not through genetics but through oral teaching linking one artist to the next, as from Perugino to Raphael or from Verrocchio to Leonardo da Vinci. He went on, "As long as some painters continue to be interested in our ideas or our works, we will not be dead."

It seemed to me that Matisse's body of work alone was enough to ensure his immortality, but he was adamant that it was equally important for an artist to remain alive in the mind of another artist and to a certain extent in that artist's oeuvre. Matisse and Pablo concurred on this point and called this the chain.

"That does not prevent each new artist from being entirely different," Matisse continued, "but he or she must also entertain a dialogue with the dead and keep them alive within himself or herself. My son Pierre [an art dealer in New York] sent me catalogues of contemporary American painters," and he handed some of these catalogues to Pablo and me. At that time we had not yet heard of Arshile Gorky, William Baziotes, Robert Motherwell, Jackson Pollock, and Adolph Gottlieb, but Matisse was already interested and so fervently alive, so open to the future. "What do you think that they have incorporated from us? And in a generation or two, who among the painters will still carry a part of us in his heart, as we do Manet and Cézanne?"

All of a sudden, I understood what he meant and what he was after: a permanent metamorphosis, yes, but also each artist being nourished by his love and understanding of the pilgrimage of his predecessors, a long chain of visual tradition leading from the Magdalenian designs in prehistoric caves to as yet unknown developments far ahead in the future. Similarities, meanderings, zigzags, and contradictions all bringing a new leaf to the tree of life.

Pablo glanced at the catalogues and shrugged his shoulders. Unlike his friend, he had not visited the United States, and even with all the art dealers and collectors he had in New York, whatever happened there remained a remote abstraction. The topic was dropped in a philosophical manner. "Well," Pablo said, "a new subject matter, a new painter!"

"What do you mean?" inquired Matisse. "Isn't it rather 'A new painter, a new theme'?"

This was a deadlock. It meant, in fact, that for Pablo the concept came first, and that if you knew what to paint, you always knew how; whereas Matisse felt that it was the artist's temperament that led him to discover the theme best suited to show his finest qualities to advantage.

They both glanced in my direction. I knew that they expected me to play my part. "Don't you think this debate is getting a little bit rhetorical—a kind of chicken-egg problem?" I said. "When we are using words apropos of visual arts, isn't it only a farfetched equivalence, or at best a fiction? Isn't painting the art of silence?"

"Well, you got out of a judgment-of-Solomon type of situation fast enough, but the art of silence.... What! This is only a sophism. During the Cubist period we even introduced words as well as collages in our canvases," said Pablo.

Matisse looked at me with a benign smile, as if I could ask him any question I wanted. For him I had scored with the art of silence.

I asked if we could possibly be shown some of his most recent drawings. He was happy to oblige, and Lydia brought a large portfolio full of studies of one model. A large number of simple linear variations attested to a splendid freedom of the imagination and the hand. The open, flowing lines transformed the white of the paper into glorious light. The proportions varied, but character was always present, each time with a different emphasis. A cheek could be ripe as a peach, the chin voluntary, the neck elongated, and in the next sketch none of these features were stressed but linear notations accented eyebrow, eye, and nose. On the next sheet of paper the undulating pattern of the hair echoed the sensuous bow shape of the mouth. Nothing was taken for granted; there were no lazy repetitions. Each time Matisse had discovered his model anew with controlled mastery, but mostly with surprise and delight. He liked to think that the multiplicity of his thoughts revolved around the unity of his feeling.

Pleased with my deep attention and obvious rapture, he made some comments about how linear notation should be musical and open (so as to allow the passage of light), and stressed that lines never express contours but volume.

I remarked that some drawings were expansive and dilated, while in others the volumes went hurtling into each other as if possessed by a centripetal motion. He answered that these differences could reflect not only his own mood but the lesser or greater self-absorption of the model. Pablo commented on the almost complete absence of straight lines. Were they not necessary to stabilize the design? Matisse disagreed; for him they were not organic in character to depict a living being.

One thing I did not dare to discuss but that I could not help but think of was all the rooms and corridors that were left in almost total darkness at Le Rêve, Matisse's home in Vence. Was it possible that the artist who juxtaposed such bright tones, the painter who seemed to have banished the contrast of light and shadow in his paintings and replaced them with the interplay of different sets of complementary colors, could enjoy closed shutters in his home, allowing the sun to penetrate only in restricted areas? For me it evoked the miserly ways of provincial people, who seldom allow sunlight into their sitting rooms for fear it might fade the curtains and the upholstery.

This *camera oscura* effect was more understandable in Pablo Picasso's painting studio in the rue des Grands Augustins in Paris, where the doors, beams, and ceiling were black and most windows were still boarded, as during the war, with the exception of one large window to the left of the easel, which Pablo opened to concentrate light on the canvas in progress. Given his desire to enhance contrast and dramatic effect, the darkness seemed to be in the order of things and quite in keeping with his temperament.

At that time I had not yet seen many of Matisse's most important paintings in which black played a major role and even dominated the structure of the composition, but I had read a letter from Vincent van Gogh to Émile Bernard in which van Gogh, describing the checked black-and-white apron of a woman from Arles, wrote that the contrast of black and white had to be added to the contrast of the other sets of complementary colors. He declared that the two colors should be used unmixed, right out of the tube, not to give an equivalent of dark and light but to provide nonatmospheric local tones for any objects in the picture. In art, nonatmospheric means not taking into account the graying effect of perspective. The local tone of an object, given its distance from the painter, is its general overall hue as observed in an even light, not at the point where it receives the brightest light, the accent, or its darkest shadow. Seen from a distance, a bright red becomes pink, for example.

This assessment was contrary to the belief held by the painters of the Impressionist school, who had banished pure white and black from their palette, saying that these colors did not exist in nature (outdoors). They replaced white with pale blue in the morning and with mauve, salmon pink, or orange through the warm hours of the afternoon. Instead of black they used ultramarine or purple.

During another short visit that Pablo and I paid to Matisse one afternoon, the two friends engaged in a lively discussion about the painters of the past and who among them had been most important in their own development. Gustave Courbet was honored first, for his anticonformism, for his fight against the academic establishment, and his robust appetite for life. Next to Courbet, Édouard Manet got his share of laurels. It was a duet of unrestricted praise for a painter who could set large areas of gray and black against any delicate pink or lemon yellow he wanted to enhance. Each of them acknowledged what a constant source of inspiration Manet had been to him throughout his life. Matisse referred to some of his own still lifes as a proof of his devotion to Manet, as did Pablo. For Picasso, Manet could do no wrong, especially since in his youth the French master had had a strong inclination toward Spanish art.

I contributed to the discussion by saying that even though I understood Manet's artistic and historical importance and loved his intimate and formal composition, I thought that in the *Execution of Emperor Maximilian* he had not reached the monumental dramatic strength of Goya in his *Tres de Mayo*.

"Yes, but you see," said Matisse, "he disengaged pure painting from subject matter, and that is why we are his heirs. His themes have an abstract presence, a dreamlike quality. Their sensuousness is post-Baudelairian, not directly evocative. He has flattened the forms, reduced shadows to the linear contour that accompanies the shape, and most important, he knew the importance of black as a color. Pissarro, the pure Impressionist, admitted that Manet was stronger than them all because he could make light with black.

"Do you know what happened to me when I went to visit Auguste Renoir for the first time at his home Les Collettes, on the hills close to Cagnes? After he very kindly showed me some of his recent works, mostly landscapes full of atmospheric qualities, in which he did not fail to point out his use of emerald green and ultramarine blue, he asked to see the canvases I had brought along. At first he did not say anything, as if taken aback. He looked puzzled, perplexed, then he made up his mind to open up and said, 'To tell you the truth, this is not at all up my alley. It goes against all my beliefs, all my achievements, even against my personal sensitivity. But I hold that you are a real painter, because you do something I could never do: use pure ivory black in large areas and make it stand on its plane as a given local tone. In your pictures, black is a color, black does not recede, it does not create a hole in the surface of the canvas, it is solid. I can't understand how you manage this effect, but I do understand that it implies real talent.' "

After this unexpected acknowledgment and the invitation to return, Matisse packed his things and left, feeling affirmed by his elder's recognition even if it had been formulated with a certain amount of reluctance. I thought that the story was quite illuminating. After that first encounter, Matisse went to visit Renoir several times, and he felt the visits had a bearing on his subsequent evolution.

Pablo contributed an anecdote of his own, to the effect that when Claude Monet (at the time he was painting waterlilies) had heard about Cubism, perhaps through Ambroise Vollard, his pronouncement had been, "As long as they have a different approach, they must be right."

Praising Monet's perceptiveness, Pablo concluded by quoting Cézanne's well-known remark, "Claude Monet was only an eye, but what an eye," now making it his own.

I have always been amused by the role of quotations in painters' conversations, such as "A gray day provides the best light" (Leonardo da Vinci) or "When the form reaches its plenitude, the light reaches its greatest intensity" (Cézanne). Of course, we all knew such key phrases. In Europe they were implanted in the minds of art students as soon as they were ready to use their first piece of charcoal. Later they became a part of the artists' intellectual bric-a-brac, even when they were meaningless or enigmatic. They cluttered the artists' minds as African masks, dried thistles, pieces of driftwood, and other paraphernalia cluttered their studios. They became the coins of the realm, they acted as passwords in secret societies. According to the quantity and the quality of the quotations that one could memorize, one was held in high esteem or was not so well regarded.

Of course, among painters, key sentences were a secondary consideration. Genius or talent came first, but nevertheless quotations were welcome. Such formulas were always readily exchanged in conversations; they were a cultural asset. Passed on through oral tradition, they were used in a highly ritualized fashion even by the most radical artists. At times quotations assimilated at an early age became bothersome, and one had to make a conscious effort to identify the specific item that had become an obstacle to one's development and get rid of it altogether.

The same was true of the dialogues between Matisse and Picasso about painters. Both wanted to verify that the very foundations of their artistic friendship were on solid ground: *a mutual understanding of the same artists and the same principles.* Their exchanges had a soothing and affirming effect on both of them.

To come back to the importance of black as a color in Henri Matisse's work and the lack of light in most of the rooms in his home: I went on building different hypotheses. Colors have a way of developing in the dark, because all one's senses are attentive and focused, and objects begin to glow in chiaroscuro. Perhaps that was one explanation of Matisse's dark rooms. But in fact, the real explanation came from Claude Duthuit, Matisse's grandson. He told me that when Matisse was

Françoise Gilot. *Self-Portrait in Profile*, 1947.

about forty years old, he experienced some blackouts that led him to think that he might lose his eyesight altogether. As one can imagine, this was not a pleasant discovery. His reaction was unusual. He started learning how to play the violin, a skill he found hard to master, since

Henri Matisse. *Portrait of Marguerite* (*Marguerite*), 1906.

he had been a reluctant pupil as a child. He wanted to make sure he could still soothe his soul, find an outlet for his feelings, even if his defective eyesight prevented him from being the artist he wanted to be. The other reaction was to lessen the demands made on his eyes by resting in semidarkness. He kept both habits even when the danger was averted.

I am told that Matisse became a fine musician, a feat that can be sensed through the exquisite tuning of his chromatic scale. When looking at the paintings with the solid, ominous black areas, usually vertical, one finds that the knowledge of their origin in a well-mastered personal drama makes them even more moving. What daring, what concision, what stoicism in *The Door* (1914); the painter of *The Joy of Life* knew how to confront his own inner drama, how to conjure fate, how to open his heart even though each dawn might be the last to bring back light and color. In the alchemical process, lead or black earth was the raw material used to initiate the first phase of transformation, and Matisse was a true alchemist. He did not fear darkness; he embraced it as the maternal and primordial source of creation.

In his pictures, black is often accompanied by blue, his favorite color. Often the violin and the violin case, lined in blue, sat quietly in darkness below an open window partly obscured by shutters and curtains. Life was suspended, life was sad and still, as in the verses by Baudelaire in "Harmonie du soir":

> *Le violon frémit comme un coeur qui on afflige,*
> *Un coeur tendre qui hait le néant vaste et noir.*
> *Le ciel est triste et beau comme un grand reposoir . . .* *

In a 1906 portrait, Matisse painted a black velvet ribbon, inherited from Édouard Manet's *Olympia*, around his daughter Marguerite's neck, to hide the scar of a tracheotomy that she had undergone during a grave illness. Black was a color, it was *the* color, it was the pitch to which all else was tuned. Black was at the beginning; all else proceeded from it. After the night wore out, at daybreak, light invaded the immensity of

---

*From "Evening Harmony," in *Les Fleurs du Mal*:

> *The violin quivers like a saddened heart,*
> *A tender heart that abhors the black, empty void.*
> *The sky is gloomy and beautiful like a large abandoned altar . . .*

the sky. Light was blue, and Matisse allowed that color to suffuse his universe.

But of course each evoked its opposite. Black called on white, blue on orange, soon followed by purple and yellow and linked by the middle contrast of red and green. Then it was the beginning of a dance; triangular relations were established from light purple to well-tempered green, the eye began to move from here to there and back here again. Red invaded the room, it became three goldfish in a globelike aquarium, soon to be superseded by the turquoise leaves of nasturtiums or set in place by a daring system of curves and exaggerated details.

Letter from Henri Matisse, "Cheers for Saint Françoise's
Day," 1948 ("Vive la Sainte Françoise de l'an mil neuf
cent quarante huit").

Some Letters

MATISSE corresponded with quite a few of his friends, but rarely with Picasso. Perhaps it was because he did not feel entirely at ease with Picasso, but I don't remember any letters being exchanged between the two men between 1946 and 1954. It was as if neither of them could afford to be spontaneous with the other; there was too much at stake. Remaining formal and keeping a safe distance seemed to be the best strategy on both sides.

Yet an intense curiosity about what was going on in the other artist's mind spurred them both toward new encounters. They had to discover new ways to keep the relationship going without seeming to stoop to a need for companionship and at the same time managing to avoid the frustration of long silences. The telephone had its advantages; since most messages were relayed by go-betweens such as Lydia and Madame Ramié, it acted as a screen as well as a means of communication. But one did not always find the right person at the right moment. Something else had to be invented, and Matisse was the first to find a different channel that could be used to the best advantage. Perhaps he came upon it by chance when he decided to write directly to me.

Each morning at home we had a ritual. Upon receiving the mail from the postman, I went to Pablo's room to hand it to him. One day I recognized the famous handwriting on an envelope on top of the pile. It was addressed to me. Not expecting any more personal attention from the master in Vence, after his photos and the gift of the cutout, I eagerly opened the envelope and beamed, unable to conceal my delight as I held the unfolded cutout in my hands. What an enchanting surprise! It read: "Cheers for Saint Françoise of nineteen hundred and forty-eight."

Pablo in turn grabbed the message and was really astonished. There was a bit of commotion at home that morning, on account of the beauty of the cutout but for another reason as well. It was usual in France to celebrate someone's saint's day by sending wishes that referred only to the name of the patron saint, omitting the word "day" or "fête," whereas in Spain the word "verbena" figured as an essential part of the good wishes. This led Picasso to believe that the letter referred to my own sanctity and not to the saint's day.

"First Matisse saw you as a kneeling figure and now as a saint— that's really too much! He really does not know you! If he had to cope with you, he would have a different opinion. No wonder he is deluded, since you always use such a sugary voice when you talk to him, keeping for me the vinegar of your sharpest comments ... Do you think he intends to say that you are a saint to bear with me, with my whims and my tantrums?"

I reassured him: "But of course not. This formulation is frequent in French; our language is elliptic."

Pablo shrugged his shoulders. "All right, all right, don't become technical. Nevertheless, he could have written to me rather than to you. Am I not his friend?"

I assuaged him further: "Yes, you are, but even though you carry about six Christian names, none of them happens to be honored today. You know very well that Matisse meant to be nice to you by celebrating the name of someone that you have chosen."

So the topic was dropped and everybody was happy for the rest of the day, especially me; it was such a joy to contemplate this delicate token of friendship. The cutout was both playful and thoughtful. Probably Matisse intuitively felt how lonesome I was and how difficult a situation I had to face day after day, coping with Picasso's unpredictable moods and the open or disguised hostility of many of his sycophants, who disliked me because I saw through their schemes. They always praised Picasso to the skies, usually with some ulterior financial motive.

It was impossible to look at the few friendly words and at the deftly cut plant forms without being deeply moved. Matisse's thoughtfulness, like a glimpse of the garden of Eden, comforted me and reinforced my self-confidence. Yet I did not know how to convey my gratitude. I was faced with a dilemma. On the one hand, I pondered how I could presume to address such an Olympian figure as Matisse, and on the other hand I was concerned about Pablo's reaction to any initiative on my part, since he was as territorial and possessive in friendship as in love. I came to the conclusion that sending one of my white gouaches rather than a thank-you note would be less subject to criticism and suspicion as far as Pablo was concerned. It was not hard to imagine Pablo's reaction if Matisse quoted some extracts of a very admiring letter of mine during our next visit to Vence! And it was not difficult to imagine the aftermath. Since I had to stick my neck out, I felt that sending a gouache had more chances of meeting with Pablo's approval, even if Matisse later made mincemeat out of my efforts.

After a bit of procrastination, during which I wondered if I had made the right decision, and after asking Pablo's opinion and getting his wholehearted permission, I finally selected a rather abstract self-portrait and sent it by normal mail, rolled inside a tube that unfortunately was not rigid enough and reached Vence in poor shape. Unaware of the mishap, I waited for an answer with butterflies in my stomach.

Pablo was as anxious as I was about Matisse's response to the gouache. When its arrival was not acknowledged, he became concerned that it might have been lost in the mail and that he would lose a chance to have Matisse's opinion about my work, so he inquired about it the next time he met his friend. Matisse must have been embarrassed not to have written earlier. This explained the tone of his letter dated April 22, 1948.

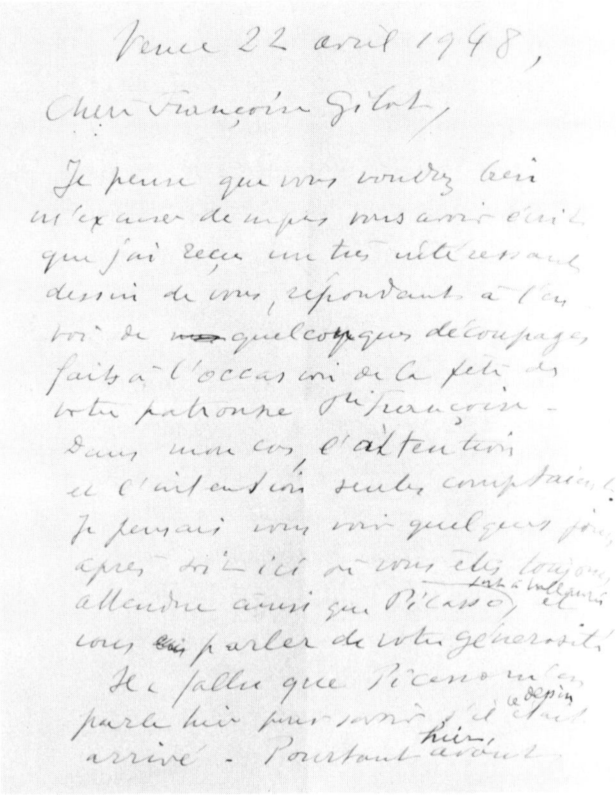

Vence 22 avril 1948,

Chère Françoise Gilot,

Je pense que vous voudrez bien m'excuser de ne pas vous avoir écrit que j'ai reçu un très intéressant dessin de vous, répondant à l'envoi de quelconques découpages faits à l'occasion de la fête de votre patronne Ste Françoise. Dans mon cas, l'attention et l'intention seules comptaient. Je pensais vous voir quelques jours après soit ici où vous êtes toujours attendue ainsi que Picasso, et vous parler de votre générosité.

Il a fallu que Picasso m'en parle hier pour savoir s'il était déjà arrivé - Pourtant avant hier avant

Letter from Matisse to Gilot dated April 22, 1948.

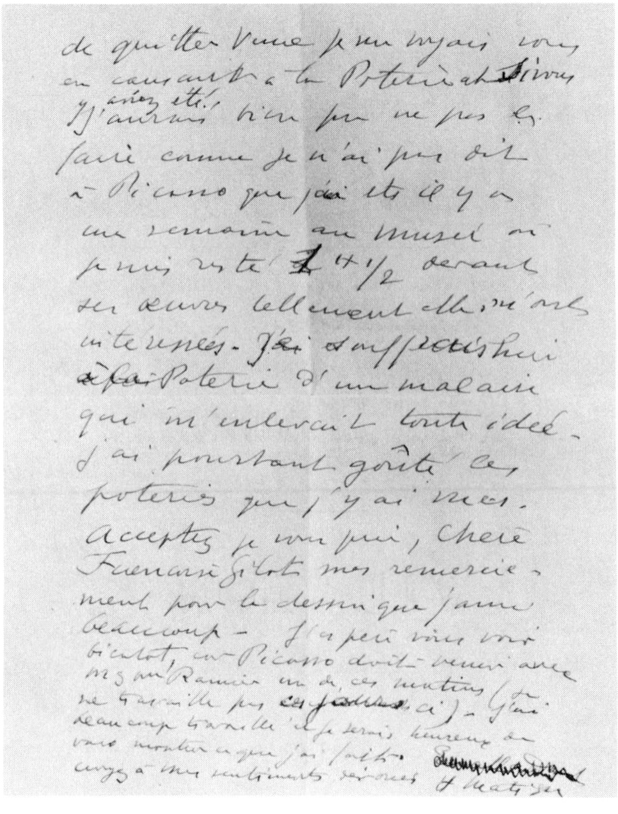

de quitter Vence je me voyais vous en causant à la Poterie ... y avez été! J'aurais bien pu ne pas le faire comme je n'ai pas dit à Picasso que j'ai été il y a une semaine au Musée où je suis resté 1 h 1/2 devant ses œuvres tellement elles m'ont intéressé. J'ai souffert hier à la Poterie d'un malaise qui m'enlevait toute idée. J'ai pourtant goûté les poteries que j'y ai vues. Acceptez je vous prie, Chère Françoise Gilot mes remerciements pour le dessin que j'aime beaucoup - J'espère vous voir bientôt, car Picasso doit venir avec Mg. Ramié un de ces matins (je ne travaille pas ces jours-ci) - J'ai beaucoup travaillé et je serais heureux de vous montrer ce que j'ai fait. Croyez à mes sentiments sincères

H Matisse

Vence   22 April 1948

Dear Françoise Gilot,

Certainly you will forgive me for not having written that I received a very interesting drawing of yours in answer to some rather plain cutouts made to celebrate the day of your patron St. Françoise.

For my part, the thoughtfulness and the intention alone mattered.

I believed that I would see you a few days later—either here where you and Picasso are always welcome or in Vallauris—and that I would speak of your generosity. As it happened, Picasso had to inquire yesterday about the drawing and ask if it had arrived.

Yet yesterday, before leaving Vence, I fancied myself discussing it with you at the potter's workshop, if you had been there. I might also not have done so, in the same way I did not tell Picasso that a week ago I went to the museum and spent an hour and a half in front of his works, so deeply was I enthralled by them. Yesterday at the pottery I suffered from an ailment that wiped out all ideas. I appreciated nevertheless the ceramics that I saw there.

Please accept, dear Françoise Gilot, my thanks for the drawing, which I liked very much. I hope to see you soon since Picasso is due to come with Madame Ramié any morning now (I am not at work here). I worked intensely and I would be happy to show you what I did.

Believe in my devoted feelings,

H. Matisse

It was too bad that Matisse had not felt well during his visit to the Madoura pottery in Vallauris the previous day. It must have been one of his first trips to the place where Picasso made all his ceramics. Also, there was a lot at stake for Matisse; he had a project for which he needed both technical craftsmanship and an atmosphere of love, friendship, and devotion, and he wondered whether Pablo would welcome his presence at the pottery. For the decoration of the Dominican chapel in Vence, Matisse was planning large ceramic designs on some of the walls, and he wished to use the facilities at Madoura to experiment with rather large tiles of red biscuit (clay that has been baked in the kiln once). Their upper surfaces were to be dipped into liquid white enamel. Once they were dry, he would be able to draw with a dark oxide on the prepared surfaces before they were all fired again in an electric kiln at the proper temperature.

Madame Suzanne Ramié, the artistic director, and her husband Jean, who owned the factory and dealt with the firing techniques, welcomed the project, but Matisse must have felt ill at ease, since a year earlier Pablo had hinted that he did not welcome Marc Chagall's presence at the workshop for any sustained amount of time because he needed the Ramiés' full involvement and dedication.* Madame Ramié had probably referred to that difficulty before Matisse came to Vallauris, so that if, once there, he had a malaise, it might have been due to anxiety as much as to his poor health.

In any case, Matisse did not need to worry, because Pablo's feelings of friendship were genuine. He greeted Matisse warmly and made it clear that as far as he was concerned, his friend was more than welcome to work at Madoura. In fact, the elder master could count on him if he could be of any help. There was no ambiguity in his attitude then or later, and it was one more proof of Matisse's exalted status in Picasso's mind, since he would not have dreamed of sharing the facilities with anyone else.

As I have said, the tiles of red clay had to be baked once before being dipped in the powdery white enamel mixed with water and arabic gum on which Matisse could draw before they went back to the kiln. These hand-performed processes required dexterity and patience. Once the tiles were shaped they had to dry without distortions, and they were not supposed to split or crack while drying or later in the kiln. Only perfect tiles were acceptable. That was the reason that Pablo was to accompany Madame Ramié when she took the first batch of successful tiles—to make the happy event a little bit more of a celebration. Given the large size of the tiles, the nature of the clay that had to be used (to allow pink undertones under the white enamel), and the fact that Matisse did not want any *chalmotte* (crushed or ground baked clay amalgamated to raw clay to strengthen the tile), which would have simplified the drying process, thus preventing warping, but would have made the surface less

---

*As soon as Picasso started to work at Madoura, his new activity was publicized in the press, and other artists became interested in working there. The pottery acquired instant renown.

even, manufacturing enough perfect tiles was quite a problem. The potters tested several different kinds of clays as well as different ways to make the tiles, but unfortunately, the results proved to be quite disappointing.

In the same letter to me, Matisse also mentioned having spent time at the Museum of Antibes in the Grimaldi Castle, a fortress built in the thirteenth century, studying a collection of Picasso's paintings and ceramics. On a subsequent visit he showed us a sketchbook revealing his curiosity about and interest in his friend's work. Matisse seemed to have especially appreciated the way in which some curvilinear torsions led the eye to visualize together those planes that simultaneously showed a front and a back view of the same figure. In his interpretation, the massive architectonic solidity of Pablo's forms lost their rigidity without losing their strength.

The memory of the conversation of February 1946 about his *Blue Nude*, in progress that year, had lingered in Matisse's mind (see page 24). Picasso had stated then that the local tone of an object could depart from observed reality only to the extent of a similar transposition in form. The monumental figures at the Museum in Antibes were quite abstract—all the shapes were far from imitative—but colorwise, though unnaturalistic, they looked more like pictorial renderings of imaginary sculptures than like the passionate recreation of a female nude. By studying them, pencil in hand, Matisse gained an insight into Picasso's use of the arabesque as a dynamic vortex defining volume, not only as an organic rhythm related to the lyrical power of color interplay on the surface of the canvas.

Yet Picasso's spirit of geometry did not satisfy him. The subordination of color to form, far from providing an answer to his preoccupations, was foreign to his vision. Colors had to determine each other's territory by their relative power of expansion. Colors were the wild beasts, interacting directly, creating shapes by the way in which they successfully ate up each other.

In the following letter, dated April 26, 1948, Matisse commented on my abstract self-portrait, which had been delivered to him in such bad condition that Lydia had had a lot of work ironing out the creases and restoring it thoroughly. When he wrote that it looked like him, he meant like one of his own drawings, but he implied at the same time that it did directly resemble some features of Lydia's face even more than his style of depicting her. With his acute sense of humor, he certainly enjoyed the ambiguity of placing himself, Lydia, and me at the corners of an equilateral triangle: Lydia's archetypal beauty as essence, his own creation as expression, and my work proceeding from both as spirit.

Vence   26 April 1948

Dear Françoise Gilot,

I am looking at your drawing. For the last three days it has been attached with fine pins to the door in front of me; in other words, I live with it almost all the time.

I like it very much, it is very noble, executed with great distinction and very well "designed." At first it was impossible to see it clearly because the postman brought it with its mailing tube crushed from one end to the other. It would not stay unrolled, its strong paper was wrinkled every two inches. To straighten it we put it inside a portfolio, but to no avail; it had to be pressed carefully with a warm iron on account of the gouache paint, and finally, fixed to the door in front of me, it is visible. It is presumptuous of me to say that it looks like me, especially since it has a beautiful plane between the upper part of the eye and the base of the nose that does not belong to me but to someone who is not far from me.

I am sure that you will also find it very beautiful (the drawing and the plane) when you come to visit me.

Are you now allowing me to hope, dear Françoise Gilot, that you will show me your work? Given my difficulties in leaving the house, could you not trust me for a few days with some of your drawings, so as to let me see them at leisure? I thank you in advance. Thanks again, see you soon.

Your devoted

H. Matisse

This gouache was not photographed, and I don't know what became of it, but I remember that I drew it with a graphite pencil in the still-

Letter from Matisse to
Gilot dated April 26, 1948,
Vence.

damp white tempera, thus producing an intalgio effect. I favored that technique at the time because it involved a perception of third dimension and texture that bare paper did not provide. I envisioned some of these sketches as projects for sculpture or bas-relief rather than as destined for further elaboration in painting. The relationship of form to empty space and the interplay of graphic rhythms in the total rectangle were my main concerns.

When I read Matisse's letter aloud it did not meet Pablo's approval. He did not like to think that my self-portrait could evoke Lydia, much less resemble a drawing by Matisse of his favorite muse, since he thought that I had already developed my own style. This epistle acted like banderillas on a fierce bull. Pablo's large head and shoulders bent dangerously forward while his feet stamped the floor as if he were ready to charge, but I knew that he was kidding. He was not really angry but enjoyed complaining that Matisse behaved as if he did not exist. In fact, Matisse's curiosity about my drawings and gouaches was rewarding to Pablo. Who else among painters of his generation could boast about such a meaningful relationship with a young artist? Wasn't he the most progressive and broad-minded figure in the art world? Hadn't he already accepted Dora Maar's career as a photographer and painter? (He was right; no one else in his generation would have stomached such a relationship without condemning the other person to failure in advance.) At such times he felt like the proud owner of a promising filly, so he was eager to know Matisse's opinion.

Having to work near Picasso day after day could have been devastating, but at that stage I was sensible enough to consider my evolution on my own terms, focusing on my own ideas and their possible positive or negative results rather than comparing myself to him. What mattered was to feel and think, to experience and not let myself be overwhelmed by my elders' achievements, however glamorous and magnificent. Earlier in life they had undergone their own trials and tribulations, and it was by meeting the difficulties with complete integrity that they had ultimately solved or transcended their own inner conflicts. Yet the circumstances of my life were what they were, and I could not indulge in slow-motion soul-searching. As if placed in a hothouse, I had to grow fast and be the very image of self-confidence. Already a painter when I met Pablo,

I had in 1946 strongly affirmed my right to keep on working, and by my steadfastness I had secured my ability to continue undisturbed.

On the whole Pablo was pleased to have a companion with whom he could talk at length about art and about his work in progress or my own. That was quite an achievement, and it was not lightheartedly that I braced myself to submit to Matisse's test. It was not in my nature to shy away from a challenge; being a gambler at heart, I soon became prepared to play double or quits. Undaunted, I started assembling a number of recent drawings and gouaches in a portfolio. This done, I showed them to Pablo, who liked the selection and was favorably impressed that I did not back out to make excuses to avoid the possibility of a negative judgment on Matisse's part. Of course, I knew that such a judgment would allow Pablo to reconsider his positive attitude and oppose my future endeavors.

Not being devoid of a sense of humor directed at myself, I was able to consider my possible discomfiture and to laugh about it in advance. So in response to Matisse's invitation to show him my drawings, I sent a rather tongue-in-cheek letter comparing my obligation to satisfy his curiosity to the ordeal of the burghers of Calais, the subject of a famous sculpture by Auguste Rodin. The sculpture depicts a historical fact of the Hundred Years War, a sorrowful group of dignified citizens taken as hostages who walk clothed in nothing but long shirts, carrying around their necks the very ropes with which they are to be hung by order of the Queen of England, in reprisal for the rebellion of the city.

I knew that Matisse had always had a great regard for Rodin. In his youth he had purchased from Ambroise Vollard the original plaster for the bust of Henri Rochefort for the sum of 200 francs, along with Cézanne's *Three Bathers* for 1300 francs. After making an initial deposit of 300 francs, he paid for both in monthly installments for a year, at a time when he and his wife were in dire financial straights. In 1908, when he moved his studio and his art school to the former Convent of the Sacred Heart (originally a part of the Hôtel Biron), he became Rodin's neighbor and had the opportunity to meet him and to become even more aware of his work. So I was sure that the tragic group was familiar to him, and I thought that the allusion to *The Burghers of Calais* would make him smile and that he might perhaps change his mind and answer that if I felt that way, there was no need for me to bring any drawings. If I believed that I could get off the hook that way, I was wrong!

Vence   30 April 1948

Dear Françoise Gilot,

How chagrined I am that you should write about your next visit and your drawings: "and myself, an unfortunate one, the noose around my neck, a portfolio under my arm."

If only you knew to what extent your reaction disagrees with the great pleasure your drawing, now in front of me, gives me. When you come you will certainly feel how sincere I am.

My kindest regards to Picasso, which I want you to share (the regards).

H. Matisse

Matisse seemed to take my words literally. He assured me that my works would be considered in a friendly rather than a critical manner. But he was certainly not aware of what I had implied.

Yes, it was an ordeal to leave a portfolio full of my drawings and gouaches at his home, knowing that they would probably become a topic of conversation among Matisse, Picasso, and myself during the following visit. Matisse was seventy-eight years old then, and Picasso sixty-six; both were world-famous. I was only twenty-six years old—very young indeed for a painter. I had succeeded in continuing to work assiduously every day ever since I began sharing Picasso's life in May 1946, stopping only for two weeks at the time of Claude's birth. I had earned acceptance of my status as a painter, thanks to my dedication, single-mindedness, and independence of mind. But nothing was ever on stable ground with Picasso, and if Matisse did not like my work or, worse, did not say anything, I knew that I would lose face in front of someone who liked winners and despised losers. Anyway, the die was cast. With or without inner trepidation, the key was to muster inner strength, appear unconcerned, and when the moment came, hold my own with the titans.

Matisse had gone on to say how sincere was his regard for the gouache I had sent him, or rather, what pleasure he felt when looking at it, but since his appreciation for that one did not necessarily mean

Vence 30 avril 1948

Chère Françoise Gilot,

Comme je suis contrarié que vous m'écrivez au sujet de votre prochaine visite et de vos dessins :

et moi, malheureuse, la corde au cou, un carton sous le bras

Si vous saviez comme ça va peu avec le grand plaisir que me donne votre dessin que j'ai sous les yeux — Vous sentirez certainement quand vous viendrez comme je suis sincère.

Mes bonnes amitiés à Picasso, que je vous prie de partager (les amitiés.)

H. Matisse

Letter from Matisse to Gilot dated
April 30, 1948, Vence.

that he would like the others, his praise did nothing to abate my anxiety. I also tortured myself on account of the ambiguity at the end of his message. He expressed feelings of friendship for Picasso that I was supposed to share. Yet possessed of an irrepressible impish spirit, he had added the word "regards" a second time between brackets to make the message even clearer. Obviously his friendship was to be shared between Pablo and me. But the underlying message was that Picasso, in turn, must be shared between Matisse and me. It was unlikely that I would share Matisse's friendship with Pablo, since their relationship had such a long history, and it would be impossible to share Pablo himself with Matisse, since Pablo, like the wind, was not to be possessed by anyone. Wasn't he the man who had said, "From my solitude I come, to my solitudes I shall return"?

I think Matisse subconsciously harbored the belief that I could improve and stabilize his relationship with Pablo. Georges Braque seemed imbued with the same hope, as if I could truly be a link to their elusive friend, as if I could be the catalyst for some unfulfilled expectations. Men of that generation had a tendency to put women on a pedestal, particularly when the women were young and beautiful, so these painters certainly believed me to be on top of the world and all-powerful. This idealized vision contributed to an aura that was flattering, for sure, but hardly attuned to my reality. Life with Pablo was a permanent roller-coaster; one day I would be praised to the skies, and the next morning I would find myself mercilessly criticized, as if I could do nothing right. As they say, there's nothing new under the sun; my father's moods had been just as uneven, so I kept a measure of equanimity by thinking that when men were not excessive, they were usually mediocre.

My tendency to draw parallels between Pablo and my father was unfortunate. Pablo, in his own eyes the eternal adolescent, did not perceive that I unconsciously cast him in a surrogate father role and that since my relationship with my father had been adversarial, the forecast for our future was shrouded in dark clouds. Though as a child I much admired my father's intelligence, I felt fiercely competitive with him. It was my way of endearing myself to my mother, whom I adored. I also feared that otherwise I would go unnoticed by them both.

In a letter dated May 16, 1948, Matisse began with a free and playful interpretation of one of my gouaches, a portrait of my son, Claude, flying.

> Dear Françoise Gilot,
>
> I am very moved by the trust you manifested in lending me your drawings, which I can now look at in leisure. I am not the only one to appreciate them, because one of my friends would be very happy if you would allow her to acquire the one that I indicated at the beginning of this letter. Will you please excuse me for my sketch.
>
> I intend to leave on June 4, that is, very soon. I want Picasso to come and get the pigeons. I have a temporary cage that will enable him to carry them. It is a parrot's cage. I hope that nothing will prevent you from accompanying him to take back your drawings.
>
> I want to express and convey to you both my affectionate regards.
> Henri Matisse
> Lydia is very pleased with her ring and she thanks you for it again.
> Vence   16 May 1948

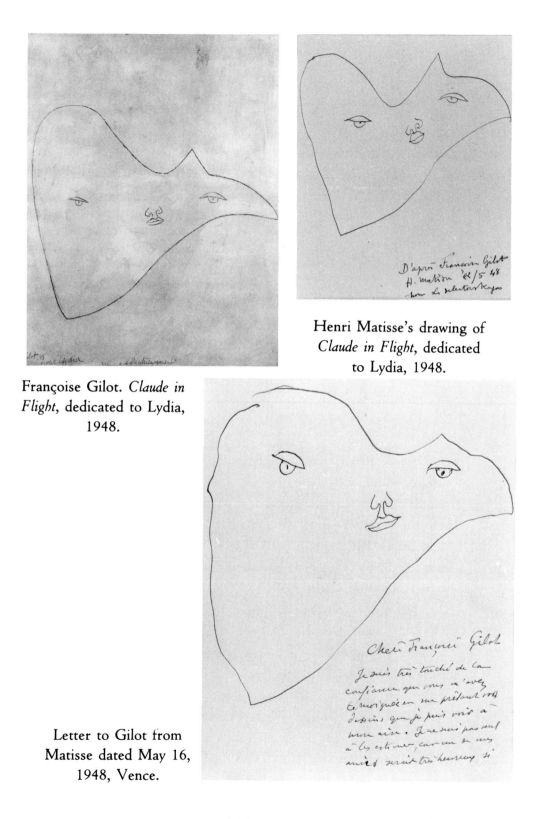

Françoise Gilot. *Claude in Flight*, dedicated to Lydia, 1948.

Henri Matisse's drawing of *Claude in Flight*, dedicated to Lydia, 1948.

Letter to Gilot from Matisse dated May 16, 1948, Vence.

Second page of letter,
May 16, 1948.

Because I was so much younger than Picasso, people believed that I had to be influenced by him as a painter, but this assumption was groundless at the time. I did not care about ownership of symbolic ideas, themes, inventions, about who did what first. But having been harassed by inaccurate critics for a style that I developed progressively on my own, according to the needs of my inner drive, it was interesting to find objective elements of truth.

Most of the gouaches in the portfolio I showed to Matisse in 1948 symbolically evoked my son, Claude, in flight; others showed my own face as a bird soaring in whiteness. Even in my still lifes of that period, objects were enveloped in the lyrical movement of flapping wings. What was the origin of these metamorphoses? For one thing, Claude as an infant was so round and supple that he seemed to bounce like a rubber ball each time he fell; as for myself, my dreams of creation were the birds that nested in my head. My ideal was to reach a hieroglyphic simplicity.

Matisse called all of my gouaches "birds." He said, "Whenever Françoise paints birds, however remote from reality they may be, they fly." Whether they flew or not, all my gouaches and drawings of that period were very melancholic, lacking a vitality that I had possessed until 1947 and was to recapture a few years later. Looking at the playfulness of Matisse's free interpretation of *Claude in Flight*, I understood the truth of the adage that it takes a long time for an artist to become young. Whatever the mature artist touches is alive. Sketchy or more elaborate, the indications are never a simple juxtaposition of signs. They lose themselves in the whole, they interact, they reach a dynamic equilibrium, they dance.

I soon learned that Matisse's friend who wanted to purchase the gouache was Lydia Delectorskaya. Before I knew that she had any appreciation for my work, I had sent her a ring with a yellow-ocher chalcedony or jasper in a simple silver setting. Since its caramel color was very sedate, I thought it would not detract attention from her eyes, while it would relate to her chestnut hair and contrast with the snow-white quality of her complexion.

In the spring of 1948, Matisse was ready to move back to the Hôtel Regina, in Cimiez, but the regulations there prevented him from bringing along some of his pet animals. Pablo was well known for his love for doves, turtledoves, and birds of all feathers. Matisse thought that Pablo would enjoy the company of the beautiful white pigeons which had been living in Vence. Among them, three of four had their tiny feet fully covered with large feathers, and they were both handsome and ornamental. Pablo of course agreed to go and get them as soon as possible. He was also delighted by Lydia's acquisition of my gouache and by Matisse's comments. I was of course elated by this positive turn of events, which upgraded my work in Pablo's eyes and augmented my freedom of action.

I was also in a happy mood because Claude was such a good-natured baby. The first word he said was neither "papa" nor "mama"; it was "red," the color he liked best and wore most of the time. Even though there was no need for Pablo's usual panacea with women—having a child—since all was going well, Pablo began to think that all would be even more perfect if we decided to have another child. I was so enamored with Claude that it seemed right to plan to give him a companion.

Pablo was working mostly at the Madoura factory, where he was producing an amazing array of ceramic plates engraved while fresh and decorated through inventive techniques with oxides, glazes, and enamels. Each firing of the kiln revealed his achievements and enticed him to go ahead.

In May 1948 we left Golfe-Juan and moved two miles inland, to a rather ugly and very small house in the hills close to Vallauris. It was not appropriate at all, but at the time we were unable to find anything else, since people seemed unwilling to sell or rent anything to "foreigners" such as ourselves.

There was hardly any room for us, but fortunately there was a chicken pen in the garden to which the white pigeons, Matisse's protégés, were delivered. They could be housed there temporarily until we built an appropriate aviary (which of course was never built). A short time later, during a walk, I found a tortoise running on a small country road. I ran after it, took it back home, named it Héloïse for some reason, and decided to give it to the pigeons as a companion. Claude, then one year old, enjoyed going into the pen and playing with the birds and the tortoise, which he called "la torture" instead of "la tortue." At times some rather large country mice would be there too, eating all the corn.

The pigeons looked very disdainfully at their new habitat and even more so at Héloïse and the country mice. If their tiny brains could remember, they certainly missed their beautiful aviary and the freedom they had often enjoyed at Le Rêve in Vence. Matisse's cats were probably well bred and well fed, but the skinny stray cats of Vallauris dreamed of having at least one good meal, which they might have if we let the pigeons out of their shelter for recreation.

As I expressed some concern for their well-being, Pablo came and looked at them once in a while. He was of the opinion that pigeons were well able to defend themselves and didn't have such peaceful inclinations in the first place. He had studied, known, and owned pigeons all his life, and for him the fable of the two pigeons loving each other tenderly was just a fable. Exaggerating all their shortcomings, he pretended that they were the cruelest birds of all.

In fact, one morning a year earlier he had found his favorite she-pigeon (the one who came to rest on his shoulder at the top of the stairs in his studio at the rue des Grands Augustins) dead, with a large open wound at the neck from which gushes of red blood had stained her white plumage. I thought a rat had climbed the spiral staircase and was the guilty party, and I said so.

"Do you suggest that there are rats in my studio? It would be horrible—they could eat up my canvases!"

"Well, it is quite possible that one came up from the publishing house on the ground floor. This is an old area of Paris, and it is well known that rats hate pigeons, with which they compete for food in the streets."

Pablo was not easily convinced, and he went on enumerating the existing or potential vices of turtledoves, doves, and pigeons—their homosexual practices, their selfishness, and a long list of other defects, largely anthropomorphized, which contradicted his fondness for them.

During our next trip to Paris, in the autumn of 1948, Pablo went back to the Mourlot workshop to pursue his experiments in the lithographic medium. One day he wanted to impress Monsieur Toutain, his master printer, with his dexterity in making a beautiful transparent wash diluted with mineral oil instead of water to avoid the usual "toad's skin" or sediment-like deposits. He began with an extremely light homogenous wash, using a large paintbrush, and gave it design and shape from outside with strokes of dark tusche until the famous bird finally emerged from the completely black background—an original lithograph known later as *The Dove of Peace*.

In fact the bird was a pigeon, and it had been in existence for quite a few months when Louis Aragon saw it at Picasso's studio in February 1949 and asked that it be made into a poster. For the purpose at hand the pigeon image was transformed into a dove. Aragon had always been a devoted admirer and a great friend of both Matisse's and Picasso's, and without knowing that the bird-model had belonged to Matisse, he was instrumental in immortalizing one of his friend's pets through Picasso's craftsmanship. Picasso's father, Don José Ruiz Blasco, was himself a good animal painter and specialized in portraying pigeons in a style akin to that of Courbet, with an emphasis on modeling and dimensionality that bordered on the surreal. Before Pablo was ten, he knew everything there was to know about birds and often helped his father, whose eyesight was declining, to finish the bill or legs and feet of these creatures. This was why *The Dove of Peace* was so lively and spontaneous; it was the result of a lifetime of knowledge.

The following spring, around 8:00 P.M. on April 19, 1949, the very day when the poster appeared on the walls of Paris during an international congress for peace, another type of dove was born: my daughter, Paloma, whose name means "dove" in Spanish. Much later still, when my son, Claude, began to study photographic techniques at a studio on rue Delambre, one of the first photographs he enlarged was a well-known snapshot by Henri Cartier-Bresson of Matisse and his beloved long-feathered pigeons.

As to the parrot's cage, it was returned to Matisse, and it was only much later, in the 1960s, that parrots began to appear in my paintings . . . but that is another story.

Between Montparnasse and Cimiez

I N JUNE 1948, Matisse decided to leave for Paris, while his furniture, his canvases, and his other belongings were moved back to his large dwelling quarters and studios on the upper floor of a majestic apartment building called the Hôtel Regina, at Cimiez, in Nice. This was a good opportunity for him to stay awhile at his apartment and studio at 132, boulevard du Montparnasse. Whether in Paris or its suburbs, Matisse had always been a confirmed resident of the left bank of the Seine. From his first dwelling at 19, quai St. Michel, to his art school at the Convent of the Birds and then at the Convent of the Sacred Heart, to his large studio in Issy-les-Moulinaux and his present comfortable abode, he never migrated to the right bank or to the heights of Montmartre.

When in Paris he was well equipped for work, and apart from painting in the peace of his own studio he often went to the Fernand Mourlot workshop in the rue de Chabrol, in the north of Paris, to make lithographs. He also enjoyed seeing important art exhibitions. He could replenish his stock of canvases, tubes of paint and gouaches, and good-quality rag paper at Lucien Lefèbvre-Foinet, a most renowned place for art supplies located at 2, rue Bréa, nearby. The owner, Maurice Lefèbvre-Foinet, was a well-known collector, and personally advised many famous artists regarding the chemistry of color and other technical matters.

TO PABLO PICASSO
REGARDS FROM HENRI MATISSE
FAR AWAY FROM THE ROAD TO SAINT JEANNET
THAT NONE EQUALS, STILL IN PARIS
IN THIS JUNE 1948

The next piece of mail from our friend and impish genius combined words and sketches of flowers. For once it was addressed to Pablo directly. Each of the five flowers stretched out its five elongated petals; they were distributed on the paper in a drill, a regular pattern akin to the calligraphic distributions in some of Matisse's paintings. Toward their hearts the links were open to allow the passage of light. The capital letters of most of the words meandered where they could between flowers like a playful sardana, a Catalonian folk dance in which people hold hands and move in a spiral.

Pablo was gratified to be the recipient of this floral epistle, but cheerful though it was, he found it too concise for his taste. There was no indication of what his friend was doing. Of course Matisse was better off in Paris while his furniture and belongings were moved from Vence to Cimiez, but at the same time, why should he be there just when we happened to be on the Riviera and might have enjoyed some contact with him? Why did Matisse stay away? Pablo knew that it was foolish to be disappointed, but this knowledge did not ease his need for companionship, even if his meetings with Matisse in the normal course of things were not as frequent as he wished.

The following letter, dated June 25, 1948, addressed to me but meant for us all, was very warm and affectionate, emanating a youthful enthusiasm.

Letter from Matisse to Picasso, June 25, 1948: "To
Picasso, regards from Henri Matisse, far away from the
route de Saint Jeannet which nothing else equals, at Paris
this June day, 1948 (À Pablo Picasso . . . les amitiés
d'Henri Matisse. Loin de la route de Saint Jeannet que rien
de vault, cependant à Paris en ce juin 1948)."

Friday, 25 June 1948

To Françoise Gilot and to her young Hercules, they are beautiful to look at, three times hurrah!

Dear Françoise Gilot,

I hope that the three of you are in good health and I send you my best regards and Lydia's. I want to congratulate Picasso on the generosity he just showed on behalf of the Jews. A huge success owed to a giving heart, neither of which astonish me in any way. There will soon be an auction to benefit children the world over. I learned by chance that the organizers of this movement still have not heard from our Pablo. There may be a misunderstanding about what he wants to give. I know that he does not question the quality of my fondness for him, so I allow myself to ask you to think about the matter on my behalf. The auction will take place next July 5. When I see you I shall tell you some unbelievably funny stories about the contagion affecting some artists who, after managing to refrain from a generous act, hasten to donate as soon as they learn that pals like you give with wide-open pockets. Lucky you, to be far from Paris, where the weather is nasty. I wish I were close to coming back to route de St. Jeannet.

How are the small curly white ones?

To you with all my heart

H. Matisse

Matisse was probably enjoying a time of intense and fulfilling creativity, but Pablo, far from being placated by the message, began counting the petals of the five flowers in my letter! I didn't have more blooms, but they had more petals, six or seven each! This was ludicrous, and he laughed at his own absurd childishness. "I'll bet you that Matisse is having a good time in the company of some bad painters," he said. (*Bad* did not necessarily mean artists without talent, but simply those whom Pablo didn't approve of.) "Or even going to see the Bal des Quatz Arts or some other bohemian social event that I can't stand. And of course he won't describe any of it, because he knows I disapprove of such reveling in the company of the clowns of our profession. This happens perhaps because he spent some time at the School of Fine Arts under Gustave Moreau. Even if he was not regularly enrolled, he has kept the tastes of a *rapin*." A *rapin* is a painter's assistant or a young

Letter from Matisse, June 25, 1948, continues.

student who does menial work at the School of Fine Arts to replace tuition—by extension, a second-rate artist.

I intervened. "You know you don't mean what you say. The word *rapin* applied to your best friend just is not fitting, and if he enjoys being a part of a carnival-like event which reminds him of his youth, why should you frown on such an innocent pleasure? It's funny to see how moralistic you can be when your friends indulge in things you dislike. Maybe Matisse does not share your taste for bullfights, but he understands that that's a part of your cultural background and therefore natural for you."

Pablo retorted, "Indeed, I despise 'innocent pleasures.' As to the bullfight, it is a highly ritualized event that has come to us through the ages, from Crete—a sacrifice to the sun, a game of life and death, not a histrionic display."

I remained silent, thinking that Pablo was not adverse to histrionic displays when they suited his fancy.

Matisse was fond of my young son. He nicknamed him "the young Hercules" on account of Claude's early ability to make fists of his hands, grind his new teeth, and roll menacing eyes whenever requested by his father to look angry. Claude made his "angry look" once or twice spontaneously when eight months old, and then afterward was able to repeat the feat at will, since it seemed to amuse his father and grant him attention and kisses. I was not in favor of having this play-acting become a habit, but since Claude was really a very easy-going and good-tempered baby and since the fake tantrums amused everybody, I usually did not intervene, except when Claude was asked to perform too often in one day and eventually became really highly strung and irritable.

In the course of his letter, Matisse referred to Picasso's generosity to Jewish children or to the Jews, since the word "children" was crossed out in the text. Picasso was often asked to give an original work to be auctioned for the benefit of charitable institutions. Matisse was mentioning the positive outcome of that auction intentionally, to encourage his friend to a new act of generosity meant for the welfare of children the world over.

Often the organizers of such benefits made entreaties to a well-known painter, asking him to help get the works of another painter. They used the mutual friendship of these artists to advantage and often were successful in gathering a sizable number of important works. In the end, all the artists had to comply or, if they found the cause unworthy, to decline, simultaneously. From the tone of his letter, it was obvious that Matisse had been persuaded to become the advocate for such an event. Picasso's participation, he added, would shame other artists into being more generous.

The organizer of the benefit was Ida Bourdet, Claude Bourdet's* wife and a well-known patron of the arts in French cultural circles. She had been campaigning among the artists for donations to the United Nations Aid to Children Fund. After a day's exhibition at the Galerie

*He was a well-known figure of the French intelligensia, the son of Édouard Bourdet, a famous playwright, and of Catherine Pozzi, a talented poet. He became the editor of the weekly newspaper *L'Observateur* and a founder of the Parti Socialist Unifié (P.S.U.) after the war.

Henri Matisse talking to Ida Bourdet in
front of Picasso's painting *The Blue Owl*,
June 18, 1948.

18 Juin 1948
Chère Madame Bourdet,
Je suis tout heureux de vous avoir donné un de mes meilleurs tableaux pour la vente de l'UNAC. Ne puis-je ainsi espérer apporter une aide sérieuse au but de si grande générosité, bien naturelle pourtant, que vous désirez atteindre en ce moment.

Mille mercis,
Respectueusement vôtre
H Matisse

Letter from Matisse
to Ida Bourdet,
June 18, 1948.

de l'Élysée, the paintings were to be auctioned at the Galerie Charpentier on July 5, 1948, through the good offices of Maître Maurice Rheims.

Claude and Ida Bourdet had met Henri Matisse in 1940 through mutual friends: André Gide, Simon Bussy and his wife, Dorothy Bussy, who was Lytton Strachey's sister and herself a writer of note, mostly famous for her novel *Olivia*. The Bourdets' home in Vence, named Les Collines, was near Matisse's villa, Le Rêve, on the same side of the route de St. Jeannet, and the friendship probably developed during the tribulations of World War II, when Claude Bourdet, one of the founding members of the underground movement Action, was deported.

One of Matisse's salient characteristics was his devotion to friendship in general and to his friends in particular, so it was no wonder that he responded warmly to Ida Bourdet's appeal and helped her to obtain more works of art. Eighty-six pieces were finally donated, including a Pascin, a Maurice Denis, and a Signac, which were given by the families of these deceased artists. He wrote her:

June 18, 1948

Dear Lady and Friend,

I am quite happy to have given you one of my best pictures for the UNAC auction. Can't I hope in so doing to be really helpful in the achievement of the very generous yet natural goal you presently desire to attain?

A thousand thanks.

Respectfully yours,

H. Matisse

In the last part of his letter to me dated June 25, 1948, Matisse criticized some artists' lack of generosity. They donated works for a good cause only when they learned that the auction would bring their works to the spotlight, thanks to the participation of their famous colleagues. This comment showed that Matisse joyfully anticipated sharing a bit of gossip, even though with him gabbing was infrequent, always good-natured, and never nasty.

Since the weather was bad in Paris, Pablo could not understand why his friend lingered in town any longer. Right away he was suspicious. For him friendship was almost as exclusive and passionate a feeling as love. He felt entitled to be possessive and obsessive. So he complained bitterly, as if he had been abandoned and left behind and was again experiencing what he had felt as a child in Málaga when, after taking him to school, his father would go to some of his friends' studios to enjoy artistic companionship. Pablo's intense competitive spirit might have been triggered early on by witnessing his father's interest in colleagues who toiled on such gigantic canvases that they had to assemble their models in the bullfight arena and work there on their decadent historical monstrosities. As the past for Pablo was always re-enacted in the present, he was intensely jealous.

Fortunately, at the end of his letter Matisse referred to "the small curly white ones," meaning the pigeons that he had given us. Since Pablo's father had been especially fond of painting these animals, Pablo as a young boy had managed more than once to take one of them to school, hidden under his shirt, rationalizing that his father would come back for the pigeon if not for him. In the same way he welcomed the mention of the birds as a token of hope and enduring affection.

Amazingly, for someone who had achieved so much and was so well recognized, Pablo was never emotionally secure and assured of his self-worth. He went through bouts of anxiety and was in constant need of reassurance, even though he made fun of this disposition himself. This was an aspect of him that was very endearing, because he could easily have been very haughty.

Matisse's letter of July 7 was adorned with two floral patterns that seemed to radiate sunlight. The upper one had six petals that ended rather like the extremities of the heraldic cross adopted by the knights of Malta. The lower one was multifoil but similar in design. The use of capital letters on some words was emphatic, and the tone was very affectionate and bombastic.

> 132, boulevard Montparnasse
> Wednesday, 7 July 1948
>
> Dear Françoise Gilot,
>
> FIRST, GLORY TO PABLO, who gave a beautiful painting to UNAC. If it did not go for twice as much as the first bidding during the auction, it is because the beautiful blue of the bird looked black at night, even under the artificial light that was on during the day of the exhibit.
>
> NEXT, warm regards for the three of you from Lydia and myself. *Fortunate* mortals who are not shivering like all of us in Paris.
>
> We are longing to see the small Hercules again. The sun, the palm trees, the olive trees, the bouillabaisse, and the sea.
>
> BE
> MERRY
> BE
> HAPPY
>
> HENRI MATISSE
> for LIFE

First, Matisse thanked Pablo for his important gift to the United Nations Aid to Children Fund. During the auction, Matisse's painting alone had brought almost one fifth of the total proceeds. He must have been elated to think that his work had helped a good cause to such an

Letter to Gilot from Matisse, July 7, 1948.

extent, and he must have been aware that other artists—Derain, Braque, Laurencin, Dufy, Rouault, Utrillo, Vlaminck, and Chagall—had been left far behind, either because they had been less generous or because their works were not as appreciated by the public.

Since Pablo had donated his oil rather late, his name had not appeared in the catalogue. What's more, the painting itself, of an owl perched on a chair in front of a mirror, was neither dated nor signed. Even though people were aware that it would be dated and signed by the artist during his next trip to Paris, it did not do as well as it could have and brought only 800,000 francs, much less than could be expected for a canvas of that size. Perhaps the subject was not appealing and the composition too syncopated for the general taste at that time.

In any case, Matisse was left with the task of telling his friend how and why *The Blue Owl* had not done too well at the auction. It probably bothered him, since he had asked for the donation and might have felt in some way responsible. In a characteristic forthright manner, he confronted the issue without reticence and with a sense of humor, calling the blue bird in the picture *zoizeau* instead of *oiseau*. It was a familiar colloquialism; from the pronunciation *un(n) oiseau, des(z) oiseaux*, people would end up saying *un zoizeau, un zozio*, or even *quel drole d'ozio* to be funny.

Such colloquialisms were already out of date, but I remembered my grandfather using other malapropisms on purpose, to be facetious. The popular author Georges Courteline obtained the same comic effect in one of his plays by having one of the characters mispronounce *angora*, which became *un zangora, le tangora, des nangoras, un langora*, and so on. Alphonse Allais and Maurice Donnay, in playlets designed to be performed at the Black Cat, a famous caf-conc, or cafe-theater, and Aristide Bruant, in his songs (he was immortalized by Toulouse-Lautrec), deformed words to get easy laughter from their audiences.

It was amazing to see how much space birds occupied in Matisse's and Picasso's correspondence. Birds seem indeed to have been a common denominator for Matisse, Picasso, and me. Both artists always kept birds at home—Matisse mostly exotic species, Pablo the more ordinary kind, except for the owl. In my grandmother's garden in Paris, my father's aviary had enchanted my childhood. He had often brought back seabirds such as curlews from Brittany, to tend a wound or a broken wing and keep them until they could be released the following summer. I had also been trained to recognize the different wildfowl in flight.

Birds in flight symbolize freedom; that might be why we shared that fascination. According to Sigmund Freud, they also carry a phallic or erotic content. It therefore became easy to associate the joke at the beginning of Matisse's letter with the hedonism and sensuousness of its end, where Matisse evoked the sun, the palm trees, the olive trees, the saffron-colored fish soup, the sea, and the radiance of his wishes of joy and happiness for us.

These letters showed Matisse as open, outgoing, enthusiastic, and eager to see life in the brightest colors imaginable and to share his intuition of joy in expanding ripples. The letters were also incantations destined to protect his friends' happiness, because he knew only too well how fragile and short-lived these carefree moments could be.

Matisse's sojourn in Paris came to an end, and in time Lydia called to say that the painter was installed in his more spacious quarters and would see us when it was mutually convenient. Nice was not far from Vallauris, but our visits to Matisse often turned out to be quite an expedition. We could have gone there in the morning and been back in time for work, but usually Matisse was not yet ready, and Pablo not being an early riser, the visits had to take place in the afternoon, which

Envelope from Matisse with drawings, 1948.

meant losing a day's work. So we had to put these excursions to the best possible use.

We sometimes chose to see a physician first or to have a dentist appointment around eleven in the morning if the need arose, then bought some *calissons d'Aix*—diamond-shaped sweetmeats made of marzipan, a speciality from Aix-en-Provence, probably of Moorish origin—or some candied fruits at a well-known shop nearby. We might even indulge in purchasing some new clothes and loafing around in the fashionable part of town. We invariably ended up at the flower market at Les Ponchettes, filling our eyes with colors and inhaling delicate fragrances before wandering through the old part of town in quest of antique shops or some Provençal bistro in which to enjoy good local cuisine. The streets were narrow, and the shops displayed multicolored arrays of groceries, vegetables, fruits, fish, and game, as well as the usual housewares, linen, and basketry. On foot or riding wobbly bicycles, people swarmed the streets, flirting, singing, gesturing, shouting, screaming, arguing, calling heaven to witness, cursing, all in the greatest disorder. We enjoyed absorbing all these fresh impressions. As Pablo liked to say, "If the things that cost nothing were very expensive, I would be ruined for sure." As soon as we had had enough of the din, we knew where to find Marcel, the chauffeur, waiting.

That summer, after Matisse came back from Paris, we were eager to visit him at the Regina for the first time. Located on a hill, as its name indicated, Cimiez was a residential part of Nice with a panoramic view of the city and the bay. The car drove up and up and around until we faced one of the gigantic hotels that had been built toward the end of the nineteenth century to accommodate Queen Victoria and English families of the gentry, who came to escape the yellow London fog and spend the winter on the Riviera. The Regina was no longer a hotel; it had been divided into large apartments.

A bit disturbed by the massive building as seen from the outside, I was even more astonished to enter a huge hall adorned with neoclassic columns, capitals, and cornices. Somehow it did not fit my image of our friend at all. But after the elevator dropped us on the landing of one of the upper floors, we rang the bell, and Lydia answered the door, it did make sense all of a sudden. The apartment was vast, with large

A room in Matisse's apartment at Le Régina, Nice.

spaces that Matisse could use as studios and other shadowy rooms opening to the right and to the left on each side of a central hall or corridor, where a six-foot-tall plaster cast of an archaic Greek *kouros* was standing. Most of the doors were made of thick transparent glass, and in my excitement I bumped my head into one of them. All the silent actors, the creatures that dwelled within Matisse's pictorial universe, offered themselves to our curiosity unprotected by their master's powerful magic. The philodendrons, the tables, the oyster-shell armchairs, and other celebrated objects assumed a dreamlike quality in the half-shadow, like ghosts in the wings of a disused theater, until their reappearance within the rarefied universe of paint allowed the visitor to ascertain which had more physical reality.

It seemed indiscreet to walk inside this den of metamorphosis, but as soon as we reached Matisse's room everything came back into focus. His larger-than-life presence radiated peaceful power and tranquillity. Though he was affable, serene, welcoming, there was something imposing about him; once there, I felt just as unsubstantial as the objects around us. Pablo himself seemed spellbound. As long as Matisse wanted us to stay, we were glued to our chairs, fully awake but in a trancelike state, and we left only when he had decided to release us and not before. Sometimes the conversation was animated, but there were also zones of silence, moments of nonverbal communication. It was a powerful medicine, and often after leaving we were not in the mood to go back home. In order to prolong the enchantment, it was better to spend the late afternoon at St. Paul-de-Vence and have dinner at the Colombe d'Or with Jacques Prévert and his wife, Jeanine, or some other friends and talk, talk, talk, about art or poetry. Otherwise there was the possibility of joining Tériade in St. Jean-Cap Ferrat or Marie Cuttoli at the villa Shaddy Rock in the Cap d'Antibes. They were always glad to hear the latest news of our mutual friend, and to gossip about the latest events in the art world.

When Picasso worked, he did so with intensity and fervor, but he also liked to take time off to recharge his batteries, and he was not always averse to enjoying the simple things in life. The next day he would go back to the pottery and to his work in progress with renewed energy and stamina. Seeing Matisse was for him a process of catharsis. I guess that they provided for each other an ideal yardstick with which to measure their achievements.

For me it was not such a clear-cut feeling. Although Matisse was so natural, perhaps because of a quality of persistent innocence, it was awe-inspiring to be in his presence, and I got used to it only gradually;

it was not an experience to be taken lightly. It put ideas in motion; things started to develop in your mind that you did not know existed before. All during the conversation his blue gaze would rest on you steadily, rather in the way an entomologist looks at a cricket or a scorpion, with no other intent than objective observation; but behind the glasses his gaze was also directed inward, carefully recording his own present state of being and attending to a vaster continuum, as if Vishnu's dream of the world were dreaming itself through him. (In the Indian pantheon, Brahma is the nonmanifest permanent essence, Vishnu dreams the ever-unfolding world of manifestation called Maya, and Shiva transforms and destroys.) Matisse could talk, consider what he saw, and at the same time sustain intense concentration that bordered on self-hypnosis. He was present and yet self-absorbed, pursuing some thought of his own, perhaps unconsciously reabsorbing or reintegrating some work in progress before projecting it anew as soon as we had left. Maybe in the haphazard way the dialogue meandered, a sound, a movement, or a sentence would resound in his soul to awaken an as yet dormant harmony. It gave you the queer feeling that behind the visible appearance of things, beyond small talk and human limitations, someone was recording the scene, as if that very moment was destined to endure forever. I do not know how to describe the feeling it elicited other than by the words "life divine." The ordinary was enmeshed with the extraordinary; things were both tangible and intangible, in and out of space, in and out of time. In all this there was great beauty but also melancholy. There was serenity but also the still-remote vibration of a future farewell.

Once while I was thinking about this, as if sensing something in the air, Pablo became increasingly communicative and for some reason started to reminisce about the art dealer–publisher Ambroise Vollard and his own illustrations for a limited edition of *The Unknown Masterpiece* by Balzac, reiterating that life imitated art. He started to talk about Porbus and Mabuse, about the young painter Poussin and his lover Gillette visiting the old Freinhoffer, who had literally fallen in love with his own creation, an ideal woman whose shape he had so lovingly formed and deformed that to the eye of the viewer only one perfect foot and ankle were still recognizable, as they were all that had escaped destruction.

Matisse remained silent, his thoughts flowing in another direction, or perhaps he did not want to be bothered with the retelling of *The Unknown Masterpiece* and with hearing how Pablo's studio in the rue des Grands Augustins happened to be the very studio where Porbus had worked a few centuries before.

Seeing that he had failed to capture his friend's attention, Pablo had to engineer something stronger to stir Matisse out of his daydream. So he short-circuited his story, and out of the blue he said, "Do you know for a fact that Ambroise Vollard was killed in car accident by a blow from a bronze by Maillol, which was placed on an overlay behind him on the back seat and that violently bounced forward during the impact when the chauffeur drove into a tree?"

Pablo probably imagined that Matisse would negate the possibility that a rather small statue by Maillol had had such a lethal impact on the very dealer who appreciated Maillol's work most. But not at all; Matisse did not become emotional. Very matter-of-factly he retorted, "That's not at all what I heard. Vollard, who was very particular about good food, was traveling with a number of copper pots and pans on the overlay behind his head. So he died from his gourmet tastes, hit by his pots and pans and not by the Maillol bronze, which rested securely in the trunk. How could a work of art ever kill anyone? You come up with strange notions from time to time." Matisse lowered his head reflectively, gazing severely at Pablo from above his glasses, which were placed low on the bridge of his nose, as if he were a schoolmaster irritated by the pranks of an unruly twelve-year-old.

But Pablo was not beaten. "This is a very inglorious ending indeed, being killed by pots and pans—quite unbelievable. I prefer the legend. When life does not imitate art, it reads only like a bad novel. Saying so shows a lack of regard. I guess that you didn't like Ambroise Vollard after all."

Matisse just shrugged his shoulders and did not bother to pursue the matter. Though Vollard had given him his first one-man show, in 1904, with forty-six paintings acquired on different occasions, a deep understanding between dealer and artist never developed, as it did between Vollard and Bonnard, Maillol, and even Picasso. With his serious legal background, Matisse never took a kind view of Vollard's customary bag of tricks, and he remained immune to his spiel.

Arrangement of objects often used
in Matisse's still-life paintings.

A Merry-Go-Round
of Objects

Objets inanimés avez-vous donc une âme
*Qui s'attache à notre âme et la force d'aimer?**
—LAMARTINE

According to Gertrude Stein, "Rose is a rose is a rose," but a cup on a canvas is not a cup, is not a cup, is not a cup; a painted pink rose has no fragrance, a sphere no volume, an animal no power to move, a person no ability to talk. Different cultures have devised different imitative, arbitrary, or conventional ways to describe or depict objects in the environment, spectacles of nature, or more ambitious compositions, including the human form.

Most of Henri Matisse's work, without being realistic, was figurative. Far from surrendering to exaggerated theoretical concerns, he could have joined Colette in saying, "If you knew how I embellish everything I love and all of the pleasure I get out of loving! If you

---

Inanimate objects, do you have a soul
That attaches itself to our soul and binds it to love?

could understand the mixture of strength and weakness with which the things I could love fill me! It's what I call the caress of happiness." Fishbowls, pewter jugs, mugs, fruit dishes, pitchers, vases, amphoras, tobacco jars, plates, opaline cups, teacups, draperies, textured fabrics, copper caldrons, glasses—familiar household objects danced a recurrent, elusive saraband in his pictures. They could be sketchy; they could be altered in shape, color, size, proportions. Each time they could be combined with one another differently, thus acquiring different connotations. Like words in a sentence, they belonged to the painter's vocabulary; and like favorite key words within a poem or an essay, they were repeated to ensure rhythm and continuity.

They helped the painter to tame the void of the white canvas. Whether or not Matisse originally acquired these objects for their beauty or usefulness, in time a link of sympathetic harmony seemed to have tied them to his soul. Some came from the hands of some provincial potter; some were refined products of high craftsmanship. Through time, they all became a part of his inner universe as well as a part of his familiar environment. They crossed the boundaries of external reality and by osmosis permeated his oeuvre. Domestic or elegant, they belonged in several paintings while simultaneously sitting still in the studio.

Matisse's ability to invest manmade artifacts with his own inner life also allowed him to make the familiar things around him appear and reappear like the figures of a merry-go-round, revolving faster and faster to the accents of a lyrical band. Fruits, flowers, creepers in a pot, two or three goldfish in an aquarium joined the dance to augment the wild vitality of the whole, to develop magic echos of sympathy between elements belonging to different realms. Several small round nasturtium leaves could reinforce the circular shape of a large ceramic plate, some lemons give emphasis to the bulge of a vase. "An oriental coolness clings to the walls, and the sparse pieces of furniture breathe at their ease. Only in this sun-steeped country can a heavy table, a wicker chair, an earthernware jar crowned with flowers and a dish whose thick enameling has run over the edge make a complete furnishing," as Colette put it.

Often the artist seemed childlike and more primeval (in the sense of being closer to the origins) than his contemporaries; thanks to his unique sensitivity he could animate all of nature and find echoes and correspondences between all things. Birds, plants, and other objects that surrounded him enticed Matisse to work. While his eyes carelessly or carefully caressed their well-loved and well-known surfaces, the creative impulse sprang toward a new vision. For him a still life was not a minor theme. Many of his strong works simply depicted artifacts of different sizes, substance, texture, color, and form and their interactions with natural forms. His resourcefulness in combining unusual viewpoints (from above, from below, along a diagonal) matched his fantasy in coupling the most unlikely pairs. In the freshness of the groupings, the various objects seemed as bewildered by their unexpected proximity as the famous encounter of a sewing machine and an umbrella on a dissecting table, advocated by Lautréamont and much later by the Surrealists.

Conflicting forms and volumes were subjugated into serene, if potentially explosive, coexistence. Each object had a part to play; each thing was determined to be itself, come what may. Matisse, like Merlin, threw them all into the magic carousel of his art, sometimes separately, sometimes all at once. With his brushes he made them whirl; with his wizardry he bound them together, and they obeyed. Leaning right or left, upward or downward, changing scale and color if necessary, they revolved and revolved until the give-and-take of a rhythmic acceleration made them both receptive and active each to each, all to all, and to the negative space around. The identity of each component was retained and at the same time melted into the lyrical oneness of the whole. Charm was a charm, was a charm. . . . There was no abracadabra, no formula, no recipe, but it worked. No one can resist a still life by Matisse. They are so delectable; it is like a frenzy, you absorb them, you eat them up—you don't look at them, you lick them with your eyes, and they taste of ginger and cardamom, of orange blossoms and turmeric, they assuage an inexhaustible hunger and quench a spiritual thirst. They make your pulse beat faster, they make your head spin, and soon they make you childlike. In the joyous din of the fairground, you ride the hobbyhorse of Matisse's fantasy on the merry-go-round of your own imagination.

Many twentieth-century artists have enabled us to share the potential lyricism dormant in the things of daily experience, thus enriching our perceptions. But depending on the theme, the hierarchy of subject matters and their relative importance were very different earlier in the Western tradition, up to the end of the nineteenth century. Religious and historical compositions in which actions and passions were displayed on a large scale came at the top of the list, and only recognized masters could tackle such themes. Just below came the landscapes, the *scenes de genre* and animated landscapes for which the scale of the canvas did not need to be so grand or the accumulation of figures so heroic. Next came portraiture (at which quite a few women excelled, because psychological accuracy was deemed more necessary than purely physical resemblance or idealized likeness). Last of all came the "embellishments," the still lifes (often from the hands of a master's young disciples). In the artists' studios of the Renaissance, the assistants, who entered apprenticeship at around ten or twelve years of age, worked their way up from the adornments on the borders or inside the canvas to faraway landscapes and figures in the distance (like some silhouettes executed by El Greco in some of Tintoretto's paintings, or angels that Leonardo da Vinci executed for Verrocchio)—when they were not busy grinding lapis lazuli or preparing huge pots of flesh tone for use in the shade, the half-shadow, and the light.

This historic perspective shows what a transformation has taken place, thanks to forerunners such as Rembrandt, Goya, Courbet, Manet, Cézanne, van Gogh, and Gauguin. The real precursor was Chardin, but it was only retrospectively that his works were recognized as the masterpieces that they are. The same is true of the Dutch still lifes, the displays of the spoils of the hunt by Oudry, the appetizing flowers and fruits by Louise Moillon, the superb "vanities" by Dutch, German, and French masters and by Zurbarán, because these were considered to be simple decorative pieces or, at best, descriptive enumerations of objects.* Following these great painters, the artists of the nineteenth century tamed the public into accepting that beholding a piece of beef, a salmon,

---

*A "vanity" was most often a still life in which the objects symbolically or metaphorically evoked death. Sometimes a depiction of an ascetic or Mary Magdalene meditating in front of a skull was also called a vanity.

an asparagus, an apple, or some sunflowers or exotic fruits could be as moving an experience as contemplating a pieta or a great battle scene.

Yet ever since the ancient Greeks or the Romans, painters themselves, if not the patrons or the public, had used objects for much more than purely decorative purposes. Thanks to their known function, objects often had a strong symbolic potential, and the association of different artifacts with animal or vegetable things created images equivalent to metaphysical statements. In a "vanity," for example, the presence of a skull could convey thoughts about the impermanence of life. There was a moral lesson, leading the viewer to a stoic acceptance of his own mortality, while in a different picture musical instruments close to a decanter and a dish of fruit would evoke a more epicurean philosophy.

In the twentieth century, with the decline of historical and religious painting, the end of the Symbolist movement, and the freedom of choice in subject matter, still lifes reached equal status with other themes or nonthematic works, and great painters renewed this form of art and brought it to new heights.

From the start Matisse recognized the importance of still lifes in his own development. He copied one of books and a candle from a composition by Chardin and others from de Heem. Soon the theme of the sideboard or dinner table covered with appetizing food made its appearance. He endowed a chocolate pot, a decanter, or a plate with his own sensibility, his own feelings. He wrote much later, "All my life was spent that way. A time of despair followed by a blissful moment of revelation that allowed me to achieve something that went beyond methodical reasoning and later left me as helpless as before in front of a new venture. Even though I saw that it would always be that way for me, I persisted in searching for the Ariadne's thread that must logically lead me to express what I believed to be exceptional in myself with means (colors) richer than linear drawing, with which I brought forth what moved me in nature, through the empathy I created between the objects that surrounded me, around which I revolved and into which I succeeded in pouring my feelings of tenderness without risking to suffer from doing so as in life."

Though in this letter Matisse wrote of empathy between objects and of their purpose as mediators of his emotions, he always reiterated that he did not use objects as symbols but as signs. Colette, his contemporary, had similarly stated, "My instinct is and always has been to flee the symbol, which inspires nothing in me." Colette did not want to be thought of as emulating J. K. Huysmans or Marcel Schwob, with their excessive aestheticism.

But this distinction must have been especially important for Matisse after he broke away from his master, Gustave Moreau, from his friends, the Nabis, and even from Gauguin after the end of Fauvism. Using objects as signs meant painting them only for their potential plastic value in terms of shape, size, color, and texture, like the conventional signs of the letters of a personal alphabet. In writing, the binding and combining of these abstract signs gives rise to words, sentences, paragraphs, and so on. In the case of a painting, their juxtaposition was used to combine a synthetic whole. It was never a naive enumeration but a series of significant interactions. In contrast, projecting objects as symbols would mean, for example, depicting a book as an image of learning, a caldron as the Holy Grail, a seashell to evoke the spiral of evolution.

Objects in Matisse's world, though simplified, were not exalted to become rarefied metaphors in an elaborate system of references. An oblong patch of yellow could be a lemon, but it did not lead the viewer to reflect on the essence of all acidity! Matisse was adamant and vehement about the absence of symbols in his work.

Objects were selected primarily for their plastic qualities. Individually and in relation to one another, they were not distinguished by poetic or literary references, not even in terms of their usual function. Once within a Matisse painting, a sturdy tobacco pot would become a mere sign within the Matissian universe, forever bereft of any other meaning or function, carrying no allusions to any essential, platonic, archetypal pot and forever deprived of holding any tobacco within its flanks. Perhaps it had just become a contrast in form to the round leaves of a nasturtium, an echo on a small scale of the rectangular shape of a table. If yellow, it complemented a purple drapery or played loyal liege to an orange. And yet all the viewer's senses were activated and came in sharp focus. In *Break of Day*, Colette reached the same direct sensuous appeal: "The sour scent of some peaches forgotten in a bowl reminded me of their existence. I bit into one and suddenly I was hungry and thirsty again for the round material world, crammed with savors."

Still, the line of differentiation was thin; many times a sign could easily be deciphered as a symbol. Was not red usually regarded as the color of love, green the color of hope? Was not a circle akin to a planet or to the idea of fulfillment? One wondered what would prevent the viewer from adding his or her own interpretation to any work of art, regardless of the exact field of action originally defined by its creator.

Historically, still lifes were not always a depiction of objects seen at close range; the objects were at times situated in the middle ground, and if they occupied the front plane of the picture, a drapery or a window opened a vista all the way to the vanishing point. With Matisse (except when the still life was only a detail in a painting), the intensity of color was such that it projected its content forward like a cinematographic closeup. By the painting's mere size and luminosity, it engulfed the spectator in a kind of hypnotic trance. On account of its frontality, the still life invaded all the space available around it: the room, the eye-chamber of the viewer, his retina, and ultimately his brain. Beguiled, he surrendered to the merry-go-round of objects that whirled in his mind.

The Way and
the Ways

WHEN IN the South of France, where we spent about half of our time each year, if Pablo was not pleased with his last among several canvases in progress—he used to work on several simultaneously for technical reasons—his mood started to deteriorate markedly, even if his ceramics came out of the kiln according to expectation. From calm the pendulum would swing to fidgety, back to irritable and forward to aggressive. He would then turn around with that certain set look on his face which meant that he was looking for a scapegoat on whom to unload his mounting distress. He started to find fault with minor victims. Marcel, the chauffeur, was a drunk who spent his time playing *pétanque*. The maid was ugly to look at. The meals were bad. . . . Soon enough he would complain about his eldest son, Paul's, laziness, or about his conduct. Then his anger would find more sensitive targets. Our son, Claude, would become "that brat who destroys all his toys. See how spoilt he is." Overlooking the ever-peaceful Paloma, still in her crib, he would finally turn against me and Matisse in one fell swoop.

Pablo started: "Why do you say nothing? What are you thinking about? Looking thoughtful makes you look silly, do you know that? And now you had better tell me what's on your mind!"

I sighed. "Oh, I'm just brooding over a dilemma in my latest painting."

He went on. "And probably to clear up the problem, you are reviewing all the solutions exemplified by Matisse throughout his oeuvre!"

I sat up in my chair. "Perhaps some of them, or I may be considering Georges Braque's present approach."

Pablo was not satisfied. "Let's not get sidetracked. For you, Matisse is a saint who can do no wrong, and you spend your time burning incense at his feet! But let me tell you that he is not as admirable as all that."

I stood my ground. "Well, that remains to be seen, but let us agree that I am not the only one to burn incense at his feet."

Pablo retorted, "So, you are being smart, but let me tell you one or two things about the armchairs."

"What do armchairs have to do with this discussion?"

Pablo said with finality: "I have got you there! I guess you, a radical, don't know about a statement from Matisse that sounds pretty bourgeois to me. He wrote that he dreamed of an art of balance, of purity and serenity ... an art that might be for every mental worker, be he businessman or writer, an appeasing influence, something like a good armchair in which to rest from physical fatigue."

As a matter of fact, I did find this pronouncement rather awkward. Such a metaphor was easy enough to criticize, and people had never refrained from doing so. Determined to come to Matisse's rescue as best I could, I began by agreeing that his image equating art and armchair was unfortunate. The metaphor, because indirect, was confusing. I thought he referred mostly to the soothing and all-embracing quality of an armchair; to be sure, the encompassing quality of art can be compared to that of such a chair. Also, armchairs were actual protagonists within Matisse's pictorial world. For him, they were as inviting as a feminine presence. As he painted them, they invaded the available space with their soft and curvilinear rhythms.

Pablo had plenty of ammunition. "Nevertheless, this quotation proves that Matisse's concern is to please. Therefore his art belongs to the category of the decorative."

I frowned. "No, since Matisse's goal is always the essential and not the pretty, he does not work to please—thinking that would be grossly unfair. Therefore his work is not decorative, and if he wishes to give the viewer pleasure rather than pain, it comes from the belief that art can have a therapeutic effect, helping to re-establish inner harmony, which is often endangered by the stresses of daily life."

But Pablo continued to object. "Why does he want to provide an armchair for a businessman? That's what I find objectionable. Why would his art not appeal to a simple workman, who is certainly more in need of a good armchair than his boss at the end of the day? Isn't that reactionary?"

I had to admit that the terms "mental worker" and "businessman" were perhaps elitist, simply because in 1908, when Matisse had written *Notes of a Painter*, the audience that modern artists had reached was limited to a narrow intellectual elite. Pablo knew that Matisse's inclinations had always been progressive. As early as 1905 he had become a friend of Marcel Sembat, a collector and well-known socialist politician. Nobody could accuse Matisse of being a self-satisfied egotist, much less a political reactionary.

Pablo launched an offensive. "So, you indiscriminately approve of the Venetian oysterlike seats, the eighteenth-century rococo ones, and the other elegant pieces of period furniture that abound in his canvases."

I did. "Since we are on the subject, can you tell me why in your abstract paintings the model is so often squeezed between the drastic parallel vertical lines of aggressive seats that look either like straitjackets or like coffins?"

Pablo would have none of it. "They are necessary as architectonic props, to stabilize the composition. Isn't it natural for a model to sit while posing for the painter?"

I looked up and smiled. "Perhaps for Matisse, who always works with a model, but for you, since you never work from nature, I don't see the need, except for the desire to confine the female figure within the restraining order of a cagelike contraption."

Pablo started to laugh. He loved to cross swords with me and with his other friends. He found these skirmishes stimulating, and so did I; they stretched the mind.

There was something special about his creative spirit, which could remain ablaze only with playful attitudes and gratuitous games, through dialogues and conversations. Ideas were discussed freely, not always to assess power by winning an argument but simply to keep the juices flowing. Those were charmed moments, when new ideas would surface and old thinking habits would be discarded.

Still, when Pablo had something on his mind, it did not take long before he came back to a similar topic of discussion. So a few days later he started. "Do you think that the *Rococo Chair* of 1946 is a successful composition? There is not even a suggestion of verticality or horizontality, while this oyster-shell–like monster pours out its guts outside the canvas. It gives me vertigo."

That was a difficult question to contend with. "Matisse has guts, he and only he can make sense of such a bizarre organization. Characteristically, with an extreme economy of means, the horizontals and the verticals used in this picture are the very limits of the canvas, and the octopuslike seat sends its tentacles in all directions, it radiates. It is sensuous."

Pablo did not relent. "Well, if you can stomach such irrationality, why do you criticize the logical structure of *my* armchairs in *my* paintings?"

I became conciliatory. "It was not meant as a criticism, just as a remark. While Matisse opens up, you close in. That may be a reason why you fascinate each other—you are so different, the North Pole and the South Pole, as you are often called."

Pablo grumbled some more for good measure, then went on. "Of course, we might have chosen not to use objects that exist in the outside world and to be nonfigurative, but we want the viewer to be surprised. He must learn to see the familiar from an unfamiliar point of view. Total abstraction is too far removed from people's emotions. Apropos of commonplace objects that participate in the ordinary experience of reality: these objects have a function, they are like a thesaurus of visual clichés. Assembled or disassembled, their assumed potential meaning can migrate."

I nodded. "Yes, that's really exciting. Not only do objects possess intrinsic expressive qualities in terms of their shapes, size, and colors, which can be used to emphasize their similarities or to heighten contrast, but within the composition each object has a symbolic as well as an architectonic function. Active interactions can unhinge the obvious content of the parts and release forces that go against the grain of people's habits, thus rejuvenating their visual perceptions."

Since the dialogue seemed to be drifting toward general ideas, the chairs and armchairs were pushed aside, so to speak. But the topic remained in the back of Picasso's mind, ready to be brought out as soon as the opportunity presented itself, which it did the next time we went to visit Matisse.

I don't remember how things started. Maybe Matisse motioned me to relax in one of the easychairs that are called *bergères* ("shepherdesses") in French, or on a striped silk *méridienne*, while he offered Pablo a less comfortable seat.

"So Françoise is well treated here; she can use one of the sacrosanct armchairs usually reserved for your models."

Matisse was candid: "It is true I love armchairs, I love to echo their friendly presence in my paintings, but today I am just trying to be an affable host and offer each of you what is most becoming: for her the curves, for you the straight lines. But since we are on the subject of armchairs, can you tell us about the recurrence and ominous presence in your pictures of a bulky armchair that you acquired a long time ago, when you went to live in the rue de Clichy? Why do you need it in your paintings, since most of the time you don't work from nature?"

Pablo: "What good friends I have. Françoise has already attacked me for the same reason. Because of gravity, bodies are not suspended in the air. They have to stand, sit, or recline; therefore I have to use some props, according to the inner logic of the pose. During my neoclassic period, for example, I used only large cubic stones as support for a sitting figure."

Matisse: "As for me, I think mostly of the mood I want to create. Perhaps the desire to express a feeling of intimacy that I developed in the nineteen twenties, for example, brought about the image of chairs and easychairs. During other periods the delineation of ground and sky was truly sufficient. Figures are standing, as in *Le Luxe*, or moving, as in *The Dance*, standing or sitting, as in *The Music*, or crouching like the Muslims praying in my large painting *The Moroccans*, because in the works of more heroic proportions and intent I concentrate primarily on the action taking place. Now I can even imagine figures without support, like swimmers, divers, acrobats, dancers, or the unfortunate mythological Icarus falling from the sky into the Aegean Sea."

He paused briefly, then went on. "The same definitions of space cannot apply equally to movement and to repose. We already knew how a body can remain suspended in water, but now, with the advent of airplanes, we have experienced how at the appropriate speed bodies can become airborne and remain supported through a given trajectory inside a flying machine. We have acquired a notion of limitless space, but we also find solace in the limited space of a room in our home full of the knickknacks that have accumulated in it through the years. Both points of view are not contradictory; they complement each other. We may want to go from the general to the more personal or subjective and back. When I went to Tahiti, where I discovered the beauty of the coral reefs when swimming underwater, I found out that the grass was of exactly the same green as in Normandy, and there I also positively fell in love with an armchair. Maybe its familiarity helped me not to shy away from the novelty of the environment. All these emotions, though concomitant, were unrelated but not contradictory; they all nurtured my later work."

Pablo: "What a strange thing to say. So you could fall in love with an armchair; I now understand why long ago you compared art to an armchair."

For an instant Matisse's blue eyes became steel-sharp behind his glasses, and the bulk of his body seemed to augment in volume. He was not willing to be bullied about a statement made in 1908.

Wanting to deflect the storm that was brewing, I interjected, "It may be an arduous task to discriminate between the relative merits of armchairs and other chairs in terms of strength, stability, charm, or appeal, but in painting there are two chairs that I can easily visualize

Henri Matisse. *Chair with Peaches*
(*La Chaise aux Pêches*), 1919.

in my mind, one by each of you: the Matisse *Chair with Peaches* of 1919 and the Picasso *Chair with a Vase of Arums* of 1942. I find them to be equally interesting compositions. The affirmation of straight lines in contrast with sinuous rhythms, the rectangles within the rectangles, the

Pablo Picasso. *Chair with a Vase of Arums*, 1943.

relation of the masses to negative space, make the two pictures re-markably compatible and akin spiritually. They are both splendid achieve-ments, and nobody could possibly prefer one to the other! As far as Matisse and Picasso chairs are concerned, no one could ever make a choice, and therefore, aesthetically, the viewer would have to sit on the floor!"

Both men sighed with relief, elated and mutually reinforced by such striking parallelisms in their works. The awkward moment was forgotten, and amiable conversation was resumed. They very much wished to be in agreement and to avoid subjects of potential discord. Being reminded of achievements that they respected in each other's oeuvre united them. They concurred in appreciating the two canvases I had mentioned, Pablo extolling on the daring innocence of the *Chair with Peaches* and Matisse praising the radical approach of the *Chair with a Vase of Arums*. Few artists could have created icons as spare and yet convincing in their simplicity.

Silently congratulating myself for my timely intervention and dwelling on the now-playful harmony, I asked if they equally enjoyed *The Caprices* by Goya, in which women were shown carrying chairs on their heads.

Pablo explained that in Spain and many other Mediterranean countries, people were in the habit of carrying chairs to church, to the village square, or just outside the house to enjoy fresh air, gossip, and storytelling. But of course in *The Caprices* the intention was satirical and derogatory to women. He added, "No wonder Goya was such a misogynist, after what he suffered at the hands of the Duchess of Alba!"

I let that statement go by unanswered, not pressing my luck any further, but I thought that anybody would be privileged to suffer at the hands of such an unusual woman. As in archaic Greek sculptures, the corners of Matisse's mouth curled up in an all-knowing grin, a smile that blessed frailty and all human fickleness, but he also remained silent.

During their conversations, Matisse and Picasso displayed interest in each other's methods of work, attempting to elucidate the reasons for their differences or similarities. Matisse, for example, did not overpaint. Each evening Lydia took a photograph of the picture in progress and then removed the day's work with turpentine. The next day he started again afresh, attempting a simpler, deeper, and more synthetic version of the same theme. He was concerned with the whole. He tried to get closer and closer to his original sensation, to apprehend and comprehend the mood, the mode, and the feeling that led him in a certain direction. He trusted his intuition; he concentrated until eventually he was able to conclude. He was focusing on an inner sense of truth as the canvas kept unifying, becoming more self-evident and more radiant. In so doing he was perhaps following Manet's admonition not to surcharge a painting with second thoughts and afterthoughts; all could be rehearsed first with aquatints, watercolors, or sketches, and then, when the composition was set in the painter's mind, it could be executed with spontaneity and bravura in free and liquid brushstrokes, giving a sense of immediacy and above all of purity. Matisse's pictures are thus as fragile and delicate as butterfly wings, since there are no undercoats of paint and no impasto to speak of.

Picasso, when asked if he was interested in "pictorial matter," answered, "The only pictorial matter that is of interest to me is the matter and sediments brought about by work itself," but we often find in his paintings interesting texture variations between thick and thin. He made engravings in fresh paint and sometimes added sand and other materials, which gave the pictorial surface an added interest and attraction.

Matisse was curious to know what prompted Pablo to create an image and then transform it radically through a series of interpolations, in which negative space became a positive shape and forms were erased or annihilated. All the alterations appeared capricious, unexpected, at times paradoxical, not a succession of more and more successful approximations but abrupt changes of heart. Already valid images seemed to be destroyed for the sake of inflicting capital punishment on the composition rather than improving the plastic means of expression and the strength of the overall statement. Matisse mused that perhaps since Pablo, the son of a painter, had been, like Mozart, a kind of child prodigy and had been able to achieve his goals well by the age of twelve or fourteen, later on he did not want to dismiss the easy or spontaneous answers to search for more unapproachable goals.

"Yes, that is true," answered Pablo. "How perceptive of you. What I achieve the first day can be perfectly valid, but it is not satisfying. If I can go that far spontaneously, then I must shed that result as an old skin and inquire further into the unknown, or at least the not-yet-known-to-myself. I get a second result, discard it, then a third, and so on. Meanwhile the external world is always there. Its beauty and its ugliness are consistent, that is to say, originating from some rather simple, unchanging physical laws. Whether I look inward or outward there is no relief, and whatever I do, there is no permanent release. It is as if I were blasé about my own possibilities and the environment. If it can be this way, then it is not enough. It is not this and it is not that; I must keep on trying, just to keep the experiment going until I get tired of it all. Even if the last result is not necessarily the best, I stop when my interest in the problem wanes."

Matisse then asked, "But isn't it because you do know, like a cat, that whatever somersault you attempt, you will always land on your feet?"

"Yes, that's only too true, because I was imbued early with a damned sense of balance and composition. Whatever I venture, I don't seem to be able to break my neck as a painter. Also there are moments, which I hate, when I am seized with an almost irrepressible need to idealize and embellish, which could lead toward the pretty, as if a jasmine fragrance were in the air. So I must at all times break away from tradition, break away from beauty, from the sentimentality of the blue period. I am also looking further and further back in time, wondering if something of value was not left behind. This is my drama. What about you?"

"Well, for me it is altogether different," replied Matisse. "I am not as fortunate as you are. I don't possess all that rich inheritance. I don't have a choice; it is only through hard work that I can give an impression of ease and simplicity. I must strive to erase all traces of effort and to reach clarity and purity. As far as I am concerned, I must break new ground. I cannot consider the ways; I can only concentrate on one single preoccupation. For me this is *the way*."

"Ah! You do not know how lucky you are!" sighed Pablo.

And there was a deep silence on both sides.

Windows of the Mind

THE EYE is the window of the body and the windows are the eyes of our homes; through them we receive and perceive light. Matisse once said, "The retina is but the window behind which a man stands."

The painter feeds on light. Without the sun, how could he discover color and form? Yet without the intuitive guidance and drive of the universe within, how could the artist organize and articulate his vision, how would it be possible to select the bits and pieces resembling the unknown goal he is relentlessly pursuing?

Inner space and the outside world are somehow attuned and re-sound with one another in the creator's heart. That is what the Zen Buddhist masters call the theory of the double sun: the sun out there, our life-giving star, and the light within that radiates from the heart-mind.

Matisse's eye was full of light, and Matisse's windows give us the color-light of their creator's double sun. Windows are also protective surfaces that can be alternately open and closed; they are related not only to light and air but to the wind. They are the membranes that allow varying degrees of wind, sound, and even fragrance to reach us. Windows can be sensed as powerful metaphors.

In part of a letter to André Rouveyre of June 3, 1947, Matisse wrote:

> With the kind of color correlations that I have a tendency to use in order to depict my feeling, without randomness, I find myself representing objects without streamlines of perspective, I mean seen frontally—almost aligned—linked to one another by my sentiment, in an atmosphere created by the magic interplay of color. Why not be logical and use only local tones without reflections—characters on the same plane as in a punchball game. On these elements of simplified figuration [I can] put a color springing from a sublimation of the local tone, or even altogether invented from my emotion, heightened by the presence of nature itself. But in my synthetic design I allow the occurrence of the accidental; I even take advantage of it. Some accessory parts become as useful as the most indispensable.

In painting it was not so much the abundance of production, the length of the endeavor, or the scope of the imagination that mattered to Matisse; rather, the climate or feeling heretofore unknown that the artist was able to convey in a visual form was significant.

If we were to analyze Matisse's depictions of windows, what would they mean to the viewer, what desires would they evoke? The very presence of a painting in a room always acts as a window to a parallel universe—that of its creator. So why a window within a window? Obviously, Matisse's primary concern was to reinforce the concept that picture equals window, window equals framed opening.

Now, where is the painter as narrator situated in relationship to the window? He can be outside, looking at a house with its many windows. They might be reflecting the light, or they might glow because of a source of light inside. But with Matisse, the viewer as well as the artist are inside, protected, as it were, by an array of familiar objects. Usually the environment is captured at short range; space is limited and foreshortened, depicting only part of a room at the most twelve feet deep and wide. Floor, walls, and objects are attractive and offer a richness of contrasting graphic adornments which shimmer in front of the eye.

Yet the whole array would be unbearably claustrophobic if not for a well-centered window or French door. And the effect of confinement would persist if the windowpanes were closed or if they did not allow the viewer to see beyond. Fortunately, Matisse was very resourceful, and even though his windows are seldom wide open, they are almost never entirely closed. He played with our desire for communication by juxtaposing the protection afforded by an intimate environment with the appeal of an expanse of unlimited space.

The windows or French doors are ornate; their tones are bright, emphasized with curtains, at times tantalizing with half-closed shutters that allow the light but not the scenery to penetrate. Alternately, the intricate patterns of a balcony impose one more obstacle between the limited and the unlimited.

In the *Interior with a Violin*, painted in Nice in the winter of 1917–18, there is a subtle interplay between the open windowpanes, the half-closed shutters, and the open violin case resting on a pale armchair, emphasized by bold interactions of light and dark tones. The joyous color of the outdoors is sharply contrasted with the blackness of the window frame, the shutter, and the interior of the room in the shade. The pale rectangular armchair provides an equal amount of opposition to the violin case, which is not only dark but curvilinear. This push and pull, this repetition of rectangles of different sizes, is most effective in creating tension on the surface of the canvas. The window becomes the showcase for the Mediterranean light outside, while similarly the armchair and the black case lined in an intense blue tone set off the warm hue of the violin itself. All the pictorial language conspires to give primacy both to the beauty of nature outside and to the bliss of art inside (the violin being Matisse's favorite musical instrument). While the realm of nature (the macrocosm) and art, the realm of man's creation (the microcosm), are separated by a wall of darkness, a semiopen window affords communication and interpenetration of the cosmic and the human aspects. The final resolution of the dialectic fight of opposites, is achieved on account of the complementarity of all these contrasts, so that the painting vibrates as a symphonic whole.

In Matisse's oil paintings on this theme, the viewer's eye usually travels first through a foreshortened expanse of negative space and positive forms before reaching the plane of the window, which is often presented frontally in a central position in the upper part of the painting. Framed by fluffy curtains or by an oriental drapery gathered in a loop and partially raised, gaping shutters and windowpanes direct the gaze toward the landscape outside. While there are no diagonals leading to a noticeable vanishing point, the tone or hues used to depict the outdoors and the sky are less saturated and colder than the rest of the composition, so that the view recedes optically as a result of physical laws, thus creating a sense of depth—a nonimitative way of evoking the third dimension. Nevertheless, the eye is drawn toward the horizon, toward freedom. The eye takes flight. Outside there is light, air, sky, sea, boats, shoreline, trees, gardens . . . a landscape, a cityscape, an escape.

In and of itself, the window theme is akin to the musical theme of a fugue or to Baudelaire's poetic *L'Invitation au Voyage*. But Matisse gives the room, the window, and the scenery an equal chance of capturing the viewer's imagination. Inside we are reminded of different kinds of sensual delights—beautiful objects, oriental rugs, drapes, armchairs, a dressing table, fruits, flowers, a phonograph, a violin—or we are detained by the mystery of a self-absorbed feminine presence or by the reflection of the artist in a mirror. The viewer can remain transfixed in this meditative repose, in this stillness, and yet the window is ajar; he cannot escape its focus, nor the desire it gives him to look further.

At times a woman is facing the viewer as she stands in front of the opening, or perhaps she has turned around, presenting her back while she leans forward to watch the scenery from the balcony. Is she an obstacle, or is she the muse who might accompany the viewer, the dreamer, in the exploration of the beyond? Is she a sphinx to whom he must reveal who he is, while he deciphers her riddles according to the way in which he interprets her presence? Are not the promises of sensuous and spiritual delights the sublime link to what is beyond grasp, out of reach, intangible? Beyond is the light, the appeal of the unknown, which Matisse makes irresistibly attractive by the magic of his art. The dreamer is pulled and pushed between the contradictions of a cozy, sensuous, well-protected intimacy and the limitless. Yet no judgment is

Pablo Picasso. *The Window in the Painting Studio*, 1943.

passed, no hierarchy established, no preference explicitly shown. In his paintings, Matisse does not shun the happiness of intimacy, nor does he find it incompatible with the aspiration for the limitless. Far from being in opposition, the two terms complement each other. The viewer as well as the creator can find delight on both sides of the window and in the window plane itself. The mind is impelled to go back and forth, from the sunlight to the glow of human intimacy and again into the sunlight. It is the double polarity, the acceptance of an alternating rhythm that sets a process in motion.

In Matisse's windows there is no recourse to any trompe l'oeil, no diagonals leading toward a vanishing point, yet the third dimension is experienced. The magic lies in the repetitive effect of small rectangles within medium-size rectangles within larger rectangles, of contrasts given by texture against nontexture against different textures. In other places the magic comes mostly from the interplay of colors. Each tone, by its relative warmth or coolness, determines a specific position in space; its relative intensity suggests distance or closeness.

Matisse used to say, "Each color has its gray." Such hues provide a respite; they allow the simultaneous contrast of complementary colors. An intense patch of cold emerald green is deflected from head-on collision with a vermilion red by the presence on the canvas of a less saturated yellow-green, or a mauve provides a transition between a luminescent Veronese green and a bluish cherry red. The first sensation is almost tactile, as if the whole composition occurs on a flat surface, then the pull and push of the design, textured areas, and color tension act directly on perception to release a sense of dimensionality. These are windows of the mind, a permanent source of enchantment.

A very different understanding of the same theme is expressed in one of Picasso's masterpieces, *The Window in the Painting Studio* of 1943. The first plane in view happens to be the very wall of the studio where the dormer window is located; it is literally squeezed in the upper right corner of the composition by protruding beams, pipes, and the ominous coils of the radiator. There is no suggestion of the ceiling nor of the floor. Even though the window is open, the houses on the other side of an inner courtyard and the sky are partitioned to form pyramidal shapes that, instead of leading the eye toward the freedom of the outdoors, are directionally focused toward the inside of the room, blocking the way. Since the planes inside the room are not visible (that is to say, they are pictorially absent), it clearly is an existential situation of no exit.

This picture was an important statement in relation to Picasso's actual painting studio on the upper floor of the house on the rue des Grands Augustins, where this window, located to the left of the easel on which he placed his work in progress, was the only one not entirely covered by black drapes (except for a tiny aperture further back in the room). Once evoked on canvas, even that window seemed not to succeed in conveying much hope, especially since a white rag hanging from a nail to the left of it obviously suggested the white flag of surrender.

This work spoke of an unbearable anxiety, almost an agony; it reflected powerfully the historical drama of the time and seemed also to reflect a state of psychological despondency and despair in the artist's psyche. The immaculate studio rag bore no traces of paint, as if, since no touch-ups or alterations were possible, the artist were ready to throw in the towel. At the same time this painting, arising from such deeply felt anguish, is so true that it stands among the most unforgettable icons used to symbolize the age of anxiety—our age, in which technological amenities such as pipes and radiators look rather like the malevolent curves of the Hydra, bent on our destruction.

Similarly, the rectangular enumeration of chimneys on top of the houses crammed into the window, far from being the smoke ducts of hearth fires, suggesting the warmth and intimacy of human life within the home, stood there in the desolate sky and spoke of the arid coldness of the war years. The whole seems to be a perfect illustration of the famous Spanish adage *todo es nada*, if not for the fact that in front of such total adversity the painting emanates strength, power, and energy, thus managing to convey a positive statement. In its radical austerity, the miracle was due to the quality of the interplay between sedate tones and also to the magisterial brushstrokes themselves, which reveal an extreme sensitivity. The picture itself is the only shield against the blind senselessness of war.

During the same years Georges Braque was also elaborating compositions on the theme of windows. For him, the focus was on the objects in the room; the window was most often closed, revealing only a cloudy sky or the opacity of night. It was the night of the soul, but perhaps not a starless night. The objects displayed on the dressing table were of a humble, ordinary kind—combs, soap, toothbrushes, hairbrushes, towels—and yet in their desultory abandonment they were all geared to lend the whole painting the metaphysical significance of a "vanity." Thus with Matisse we could experience an epiphany of pagan hope and desire; with Picasso, stoic strength in the face of adversity; and with Braque, a Christian lesson in acceptance and resignation.

Henri Matisse. *Reclining Odalisque with Green Sash*
(*L'Odalisque à la Ceinture Verte*), 1926.

Henri Matisse. *Odalisque with a Turkish Armchair*
(*L'Odalisque au Fauteuil Turc*), 1928.

Models, Odalisques, and Muses

SINCE the student days at the School of Fine Arts under the guidance of Gustave Moreau, Matisse had kept the discipline of observing nature with pencil or brush in hand. He did not attempt to imitate but only to decipher an enduring truth that was beyond the mirage of changing appearances. He wrestled with nature, he did not submit to it.

No object was too simple, no landscape too plain to escape his vigilant curiosity. At times he would even paint from the inside of his car. But above all, aspects of humanity captivated him; he never tired of scrutinizing the human form, as if it enclosed a potential revelation.

Far from being drawn only toward the study of female models, the young Matisse established a strong sense of structure by working from male nudes. In these, the uncompromising simplification of planes in the light reflected how well he had assimilated the lessons of Cézanne and Rodin. At times he depicted other painters, his friends and companions, at work around a sturdy man named Bevilaqua who often modeled for Rodin. Reciprocally, Matisse appeared on his friends' canvases. Joyfully they painted each other around the standing nude, thus celebrating their shared aspirations. Apart from having an intrinsic aesthetic interest, the time they spent working together reflected a trusting comradeship devoid of petty rivalry.

Later, at the time of Fauvism, Matisse made several portraits of Marquet, Derain, and several others in the group, and they reciprocated, each one emphasizing not only their shared theories but his individuality and the personality of the sitter.

Matisse's interest in portraiture expanded to his writer friends, such as André Rouveyre; to the art critic George Besson; to his collector Michael Stein and Allan, his son; to Sergei Shchukin, the industrialist who was his most important patron from Russia; to Auguste Pellerin, and later to his friend the poet Louis Aragon. He said, "I discovered that resemblance in a portrait comes from the opposition between the sitter's face and other faces, in one word from its particular asymmetry. Each line has its own rhythm, and it is this rhythm that creates the likeness."

In preliminary studies for his portraits of men he often used shadowed charcoal on paper rather than line drawing with pencil or pen. His characterizations of Shchukin and Aragon, for example, were extremely synthetic, powerful, masklike effigies, with emphasis on sculptural form. Some charcoal sketches called themes usually came first, then multiple linear drawings called variations, and finally the oils. In these different media, Matisse also made imaginary portraits of the poets of the past whom he loved best, such as Charles d'Orléans, Ronsard, Baudelaire, and he also made drawings of his friend Guillaume Apollinaire, from memory a long time after his death. (Apollinaire had died of Spanish flu in November 1918.)

In his male portraits, Matisse was not playful. In all of them structure was the chief concern. It is easy to see how well he assimilated the geometric abstraction of African masks and the lessons of Cézanne. Because of the conciseness in the execution and the apparent lack of affect, and also the color scheme, which was muted and relied mostly on black, white, and earthy tones, the work was reminiscent of Manet's portraits of Émile Zola and Clemenceau; in all these portraits the faces remained expressionless, neither sad nor joyous. The emphasis was not on subjective feeling but on character. The various interactions in all the different areas of the picture were built up in relation to the specific features of the sitter and of one volume to another. Neither Manet nor Matisse wished to impose his psychological insight in his model. Their approach was ontological, architectonic.

Matisse's trip with Hans Purrmann to Munich introduced him to an exhibition of Islamic art, where he was struck by the serenity, the permanence of its spirituality, which gave a feeling of timelessness. The graceful idealization of early Persian, Moghal, and Indian miniatures especially appealed to him. He felt that oriental people were more naturally artistic than people from Western cultures. He thought that as Western nations grew old, their art got too complicated and too soft. He started looking for a more spontaneous and youthful form of expression, welcoming the sacrifices necessary to work in a candid manner.

He had always been a frequent visitor to the Louvre, where he had copied the masters during his early years of soul-searching. After Munich he returned to it, looking for Persian miniatures and ceramics and for Byzantine and Russian icons. Once there, he also went back to the large galleries where Delacroix's major works were displayed. *The Entrance of the Crusaders in Jerusalem, The Pest Epidemics in Jaffa, The Massacre at Chios,* and *The Death of Sardanapalus* were exciting romantic masterpieces, showing that life, with all its heroic splendor, was fatally enmeshed in the coils of disease and death. *The Women of Algiers,* a less monumental picture, was more immanent, more pleasure-oriented, revealing a world where time did not count, where days flowed into each other in an endless continuum—a sensuous world akin to the oriental miniatures' hedonistic beauty.

Matisse studied Delacroix's achievements, from the rhythmical arabesques of his compositions to his bold color contrasts, with passion. He learned that in 1832 Eugène Delacroix had joined the diplomatic mission of the Comte de Mornay to Morocco, where he discovered a world of color, sensuousness, wild hunting, and equestrian bravado, a shimmering world of movement, generosity, trust, and betrayal, a proud world of untamed beauty. He stayed in Tangiers and later traveled extensively. This voyage was to have a real influence on his life as a painter and consequently on succeeding generations of artists. He made numerous sketches of riders bedecked in oriental regalia and of ferocious fights in the wilderness between animals or between men and beasts. He also drew women, mostly from the Jewish quarters of town, in picturesque attire.

Delacroix not only introduced exotic and romantic themes into the art of his time, but in terms of lyrical and pictorial magnificence, his works could be linked and equated to the greatest among the Venetian masters of the Renaissance, such as Titian and Veronese. Assuredly, he possessed the "grand manner." He brought about a revolution in color, being the first to make use of the novel theories of the physicist Chevreul about the simultaneous and delayed contrast of complementary colors, that is, of a primary to a secondary color, such as blue and orange or yellow and purple. As Delacroix said, "Give me mud, and provided you allow me to delineate it on one side with red and on the other side with green, I'll make a Venus out of it yet."

Strangely enough, while under Delacroix's spell, Matisse also became engrossed with his foe, the arch-classicist Jean Auguste Dominique Ingres, who, unable to escape the general enthusiasm for orientalism, had produced perfectly modeled but entirely unanatomical imaginary portraits of women from the harems.* These swan-necked beauties exposed their handsome backs to display a number of extra vertebrae, a fact that had powerfully disturbed the public during the First Empire and the French Restoration period but that enchanted Matisse at the Louvre. He also looked at the work of Théodore Chassériau, a gifted disciple of Ingres who had also succumbed to the general fury by turning to the camp of the Romantics. Chassériau synthesized both visions in his famous composition *Susanna at Her Bath*.

The imaginary harem women, called odalisques by the artists, provided a good opportunity to present nude women to the public. Actually, in the harems such women were considered of a rather inferior rank. The name had an appeal simply because it was euphonic in French, and from then on, odalisques proliferated on the walls of the yearly salons and of the art galleries. Later they became a favorite theme even for the academics such as Gérôme and Descamps, and no well-established

---

*Ingres was an ardent promoter of neoclassicism. Following in David's footsteps, he wanted to emulate the Greeks, the Romans, and the serenity of Raphael.

bourgeois family could do without a piece of orientalism in its drawing room. By the end of the nineteenth century, all seemed to have been said and done on the subject—done, redone, and overdone, *ad nauseam*.

Impervious to the ups and downs of fashion, however, Matisse found that orientalism caught his imagination, and he started to dream his own dream of sunshine. He felt the urge to go to Tangiers in 1912, in 1913, and again in 1914. He approached what he saw there as a completely fresh experience. For him, as for Delacroix, Tangiers was a major discovery that enlightened the rest of his life.

Many of Matisse's Moroccan works were originally purchased by Shchukin and Morosov were nationalized during the Russian Revolution, and are now permanently on view in the USSR, at the Pushkin Museum in Moscow and at the Hermitage Museum in Leningrad. They have all kept the same freshness and intensity of color that they had when they sprang from his brush. A Moroccan triptych that I saw during a 1982 visit to the Soviet Union was particularly striking. In each canvas the dominant limpid azure blue, applied unevenly on top of an undercoat of mauve brushstrokes, managed not to recede and to occupy the foreground of the canvas firmly. The figures, sparsely suggested, were endowed with a poetic quality, and they were figurative only in the most general way, not insisting on any specific individual trait but giving rather a general feeling of *presence*. An arch, a suggestion of landscape, a prayer rug, and a small pair of slippers were the only accessories allowed to embellish the utter simplicity of the whole. The painting showed how attuned Matisse must have been with Persian or Moghal miniatures, to be so much at ease with his environment. His Tangiers paintings of that period radiate not only light but a deep empathy for the Muslim world.

What was Matisse's goal? Was he following in Delacroix's footsteps? Was he emulating the purified design of Ingres, as exemplified in *The Turkish Bath*? Did he go to Morocco for the zest of adventure or in search of the exotic? Like many great painters from the north, he gravitated toward the south, toward the pink light that lent luster to all color interplay and dilated the soul. He went there and felt an increase of his powers. Under the sun, each pebble became a gem, the acuity of the senses was augmented, melancholy was averted; there was no yesterday and no tomorrow; everything could be appreciated without any sense of linear time. Matisse's dream was the Edenic dream of *The Joy of Life*; he knew that one day he would reach the phase in his evolution when his own degree of enlightenment would allow him to express a complete vision of order and beauty: luxury, calm, and voluptuous delight. He broached the subject in 1907 in a canvas that was a premonition of the quest of a lifetime. Even after the trips to Morocco, however, the theme of the odalisques was still veiled in his imagination.

Meanwhile, Matisse's representation of himself appeared more and more frequently in his own creations. Like a wizard, he came in and out of his own paintings and drawings. Early on, his self-depictions were straightforward observations—analytical at first, but becoming more and more condensed and elliptical as he invented shortcuts to the descriptive path of reality. In 1909, having acquired enough knowledge and self-confidence, he asserted his presence in a completely different manner. In a picture entitled *Conversation*, he appeared on the left side of the canvas (which supposedly encloses spiritual values) wearing striped pajamas, a serial succession of vertical lines. Larger than lifesize, his figure stood erect in the foreground in absolute parallel to the vertical stretcher bars, his feet reaching the floor plane below the picture, the crown of his head also cropped out and ending beyond the boundaries of the canvas.

This cropping of the top of the head was in absolute contradiction to the dogmas of classical composition as taught at the School of Fine Arts and other academies where he had studied as a young man. After Tintoretto and after the Japanese engravers, the Impressionists and the Nabis were the first to surprise the public with unexpected layouts in which the sacrosanct upper part of some human figures were virtually bisected in the interest of the general composition. Even then, no artist ever left only a small part or the very edge of a figure to end outside the frame line; it would have seemed very amateurish, as only beginners made such mistakes, from lack of skill. But Matisse willfully edited out the crown of the head, the brain cortex, the seat of intelligence and reason, to accentuate the vertical thrust of his silhouette and to open

Henri Matisse. *Conversation*, 1909.

the composition in the upper left part of the canvas.* He clearly meant
to say that since his intelligence and reason were all over the canvas,
in each part of it equally and in the whole totally, it could not be found
in the imitative representation of the upper part of his skull within the
picture. His profile, his whole schematic figure in striped pajamas, resembled the capital atop a classic column, supporting an invisible temple
above and beyond the canvas. Thus the verticals did not stand for

---

*In the weavings of Native Americans a thread or threads always traces a special upward
path so the "spirit" of the piece, instead of being kept captive within the intricacies of the
design, has an outlet to freedom.

abstract intellectual values; they indicated an aspiration toward pure intuition, reinforced by the deep celestial blue dominant and by the inviting opening of the window in the center. To the right, the dark, curvilinear sitting figure of Madame Matisse found an echo in the rhythms of the trees and the ironwork of the window banister carrying the earthy arabesques of life itself.

In *The Painter and His Model* (1916), the game became more elaborate, like the play within a play in Shakespeare's *Hamlet*. To the left on an easel the canvas within the canvas is emphatically presented as an echo of the model, whose eminence in the background seems threatened by the sharp vertical clash of light and dark and the monumental size of the baroque mirror. His back turned toward the viewer, entirely self-absorbed, the painter works. He is sitting in the foreground in a position symmetrical with the structure of the easel, while to the right a window opens a vista onto the outside world. As in a game of chess, black and white fight for dominance. Active and passive areas are orchestrated by the complementary colors: purple and yellow ocher, leaf-green and red. The interplay among painter, model, and painting is accentuated by the utter simplification of the whole composition— the minimal yet clear definition of each part.

In a self-portrait made in Nice in 1918, Matisse teased the viewer even further, by planting the suggestion of a still life on an easel in the background while depicting himself almost oversized, firmly sitting in the center. The artist's face is stern, his gaze behind the glasses fixed, while he is shown at work, brush in hand, on a painting that the viewer is not allowed to see. This ideal or potential object of desire, a work of art in the process of becoming, is visible to the painter alone. It is located just beyond the edge of the actual canvas, accessible only to the painter's brush and eventually to the viewer's imagination.

Matisse started this rendering of the artist at work while looking at himself in a mirror; this is certain because Matisse was right-handed, and here he appears to be painting with the left hand while holding the palette with his right one. The body's posture is relaxed; the arms and legs are open, the plexus region protrudes. The thumb coming through the hole in the palette is very large as it grasps the strong diagonal thrust of a large brush in the foreground, crossing over a darker line in the genital region of the painter's suit. The other hand, holding the paintbrush in action, also affirms its willfulness, by obliterating the inward push of an umbrella in a stand toward the still life in the background. Clearly the natural pulse of the human libido was crossed out in order to be integrated at the sublimized level of artistic creation. It was as if Matisse were confiding to the viewer the necessity of asceticism, of transforming sensual desire into a will to project the intangible, a will to attain a higher level of reality, a will to reach into the essence of art.

In another canvas, painted in Nice the following winter, the composition focused on a nude clearly delineated in the center and aptly endowed with the most beautiful and important set of curves in the whole picture. To the left the painter is at work, his back protected from the viewer's curiosity by the stern bars of a chair. His painting within the painting remains vacant, even though the brush seems ready to strike. Thus the spectator is allowed to follow the artist into the secret chambers of creation; he can follow him, yes, but he is given just the actual painting itself as a spectacle, while the creative act on the picture within the picture is left to his imagination. The communication about the act of creation remains cryptic; it is for the viewer to decide what was real.

These self-images were neither embellished nor derogatory, neither flamboyant nor ugly, neither pompous nor modest, neither fierce nor meek, neither proud nor humble, neither stylish nor deformed, neither emphatic nor just factual. If anything, the keen observation of Matisse's own features and character, aided and abetted by a marvelous sense of humor, led the artist to unexpected solutions. Matisse wanted to tease the eye and appeal to the mind. Later still, in an unforgettable group of drawings, his reflection appears in a mirror in the background and his hand in action in the foreground. With the ease of a magician, he appears, disappears, and comes back, while at the same time he displays, juggles with, or conjures away the objects he loves or his own models. Taken by surprise, tricked but seduced, viewers are right away ready to smile. Matisse successfully puts them on his side and makes them wish to belong to his universe.

His universe was one of participation, where no part of the whole was ever considered in isolation. He could easily have leaned toward total abstraction, but he wanted to keep the tension between the ideal and the down-to-earth aspects. Without yielding to the descriptive, he considered the challenge of figuration to be the hardest task, the highest goal. That is why Matisse never tired of introducing human features both in his drawings and in his compositions. Alternately he analyzed the possibilities contained in one posture and excelled in combining an arresting cluster of simplified figures. Many art lovers would have difficulty understanding why, knowing the human body as he did, he still usually worked from the model, since he had no need for a sitter as a guideline to follow and imitate.

When he started to spend more and more time in Nice, Matisse, the lucid dreamer, was about ready to people an Orient of his own imagining with the houris of an earthly paradise. He did not need many props to set the stage: a small niche where the sitter reclined, dressed mostly in pantaloons of one shade or another, with the possible addition of a brazier or a ewer, a Moroccan textile drapery with see-through embroidered window-shaped designs, a vase, some flowers, some fruit perhaps. For him, organizing the environment that he wanted to depict was like writing the scenario of a play. The initial climate he created was a prelude to the future interaction of volumes, colors, and textures that he envisioned. On account of his myopia he worked so close to the sitter, that he experienced her proximity as a living part of the pictorial space. Far from making him feel threatened or claustrophobic, the model's presence guided him toward a progressive transformation of what he perceived into what he knew to be true, as he reached out toward an enduring reality in the realm of art.

Because they were more painterly, the odalisques and other canvases of the 1920s did not possess the heroic qualities of the works Matisse achieved during the previous decade. Yet some of them, like *Decorative Figure Against Ornamental Background* (1925) and *Sitting Nude with a Tambourine* (1926), were daring and monumental. If the reproach of escapism can be granted, it would still be wrong to believe this period to be of lesser merit. Matisse was reaping the crops that he had sown and nurtured earlier. The resources of his palette were playing to full advantage. The sensuousness of the treatment was appropriate to the sensuousness of the subject matter. A body only partly undressed was more erotic than an unsophisticated nude, and the exotic setting also made the painting less of an "academy," a simple study from the nude. The painter was no longer Matisse the savage, Matisse the wild beast —he was Matisse the voluptuous, Matisse the Persian.

At the beginning of the 1920s, the art scene in Paris was paradoxical. On one side, Pablo Picasso and Georges Braque, the archradicals, had adopted a composite style alternately neo-Cubist and neoclassical. Derain shamelessly worked his way back to classicism; the rest of the Fauvists returned to traditional colors and forms or became tame. On the other side, the Dadaists and the Surrealists promoted automatic painting as well as automatic writing. They believed in irrational creations surging from the unconscious to free the individual from the stereotypes of a decadent society.

Matisse was not drawn toward the theories of the Surrealists, even with the knowledge that Aragon led a cult for him, and though he was also much admired by Tristan Tzara, he did not understand Dadaism. Most important, he never surrendered to neoclassicism; the necessity of being modern defined his position in a most consistent, unambiguous fashion. The Orient he had discovered in Tangiers and superbly integrated in *The Moroccans* was now invoked not so much as a memory but as the subjective climate of his dreams. The past splendor of Diaghilev's ballets, such as *Schéhérazade*, created in 1910, the lavish Russian sumptuousness of stage sets by Bakst and Benoît, and the fashions of the famous designer Poiret possibly also had a bearing on the origin of his odalisques.

During his days of work Matisse was like a Sufi initiate, imagining tales and parables that illustrated points of this esoteric Muslim doctrine in a playful way. The blooming of these apparently effortless but by no means easy pieces was the springtime of a new maturity, the necessary release, the flutter of butterfly wings, before Matisse's ascent to a new plane of metamorphosis. Each and every step of the ascent was punctuated by the recurring presence of favorite sitters. Even when the subjects were similar, each work stemmed anew from a knowledge that was never repetitive but always jolted the viewer with Matisse's capacity to reinvent the whole.

The French poet Arthur Rimbaud once said, "Love is to be reinvented, one knows it." And with Matisse every day started anew, as if he saw things for the first time and gazed in wonder. Painting had to be reinvented, one knew it. The artist obeyed his daemon, his forceful inner drive, which irresistibly propelled him forward.*

Matisse was dedicated to his art in the way that others are dedicated to religion. He was relentlessly forceful and willful in the pursuit of his goal. Many young occasional or professional models could not captivate his attention for long. He preferred to measure himself against women with stronger personalities. From the start of his career he did not have to look very far to find them: these qualities existed in his wife, Amélie, his dedicated companion, and in his daughter, Marguerite, who modeled for him during her childhood and young adulthood. Both women were proud, erect, with good minds of their own. Out of devotion for Matisse they had to submit to endless sitting sessions, but as a result of their good will and resilience, they appeared in many canvases.

Far from being at all pleasant or carefree pieces, these works reveal a poignant knowledge, a darker mood, a lucid but dramatic identification with the model, a possessiveness that cannot be found anywhere else in Matisse's oeuvre. There is a smoldering, silent passion, an almost tragic form of love, full of shadows and forebodings that are not as evident in the portraits Matisse made of his sons, Jean and Pierre.† Maybe Amélie and Marguerite were more patient and allowed him to go to greater depths. Both were women of substance, not decorative women; women with minds, the very opposite of the passive archetype of the odalisques that prevailed in Matisse's work during the twenties.

If the sitter is morally on equal terms with the artist, portraiture can be the most demanding and, when successful, the most compelling art form, such as the portrait of his sisters by Chassériau, the portrait of Berthe Morisot by Manet, the portrait of Whistler's mother by Whistler. But Matisse was hardly one to be rebuked by such difficulties.

---

*A daemon is the creative spirit of an individual. In classical mythology, it was one of the lesser gods whose chief purpose was to guide human beings.

†Matisse alternately made his sons appear older or younger than they actually were, which proved how much he relied on his imagination and memory rather than on factually observed reality.

He was always ready to decipher the enigma of an interesting face. As a consequence, many women collectors and their relatives commissioned him and posed for their portraits: Sarah Stein, Greta Moll, Greta Prozor, Germaine Raynal, Yvonne Landsberg. At the request of Etta Cone he made four posthumous drawings of her older sister, Claribel, from photographs, the fourth being the most accomplished, and drew six studies of Etta herself, also from photographs. It was highly unusual for Matisse to work from photographs, yet these portraits rang very true.

He never looked for beauty in his sitters, but for well-balanced or even powerful features. If his knowledge of the human figure spoke of the keen observing gaze of the anatomist, his interest in the char-

Henri Matisse's portrait of Lydia Delectorskaya entitled
The Blue Eyes (Les Yeux Bleus), 1935.

acterization of intelligent female sitters demonstrated the mastery of the psychologist. (He seemed to reserve psychological insights for his female subjects; with men he emphasized generic features rather than individual characteristics.) He did not idealize his models; he made them handsome, alive and solid, he made them real. Often he even had a sense of humor about them, which remained visible in the finished work, preventing prettiness from setting in. Women were magnified, but his lucid gaze was never indulgent or flattering. Even the professional models who retained his attention over a period of time, such as Laurette, Henriette, and Antoinette, were far from beautiful in the conventional sense. He exaggerated some of their particular features in a close to expressionistic fashion. The evocation also went further than mere assessment of visual characteristics. In Laurette's portraits, for instance, the fragrance and the weight of her dark locks were made palpable and contributed to the mood of the subject as much as the accentuated shadows under her eyes.

After a decade of meditation and relaxation, the first appearance of Lydia Delectorskaya in Matisse's studio in the late 1920s posed an entirely new challenge. She allied the active and the passive. She became Matisse's full-time secretary and at times his model. She was alive and present both in mind and body. During the 1930s and even afterward she was his essential source of inspiration. Her regular features and the statuesque grace of her figure presented themselves again and again as a leitmotif of peace and serenity. In such pictures the model was more clearly defined and even more individualized than in Matisse's studies from professional models. The almond-shaped eyes, the straight classical nose, the sinuous lips, the strange expression of an aloof kind of sensuousness, and a unique flavor of mystery were quite recognizable. Not only that, but Lydia's clarity of spirit, her integrity, led Matisse toward some of his boldest statements and most meaningful achievements. She was a muse, providing the artist with a constant challenge and a constant incentive to transcend his previous creations.

And yet Matisse had an addictive need for new faces. After his operation in 1941, his friend Aristide Maillol felt he knew how to rekindle Matisse's curiosity in the human form. Maillol had found his most vital inspiration in the person of Dina Vierny, and he wished some of his

Henri Matisse. *The Open Window, Collioure*
(Porte-Fenêtre à Collioure), 1914.

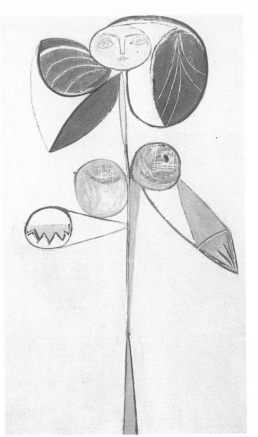

Pablo Picasso.
The Woman-Flower
(*La Femme-Fleur*), 1946.

Henri Matisse.
Portrait of Madame Matisse
entitled *Woman with the Hat*
(*La Femme au Chapeau*), 1905.

Henri Matisse. *Nice Interior, Young Woman in Green Caftan Leaning at the Window* (*Intérieur à Nice, Jeune Femme en Caftan Vert Accoudée à la Fenêtre*), 1921. Note the double "K" diagrams formed by the window and the figure shapes.

Henri Matisse. *Harmony in Red* (*Red Room*)
(*Le Desserte Rouge*), 1908.

Henri Matisse. *Interior with a Violin*
(*Intérieur au Violon*),
1917–18.

Henri Matisse. *The Artist's Studio (Le Grand Atelier)*,
Issy-les-Moulineaux, 1911.

Henri Matisse. *Sorrow of the King* (*Tristesse du Roi*), 1952.

Henri Matisse. *Sunset in Corsica (Coucher de Soleil en Corse)*, 1898.

artist friends to share his enthusiasm. Since Édouard Vuillard had recently passed away, Dina, then twenty-two years old, was sent to the French Riviera to sit for Pierre Bonnard at Le Cannet and to visit Matisse at his studio in Nice. First she was impressed by Bonnard's interesting approach. He started an oil with her; then she went to Cimiez. Matisse started drawing with delight. Along with the attractive messenger, Maillol had sent him a letter in which he said, "I lend you the vision that impregnates my work; I know that you'll reduce it to a line!"

Of course, Matisse was quite stimulated, then joyful and talkative as he set to the task. Dina enjoyed his conversation, and he made drawing after drawing. After a few days, as Dina reminded him that she had to visit Bonnard again to allow him to complete the canvas he had started with her, Matisse became adamant that her presence was necessary for a longer period of time. Jokingly, he even drew a silhouette of Bonnard in the background of one of his drawings: "So that's it. Bonnard is here behind you; let's go on."

Certainly Dina's features were evocative of many of Maillol's sculptures, but Matisse thought that she resembled Victorine Meurent, one of Manet's favorite models.* Dina's neat figure, her face with its high cheekbones, her short nose, and her slightly slanted eyes, specifically reminded him of the *Olympia*, and he insisted that he wanted to paint an *Olympia* himself. "You must be the Olympia by Matisse," he intimated.

Dina's good grace and patience were tried, yet she was persuaded to linger a bit longer. But she had a will of her own, and after a while she decided to return to Banyuls to resume her privileged dialogue with Maillol: the dialogue of the sculptor and the muse, the dialogue of the creator and the true inspiration. She was pleased to bring Maillol up-to-date news of his friends' recent researches and present interests. So there never was an *Olympia* by Matisse.

For Matisse, the beauty of a model set a process in motion. By enhancing the acuity of his emotions, it made him aware of his own

---

*Victorine Meurent sat for *Olympia*, for *Woman in a Matador Costume*, for *The Woman with the Parrot*, for *Woman with Cherries*, and for many other important works and portraits. She herself was a gifted draftsman.

lyrical aspirations. He worked with several different models to renew his interest in the human figure. He found young women whose features and characters corresponded to a definite project he was pursuing, such as the young woman from Martinique for the illustration of Baudelaire's *Les Fleurs de Mal* and a Russian girl named Doucia who sat for the fifteen portraits embellishing the deluxe edition of the famous *Letters of a Portuguese Nun* published by Tériade. For this work Matisse was perhaps also inspired by the psychological evolution of Monique, a nurse who cared for him after his operation and pulmonary embolisms in 1941 and who in 1942 posed for *The Idol* and other works. After a spiritual crisis and some soul-searching, she became a nun at the Dominican convent in Vence, on the opposite side of the street from the Villa Le Rêve. Some models, like the fair Katia and Paule, a dark-haired French studio helper, were permanent members of the household.

Matisse enjoyed the presence of women. Even though the precariousness of his health kept him indoors most of the time, he was by no means a hermit or a recluse. While he worked, the cheerful loveliness of his young models opened a window to the world. He listened to their chatter and grasped the expression of a fleeting moment. Their glorified beauty infused the shadowless freedom of his line drawings or became manifest in the simplified mastery of a radiant painting.

During sittings, a unique relationship developed between Matisse and his models. It usually did not imply any personal intimacy, but there had to be an implicit trust on both sides, a climate of serenity propitious to the artist's work. A good model had to give him more than the attitude or posture he asked for; she was to summarize the essence of femininity and thus allow his meditations to take shape. As before, he continued to work extremely close to the sitter. It was as if his eyes were touching the volumes rather than simply looking. Without doubt, his haptic sense was more necessary to him than visual perceptions alone. To help define a plausible environment, he assembled accessories around these young women which served as a logical context to the pose, thus adding substance to the flight of his imagination.

He no longer used his oriental bric-a-brac, and his sitters wore elegant French designers' dresses as they relaxed in cozy armchairs or talked with a friend, sharing a moment of intimacy by the fireplace under the protection of gigantic philodendron leaves. Matisse selected professional models who were shapely without excess and not too tall; otherwise his rhythmic lines would have to expand too far before reaching the end of a limb. He liked swanlike necks or necks resembling slightly swelling columns. In any posture, a body had to flow like a river, never suggesting complete immobility. He had a predilection for delicately jointed limbs, fine wrists and ankles. During the sessions his proximity to the models certainly accounted for bold foreshortenings or unusual angles of vision; mirrors provided him with additional aspects of the same poses.

Even if the human figure was caught in an expressive gesture (an extended or a folded limb, for instance), that gesture was nullified as such by the competitive activity of other colors, forms, and textures, until it became only a pattern among many, playing its part in the symphony of the whole. The focus of attention had to be the picture or the drawing itself. All the marks left on it contributed to its necessity, or else they disappeared during the process of creation. Abstracted, some figures reached not only frontality but perfect symmetry, as in *The Yellow Dress* (1931), *Large Blue Dress on a Black Background* (1937), *La France* (1939), *Young English Girl* (1947), or *The Hindu Pose*, as early as 1923.

The trusting comradeship that linked Matisse to Maillol and Bonnard allowed them to share models now and then as a way to sharpen their dialogue, but their mutual good will did not expand to include Picasso. Though Dina met the latter several times in 1943, he was not given the opportunity to make sketches of her during Maillol's lifetime. But conversely, it would have been unthinkable to imagine Picasso sending Dora Maar to sit for Maillol. During Picasso's early adolescence, he worked from professional models provided for him by his father, as in *Science and Charity*. Later he never used models, apart from friends and collectors who sat for portraits. He did not work from nature; therefore he had only muses, or detested ex–loved ones who became countermuses in his private inferno. He felt so territorial in that regard that he was certainly not willing to share his muses, and even his scourges were taboo.

In the past, Matisse's insatiable appetite for faces had led him to draw Josette Gris, Juan Gris's wife, and in 1942 he had made a theme-

and-variations series of Elsa Triolet, Louis Aragon's Russian wife. Usually everyone was flattered by the attention. That's why, in Matisse's mind, asking to undertake my portrait in February 1946 was equivalent to signing a peace treaty with Picasso. In his opinion, it would make the relationship between them more relaxed and intimate. Triggered by Matisse's avidity for portraiture, it could have been a psychological faux pas or perhaps a veiled but conscious provocation, destined to stir the Andalusian's possessiveness and jealousy. Pablo did not lack tact or self-restraint; he could have asked to make a portrait of Lydia, and Matisse might have been quite taken aback by the suggestion.

In the late forties and the early fifties, some of Matisse's models were art students who were enchanted to have an opportunity to talk with the master and watch him develop his ideas while sitting for him. He was very kind to them, took interest in their goals, and often extended a helping hand on their behalf. He said he needed a model as a springboard to depart from. Maybe the singularity of a newcomer's features could by itself shake away the possible repetition of idiosyncratic forms, but he also had to measure himself against a woman of substance, a muse to whom he could surrender his power.

Whether models, odalisques, or muses, women's features supplied more than a springboard for Matisse's imagination. He was a keen observer. Far from depersonalizing his sitters to fit a preconceived idea of his own, he allowed himself to be led on by the singularity of each one. He took this uniqueness into account not to dispel it but to distinguish between anecdotal appearances and noumenal reality. He battled his way into the few traits that made sense. *Exactitude was not truth*. By discarding the superficial, he could delineate the necessity of the interactions he emphasized. This was clearly revealed in the spontaneous series of drawings in which he allowed his thoughts to revolve around the axis of a concentrated sensation, becoming more and more essential as he went. In the photographs of various stages of the *Leda* painted on a double door for an eccentric Argentinian couple, the Anchorenas, for example, the willful effort toward increasing abstraction, generalization, and simplification were like a discourse on his own method of work and a tribute to his clarity of intent.

In addition to human models, many animals found their way into

Matisse's oeuvre: horses, donkeys, dogs, cats, tortoises, birds of all feathers, including parakeets and canaries, goldfish, starfish, crabs, dolphins. Upon entering Matisse's arch, they ascended to another plane; they became archetypal signs of life.

Like Matisse, Picasso always was a tireless interpreter of all animal life. He loved animals, and besides his pigeons he successively owned a mischievous monkey, a huge Saint Bernard, a gaunt Afghan greyhound, a boxer, and many other pets, some of which were immortalized by their master.

Painting was almost a birthright for Picasso; he started so young that quite naturally his first models were those closest to him: his father, his mother, his sister Lola, relatives and friends. Even then he seemed most interested in the inner life of his sitters, who often looked thoughtful and self-absorbed. During adolescence, when his family settled in Barcelona, he met young artists of his own generation who became his models, as did dancers and performers in the cabarets. While still in Barcelona and during his first sojourns in Paris, he began to focus his attention on the aged, the poor, the unwanted, all the pariahs of society, and he simplified his palette, using Prussian blue* as a dominant color. From 1901 to 1905, during the blue period, all individual human features that he sketched or observed around him fused under his brush to convey the sufferings of the forsaken and to personify his feelings of compassion. The suicide of his friend Casagemas, a young Spanish artist, added to his own experience of extreme poverty, goaded him to create tragic images of dereliction. He began to work mostly from memory, thus transcending the accidental or incomplete expressive power found in the study of a given individual. He typified without portraying excessive pathos but with extreme sensitivity, thus gaining in lyricism.

By 1905 Picasso was ready to stage the characters of his inner drama. Watching a shabby family-circus performance near the Eiffel Tower was perhaps the inspiration for his next series of large compositions, including mountebanks, acrobats, harlequins, jesters, and clowns. Their sadness was more poetic; their poverty seemed less hopeless.

---

*Prussian blue is made from potassium cyanide and is a very invasive color that in time bleeds on other tones.

Slowly a new color suffused the canvases, a very special earthy pink that heralded the beginning of the rose period. All figures remained simplified and to an extent hieratic, but they now were caught in motion or in an expressive gesture.

Picasso's life began to open up. There were art dealers such as Ambroise Vollard, Clovis Sagot, and others, who underpaid him but exhibited and sold his work. There were also intelligent collectors, such as Michael, Leo, and Gertrude Stein. Above all, the pink dawn was due to his new love for the beautiful Fernande Olivier. Born Amélie Lang and separated from a violent husband, Paul Percheron, she adopted the pseudonym Fernande Olivier and became successful as an excellent professional model. With her regal bearing and her almond eyes, she posed patiently for hours on end, and she was sought after by sculptors and painters alike. Capricious and witty, she followed all her whims and led a bohemian life.

In the summer of 1904, Picasso, who already admired her from a distance, met her on the place Ravignan during a storm. He convinced her to come to his studio, where they made love that afternoon, but she did not agree to stay. Afterward he wooed her constantly, and it was only after almost a year of hesitation that Fernande agreed to share his ramshackle studio at 13, place Ravignan. Picasso painted many nudes and handsome portraits of her. She did not have to sit for him, as she had done before, since he worked mostly from memory, but he needed the reassurance of her presence; she was his muse, a constant inspiration. Even the paintings in which she did not appear were suffused with the sensuous rose glow that emanated from her.

In May 1906 the two left for Spain together, and after some time in Barcelona, they went to Gosol in the Pyrenean mountains, where Picasso embarked on large compositions and basked in the presence of his beloved. He also did several portraits of their old innkeeper, Josef Fondevila. The sculptural Iberian structure of these studies gave him the answer he was looking for so that he could proceed boldly forward. In late August he and Fernande came back to Paris, and Picasso made a last masklike drawing of Josef Fondevila. Thus, before Gertrude Stein returned from her summer holidays, he was able to finish her portrait by fusing what he had just learned about form with the objective knowledge he had acquired during Gertrude's numerous sittings.

This was the beginning of an inner revolution. Picasso perceived that when shapes become architectonic, they acquire a reality of their own. He confirmed his discoveries by studying tribal African objects. In his work, torsos often became as tubular as tree trunks, and limbs followed abstract rhythmical patterns drawn in dynamic diamond shapes. Some people attribute this evolution to the fact that Pablo smoked opium at that time, but the drug simply helped erase his last inhibitions in regard to the artistic tradition of Western art, to the legacy of the Renaissance. If opium perhaps leveled his last doubts, if Fernande's love boosted his self-confidence, his subsequent evolution was still a direct result of the way he applied an impeccable inner logic and followed the drive of his creativity to its ultimate consequences. His new certainty surfaced in a series of self-portraits and culminated in 1907 in the controversial *Demoiselles d'Avignon*. This was the breakthrough he strove for; he was not yet twenty-six when the painting was completed.

Georges Braque was initially shocked by the barbarian violence of *Demoiselles*. On his own he found a path of simplification by following in Cézanne's footsteps, and during the same year, 1907, he developed a new style quite compatible with Picasso's accomplishments. In 1908 Cubism was born from their combined certainties. The two artists then initiated an unusual artistic dialogue, which they pursued day after day until 1914. They worked in separate studios and met in the evening to evaluate works in progress and agree on further research. The ideas they developed and shared attracted other artists, who adapted them to suit their own needs.

For Picasso, for Braque, and later for Juan Gris, this unfolding of their conceptual thinking was a quest for the ultimate, a purely abstract summation that needed neither models nor muses, just the crystalline facets of their creative minds. Token concessions to figurative stereotypes in portraits or still lifes were achieved through the integration of recognizable attributes such as a waistcoat, buttons, a pipe, collages of wallpaper or newspaper, and later typographical letters, musical scores, and such. During these years of heroic asceticism, Picasso and Braque were so selfless that often they did not even sign their canvases.

World War I put an end to this community of spirit, which could never be recaptured, even when normal peacetime life again prevailed.

In 1918 Picasso married Olga Koklova, a Russian ballerina. On the one hand he continued to amplify the conquests of Cubism; on the other hand he embarked on neoclassic compositions. A visit to Pompeii and to the Museum of Antiquities in Naples certainly had a strong impact on Picasso; he said so himself. Still, his transformation of the stylish, slim, green-eyed, and red-haired Olga into a dark-haired and dark-eyed giantess was quite improbable, unless it was meant in defiance, in opposition to Olga's standards. Was Olga the muse of this new development? She was perhaps an antimuse rather than a muse. Their smoldering antagonism soon permeated not only his giants and giantesses but his Cubist paintings, as in *The Dance* (1925).

Now and then Picasso tried to placate his wife by having her sit for him. He would make some highly idealized portraits. Quite true to life, they were examples of the masterpieces he could produce in a classical mode when he put his mind to it. Under this apparent stylistic fragmentation, Picasso was taking stock. He wanted to add his Mediterranean heritage to his discoveries; he wanted to put it in phase with the revolutionary acquisitions of Cubism. From 1920 to 1930 he demonstrated his mastery of different pictorial idioms.

But concomitant with the appearance of Marie-Thérèse Walter in his life, around 1927, a stylistic reunification began to take place. This woman perfectly embodied a synthesis of Picasso's aspirations. Her sculptural proportions, classical profile, passivity, and voluptuous rhythms combined to make her a perfect odalisque. Her presence was the incentive Picasso needed to emphasize color, light, and the arabesque, but not to the detriment of form. This was a period of great lyricism. Love and peace are what they are, and as such they endure.

Historical events took charge; conflicts arose between ideologies. Picasso felt a compelling need for a change of phase. He could not and would not remain indifferent to the outbreak of the Spanish civil war in July 1936. He also met a new muse, Dora Maar, a Surrealist photographer who soon became a painter. The daughter of a Yugoslav architect, she had spent her childhood in Argentina and spoke Spanish fluently. She had looks, she had brains, and she was talented—just the feminine complement Picasso needed to face and express the mounting tempest in Spain. She found him an artist's studio at 7, rue des Grands

Augustins, which was large enough for him to paint *Guernica*, his outcry after the bombing of that small Basque city by the Nazi air force, Franco's allies.

Entirely painted in gray, black, and white, *Guernica* was finished on time to be placed in the Spanish Republican Pavilion at the International World's Fair of 1937 in Paris. Highly abstract and austere, the large symbolic composition was astonishingly expressive and moving. This painting was the highest point in Picasso's career since Cubism. After all the studies preceding this masterpiece, Picasso continued in the same dramatic vein throughout the following years, until the liberation of Paris in 1944. Dora Maar was a constant source of inspiration, a *Muse of the Sorrows*. Many paintings were entitled *The Crying Woman*.

With the liberation of Paris, Picasso was ready for a new swing of the pendulum, away from the drama, back to a pure abstract geometry. It seems that he had a special flair that enabled him to discover the appropriate muse at the appropriate time. Each new companion consciously or unconsciously helped trigger a new phase in his creativity, as in Wagner's operas, where each character is heralded by a particular leitmotif. I observed the increased presence of elongated forms and the conjunction of green and blue in two principal combinations, a pale blue to a leaf-green or a light ultramarine blue to a Veronese green, after Picasso completed my portrait as *The Woman-Flower* in May 1946. Linear patterns also acquired importance. Some works made in the autumn of 1946 at the Grimaldi Castle in Antibes were almost purely graphic compositions, painted mostly in different qualities of white on white. I also noticed that Picasso often expanded discoveries made spontaneously in one medium with more purpose and more effect in another medium.

Picasso was satisfied with the large red lines ending in seal-like circles that he had devised for the illustration of Pierre Reverdy's poem *Le Temps des Morts*. When we came back to Paris in the autumn of 1948, he soon started a very abstract painting entitled *The Kitchen I*, using linear patterns to define the intersections of the various planes. Walls, table, door, stove, cabinets are simplified and even a growing plant is reduced to mere vertical arrows. Each change of direction is emphasized by seal-like circles, as in *Le Temps des Morts*. The result is minimalist in style and stunning in its apparent simplicity. Picasso then proceeded to make a more painterly variant entitled *The Kitchen II*, placing the same diagrams in a semichiaroscuro. In December and January he continued painting in the same fashion with very free interpretations of my face and figure, based on the same principles. The linear patterns branched out. Often they were red, as they had been in the illustration. They no longer acted as a border between one plane and another; they could come in the middle of an area of an entirely different color. They added rhythm to each area; they echoed each other and activated the whole composition.

At times some of these surfaces and patterns were treated in black and white, like a collage, while the rest of the painting had strong colors. The head was drawn in black inside a white rectangle to resemble a lithograph that Picasso had recently finished. I was flabbergasted, because the whole painting seemed to be a portrait of my mother, whom he had never met. It was uncanny: on each canvas where he tried that approach, even if the black graphism on the white rectangle was different, as were the other forms and colors, when finished it still looked like my mother and not me. It was not because I resembled my mother, since I did not. It was the black and white, which definitely had something to do with my mother's personality and not mine. We were quite amused by this incident and decided that Picasso had discovered my mother's leitmotif, even though he had never seen her. For me, he had better stick to the blue-green or green-blue combination. It worked even in the most abstract compositions, in the same way that pink announced Fernande, voluptuous arabesques were linked to Marie-Thérèse, and deep purple epitomized Dora.

Javier Vilató, a young painter who was Picasso's nephew (the son of his sister, Lola), was intrigued by this occurrence. He wanted to meet my mother. We did so, without Picasso of course, since my mother did not want to meet him, but she was very gracious to Vilató, and he was able to report that these abstract portraits indeed looked like her and that furthermore, she could have been Spanish with her dark hair, dark eyes, and very pale complexion. Picasso was satisfied. He said he had seen her in my mind, and we were all amused by what looked like a case of extrasensory perception.

The Vence Chapel

IN ADDITION to his genius, Matisse the benevolent patriarch was endowed with an impish spirit. He simply could not resist testing the limits; the word "impossible" was not part of his vocabulary. He needed to overstep the bounds, to experience how far he could carry things so as to test his own forbearance, as well as the potential adverse reactions of his friends. He could enter a new artistic venture in a state of utmost innocence; then he would proceed to build his intuitions into coherent theories. Because his sincerity was complete, he did not hesitate to put himself in extreme situations; he needed to follow his work to the end, regardless of obstacles and possible controversy.

Not only was Matisse steadfast and persistent, he was also opinionated. Because he was such a celebrity, his opinions, his choices, and his actions were often reported by the press and therefore came to public attention, even if he kept a low profile as far as his personal life was concerned. In France intellectuals and artists had a great influence on public opinion; they were considered *maîtres à penser* (master thinkers), and thus they were studied, followed, and criticized.

As Aragon put it, "Those who believed in heaven and those who did not" fought in the Resistance together, regardless of political factions. In the euphoria following World War II there was a revival of "sacred art" in France. The Abbé Devény and Father Couturier, a Dominican, were artistic advisers in the decoration of a church situated on the plateau of Assy in the Haute-Savoie, a place with many sanatoriums where students went to recover from tuberculosis. Regardless of their religious or nonreligious allegiances, Georges Rouault, Pierre Bonnard, Georges Braque, Fernand Léger, Jacques Lipchitz, and Jean Lurçat received commissions for this church, and accepted them. Matisse was also approached, and in 1948 he executed an effigy of Saint Dominic for the altarpiece, a simple black design on off-white glazed tiles, accompanied on both sides by grapes and vine leaves. It was placed at the end of the south aisle, opposite the Bonnard altarpiece, which ornamented the north side.

This first religious work had quite a history behind it. When Matisse was convalescing after his surgical ordeal and subsequent complications in 1941, a young woman named Monique came to nurse him and occasionally sat for him. Later she came to the realization that she wanted to become a nun in a Dominican convent. The one she chose happened to be in Vence, on the route de St. Jeannet, just on the other side of Matisse's Villa Le Rêve. The convent-run rest home, called Foyer Lacordaire, needed to rebuild and enlarge an oratory that served as a chapel but that had been destroyed by fire. Matisse's friend, now called Soeur Jacques, was artistically inclined, and started to design models for stained glass windows. In 1947 she took them to Matisse for constructive criticism, and he began to show interest in the project.

Brother Rayssiguier, a novice in the Dominican order, was convalescing at Foyer Lacordaire. He had ideas about architecture and was enthusiastic about modern art, so he and Matisse began a dialogue about aesthetics, symbolism, and liturgy, in order to devise architectural plans for the oratory. The structure had to be both appropriate for the religious purpose it was to serve and consonant with Matisse's views. Auguste Perret, a famous French architect and one of the painter's friends, was asked to become a consultant. Perret and Matisse met in Paris in July 1948, but the architect's suggestions were not retained, because they were not in keeping with Matisse's vision of the type of space that he wished to "enlarge" with his pictorial contribution.

In his album of cutouts entitled *Jazz*, Matisse had written: "I believe in God when I work." In that sense he concurred with the opinion of Father Couturier and the Dominican order, who believed that regardless of artists' conscious political choices and philosophical opinions, the act of painting was a religious act when truly inspired. The Dominicans, one of the most progressive and enlightened religious orders, were making a fantastic effort to promote the integration of valid examples of contemporary art into religious edifices.* Catholicism was such an integral part of French culture that when Matisse, passionate as always, became engrossed in the project of the Chapel of the Rosary, he didn't stop to consider whether such an undertaking was in keeping with his well-known agnosticism and progressive political views. Father Couturier had reassured him when he became interested in the Vence project that he could keep all his independence of mind, and time and again Matisse felt the need to reassess his freedom, orally as well as in writing.

But things were not that simple. Nothing that Matisse did could remain private for very long. His interest in decorating a chapel was publicized and gave rise to controversial debates in the press, much more so than the work done by the artists who had accepted commissions for the decoration of the church at Assy because it was a shared effort, each artist doing only a part. Henri Matisse was the much beloved and admired "grand old man" of France. Each party, each religious or philosophical group, wanted to win him, or at least hoped to claim him as an ally.

Before much of the work was accomplished there were some confrontations between Matisse and Picasso regarding how appropriate it was for the former to engage in such a project. In the summer of 1948, during a visit to Cimiez, Matisse insisted that Brother Rayssiguier show us the model of the chapel, despite Picasso's reticence and his unwillingness to discuss the topic. When he realized that Matisse's work was

---

*The Dominican order in France also published a literary and philosophical journal called *La Vie Intellectuelle*, to which many writers in the forefront of progress contributed because of its nonpartisan objectivity.

not just a simple decoration in a given space already in existence but a full-fledged architectural and environmental whole, he was amazed at Matisse's decision, and rather upset. The separation of church and state in France had been achieved early on and thus was no longer a dramatic issue for anyone, but in Spain the church had more or less endorsed and upheld the Franco regime, so for a Spanish Republican like Pablo, his friend's decision to do something for the church was controversial and unwelcome. It was equivalent to morally endorsing an institution that had for Pablo a reactionary aura.

Pablo asked Matisse if he had become a believer. Matisse answered that the chapel was giving him the opportunity to work on all the different aspects of a complete environment and that for him it was an artistic project.

"But do you pray?"

Matisse answered: "No, not really; I meditate. Always aiming toward serenity, I would say that I am closer to Buddhism than to anything else."

Pablo was not interested in meditation, nor in Buddhism. He tried another tack. "If you want to compose an environmental piece, why don't you decorate a marketplace?"

Matisse just answered that the colors of the fruits and vegetables would clash with the colors of his composition.

We left. The next time we returned, Father Couturier was present and the discussion started all over again. Picasso repeated that he found it objectionable for a nonbeliever to work on a religious project. He felt that it went against the unity of intent an artist should have, and he quoted Arthur Rimbaud: "Truth in a body and in a soul. That's what matters."

To placate him, Father Couturier exclaimed, "Ah, we know that Picasso paints with his blood," and added, "Really, there is no contradiction. We do not ask the artist to be a believer. For example, Fernand Léger and Jean Lurçat, who belong to the Communist party, both accepted commissions for the church at Assy. One made a large mosaic and the other a tapestry."

Pablo interjected, "That's their problem."

Then Father Couturier, who had known me from my school years, turned to me, hoping that I would agree with him on his Order's open-mindedness.

Even though I had great respect for him, I was in complete agreement with Pablo, and reminded Father Couturier that in historical times the Dominicans had been responsible for the Inquisition in Spain: "At that time the church imposed its views through coercion. Now, because the church is weaker, bringing people into the fold has become a process of seduction."

Picasso was enchanted by my aggressiveness, and Father Couturier smiled indulgently, as if pleased to find out that I had lost nothing of the stamina and rebellious spirit for which I was known at school. He knew that in the end, even doubt or revolt was not indifference. Picasso's opposition and mine, as well as Matisse's meditations along the lines of an unorthodox neo-Buddhism and his occasional denials of any personal religious intent—all these things were just part of the same package. Through thesis and antithesis, paradoxes and contradictions, a dialectic process spurred the artist on toward the full realization of a work of art that could not fail to make an important statement. Father Couturier could have paraphrased the seventeenth-century philosopher Blaise Pascal, who had said: "Get on your knees and you *will pray*." The father always hoped to bring artists back into the fold, but he was also sincerely interested in modern art.

Meanwhile, stimulated both by the artistic challenge and by the controversy, Matisse was hard at work, first using models for preliminary sketches and then further elaborating his ideas on huge sheets of paper pinned to the walls of one of his studios at the Regina, which by chance approximated the size of the chapel. Again he undertook many studies, abstracting and purifying his initial designs until they achieved a simplicity that satisfied him.

From the start Matisse was concerned with the technical as well as the aesthetic aspects of his future realization. He had conceived that the Madonna and Child, the stations of the cross, the Saint Dominic, and a medallion were to be executed in ceramics. As I have mentioned, he selected the Madoura pottery to test the feasibility of large handmade ceramic tiles, and Picasso, though averse to his friend's project, outdid himself to be helpful. That is why, when it became clear that the pottery could not manufacture enough perfect tiles, Picasso and I volunteered to accompany Lydia and Monsieur and Madame Ramié to Aubagne to visit several ceramic factories that specialized in tiles.

Understanding the nature of the commission and its importance, the Bourdillon factory sent the best samples, in terms of solidity, consistency in size, clay tone, and quality of handicraft. It was thus retained to make the tiles and bake them once, after which it sent them to the Madoura pottery, where they were inspected. The tiles' upper surface and sides were then dipped in liquid enamel and set to dry. In that state they were carried by truck to Matisse's studio in Cimiez, where they were assembled on the floor to match the size of one of the future panels. Armed with a brush tied to a bamboo stick, Matisse drew directly, taking inspiration from one of his designs. Afterward, the tiles were carefully carried to a truck and sent back to the Madoura pottery to be baked a second time in the electric kiln. The whole procedure was technically difficult and time-consuming, but thanks to Matisse's willpower and his assistant's dedication, the work proceeded evenly.

Matisse was caught in an ascending spiral of vision. He became more deeply involved than he thought he would, for spiritual, if not exactly religious, reasons. His designs in the chapel were to include all the sacred objects—the chalice, the crucifix on the altar, the chasubles, everything. He was a severe taskmaster; he completed many projects for the stained glass windows which he then discarded, believing that they did not achieve the unity of feeling he wanted in conjunction with the other elements of design—chiefly the enameled tiles outlining the stations of the cross, the Madonna and Child, Saint Dominic, and the medallion. The sketchy appearance of the ceramic panels, of an elaborate and refined simplicity, was a reminder of elements of the Catholic faith, already well assimilated by the clergy and the lay public during two thousand years of Christianity. Matisse not only agonized over the forms and color combinations of the stained glass windows but also over a certain intensity of lemon yellow glass that could not be found or made to his specifications. Some of the colored pieces of glass were sandblasted to become more translucent and less transparent. He cared about each and every detail.

From the outside the project was unpretentious, and looked not unlike other oratories in the region. The size of the chapel, the blue-and-white enameled Roman tiles of the roof, its low incline, and the fine steeple made of wrought iron were naturally attuned to the hilly land-scape.

Model of the Chapel of the Rosary in Matisse's studio in Nice, 1950.

While Matisse was toiling in Nice, Picasso and I were spending the winter in Paris at the studio as usual, working steadily and late into the evening, dining out at the Brasserie Lipp or in some other restaurant patronized by the intelligentsia where we were sure to meet some of Pablo's friends. Inès, the maid, used to bring the mail along with breakfast, and one morning in the heap of letters and publications I found an envelope addressed to me in Matisse's recognizable handwriting. I opened it. It just said: SAINTE FRANÇOISE   H.M. 1949. Its rosette ornaments were akin to those that Matisse planned to use around the Virgin and Child in the Vence chapel.

This little note, received on my saint's day (March 9, 1949), did not create half as much stir at home as the similar message had the

Letter addressed to "Sainte Françoise" from Henri Matisse, 1949.

198

year before. Pablo had told Matisse that I was expecting a second child, and Matisse was amazed to think that his friend was adding to his family at his age (sixty-eight) and with all his other responsibilities. He perhaps believed that my acquiescence to all of Pablo's wishes would not necessarily enhance our happiness in the long run. Whatever the reason for his kind reminder of my saint's day, I received it with pleasure in Paris, where the winter was cold and somber.

Pablo was mostly involved in making very imaginative black-and-white lithographs, including some of me in a folkloric jacket from Poland. He was also continuing a series of variations that he had started in 1947, giving further interpretations of a painting by Cranach the Elder, *King David and Bathsheba*, and other subjects. Huge stones were brought to his studio in the morning and carried away in the evening. At Mourlot they were prepared, inked, printed, and deprepared (which meant made ready for additional work), and then they were brought back to him along with fresh lithographic ink, pencils, and zinc plates, in case he felt like making other images. Charles Sorlier was the designer who came with them most of the time, along with an assistant since each stone weighed between one hundred and two hundred pounds. What he did was a feat of strength from every conceivable point of view, since he was also the go-between and was expected to give Picasso technical advice, which Picasso then set about to disprove—almost always successfully, much to everyone's amazement.

Everything was so old and dark at 7, rue des Grands Augustins, that it created a feeling of living in the past, which was excellent for concentration but led to thoughts disconnected from reality. Despite this, I worked on a series of rather sculptural drawings of my son, Claude, sitting or driving his toy car. All were rather simplified and rather sinister, whereas the previous series (in 1948) had been at least full of light, if not actually joyful. In retrospect it seems that I was very depressed, not faring well with my pregnancy.

Even though the baby was due in May, my obstetrician, Doctor Lamaze, decided in April that I had waited long enough, and the delivery took place a month ahead of time at a fashionable private clinic. My daughter was born on the very day that Picasso's *Dove of Peace* was posted on all the available walls in Paris. As a result of this coincidence she was named Paloma. She was small and very beautiful. Her birth helped restore my equanimity and put an end to my depression. A few days later Pablo was astonished to see how cheerful I looked: "My word, you do look happy," he said, as if suddenly something had gone wrong, as if the plot, whatever it was, had taken a new twist. His bizarre expression puzzled me, but I did not pay much attention to it because I was so incredibly happy. I did not know then that the birth of a female relative, his own daughter, could recall the old trauma of his sister's birth.

I stayed perhaps ten days at the clinic, decked out in pink satin dressing gowns that I had purchased for the occasion and had never worn before and receiving flowers, telegrams, and friendly visitors all day long, including personal friends whom I did not usually encourage to visit, lest they disturb Pablo. Doctor Lamaze came every day, and we talked and joked. Just looking at Paloma was divine, a marvelous moment of respite after so much tension, and I enjoyed it to the fullest.

In his letter of May 19, 1949, Matisse congratulated Picasso and me on our daughter's birth.

Regina, Cimiez   19 May 1949

Dear Friend,

All my congratulations, which I want you to share with Picasso, on the undoubtedly most charming dove, who must be making herself audible by now.

How strange things are sometimes. For the last few weeks I have been working at representing a young mother and the child that she holds on her knees, since she is seated; and seated; and despite being seated she measures ten feet high.

Even though I made no attempt at giving her a resemblance to anyone in particular, the architecture of the image being of foremost interest to me, Lydia said to me a few days ago: "When looking at what you are doing, I am thinking about Françoise and her child."

It seemed to me that she was not completely wrong, but I am not yet finished and I shall fall back into something more general before the end.

Accept, dear friend, my best wishes for the baby girl and my regards for her parents.

H. Matisse

Letter from Matisse to Gilot, May 19, 1949.

The "mother and child" that he referred to was not to be a small project: even in a sitting pose, the Virgin measured ten feet. Matisse had started by using charcoal on large sheets of white paper pinned on the walls of his studio at the Regina. As usual, he modified the initial design almost daily until he felt he had attained a pristine purity of expression, as well as the grace, balance, and wholeness he was looking for.

At a certain stage of the work in progress, Lydia apparently thought that it evoked me with a baby—Claude, probably, since Matisse was fond of him. Matisse, rather pleased with the idea, pointed out that the resemblance would disappear before the final stage of the composition, because he wanted to build an image whose message was universal rather than subjective and personal. Once he had completed a satisfying model of the Madonna and Child on paper, he could use it as a guide to draw freehand on the ceramic tiles.

Knowing Picasso as he did, Matisse was not averse to subtly teasing his friend. He knew how to trigger an emotional upheaval while appearing entirely innocent of any guile. All he had to do was set the trap. He probably had been pleased with the results of some clever moves he had made on previous occasions in the competitive games he and Pablo enjoyed playing to test each other's presence of mind. The subject of my appearance in his paintings was touchy, and he knew it full well, but here he succeeded in suggesting the possibility quite indirectly, as if by chance. The letter was addressed to me, but since the congratulations about Paloma's birth were destined to be shared with Pablo, he was assured that his friend would hear or read the rest.

The small time bomb exploded as planned.

"This beats it all!" claimed Picasso. "He calls himself my friend, but when it has to do with you, things take a strange turn indeed. The first time he saw you, he made innuendos about the desirability of making your portrait. Then, in 1947, he presented you with a cutout where you were kneeling. Afterward came the letter about your 'sanctity,' and now 'Lydia'—not him, mind you—discovers that the Virgin Mary in the work in progress looks like you!

"As to the child who resembles Claude, does that mean that his birth is the result of an immaculate conception? What's more, it is not a small sketch, the feeling of a fleeting moment; it is a huge composition to be carried out at the Chapel of the Rosary, where everyone will enjoy seeing it for sure. I feel negated—that's it, negated, obliterated from *A* to *Z*, not only as an artist but even as a father!

"And Matisse is so innocent that your likeness came about by chance! That's hard to believe. Why does he get involved in the particular if, as he says, he will return to the general and the impersonal before the end? This is adding insult to injury. Either he is inspired by you and should admit it, or he is not and should leave your likeness alone. The purpose is supposedly religious, but nothing is sacred to him. I can't own anyone or anything in peace. Between his 'purity' and your 'virginity,' I realize that no one loves me."

It was hard to put an end to such an outburst of self-pity, because I could not stop laughing. At last I succeeded in stifling my giggles to reply, "Bravo—I see that you are versed in the intricacies of the Roman Catholic faith. Anyway, take this letter at face value instead of looking for hidden meanings. Matisse felt that the coincidence of Lydia's remark about his work in progress and the birth of our second child was a good omen which he wanted to share with us. As an artist, it is his way of congratulating us and approving of our lives together."

Pablo answered, "Perhaps you are right. After all, he thinks about us, he is all-inclusive in his friendship. You have a knack for finding solutions to my attacks of anxiety. I feel better. Anyway, as Töpffer would have said, what is the particular and what is the general?* We go all the way from the head to the egg, like Brancusi, and back to the head, like me, oscillating like a pendulum. There is no such thing as aesthetics, nor pure painting. What's more, if I make a portrait of you and Claude, I want the depiction to be as characteristic at the end as it is at the beginning. Even if the outcome is far from objective reality, my intent carries a power that dominates the form and reveals the essence of the subject, its uniqueness, whatever metamorphosis took place on the way."

---

*Rodolph Töpffer (1799–1846) was a Swiss writer and artist with a keen sense of humor, whom Pablo liked to quote.

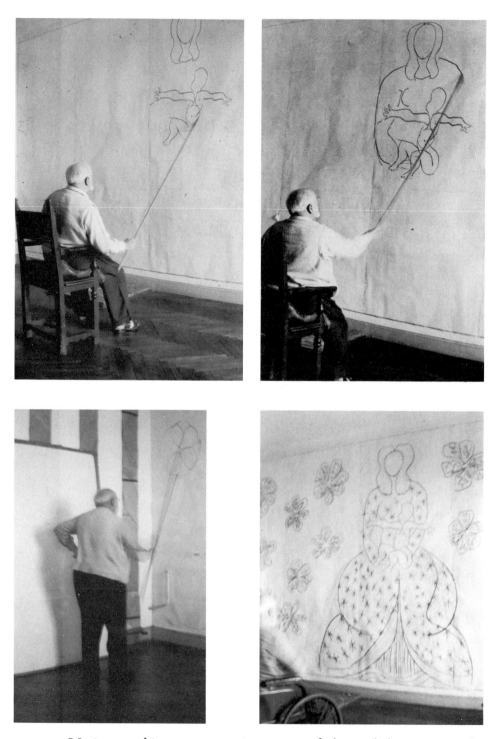

Matisse working on successive stages of charcoal drawings, studies
for the Virgin for the Chapel of the Rosary at Vence, 1950.

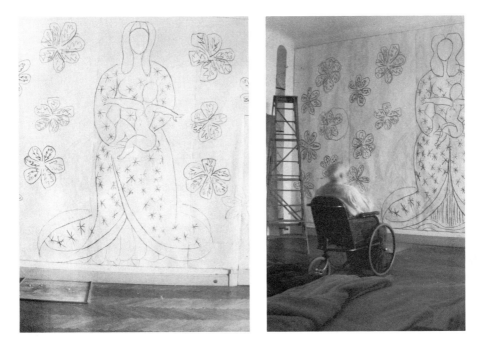

I said, "You have a good point. Why did Lydia make that remark? Did 'she think it would please Matisse? Was it spontaneous? Was she deeply interested in us as well? My feeling is that Lydia empathizes with us, and even though she is so aloof, she always seems to be happy to see us. What is your opinion?"

Pablo answered, "My opinion is that apart from their inordinate taste for caviar and champagne, Slav women are always inscrutable. I should know, I was married to one! If it was already so with Olga, who came from Leningrad, it must be even more so with Lydia, who was born in Siberia. Let's drop the subject. I am satisfied."

Pablo brightened up, invigorated by this theoretical skirmish with Matisse in absentia and by having taken indirect revenge on Slav women in general. He was ready to resume work. While setting a new canvas on the easel, he only added meditatively, referring to his friend, "When one of us dies, there are things that the other will not be able to say to anyone else ever again."

As usual, work sessions were pursued until late at night, Pablo busy in his studio, me in a different room at my drafting table, and Claude asleep in his room. After my return from the clinic, Claude was quite upset by the presence of his infant sister in his own room. Though only two years old, he spoke very cogently, and complained to Inès, the maid, that Paloma was too white and that he had wanted a red sister.

Spring in Paris was rather pleasant that year, and we went through our normal routines, one of which was attending interesting lunches at Marie Cuttoli's home on the rue de Babylone. She owned a very large duplex apartment that opened onto a garden. The huge drawing room was full to the brim with first-class Picassos from all his different periods. The *Tall Nude* by Braque (1908) and some Mirós of the Surrealist period graced the dining room, some Calders the foyer, to say nothing of the impressive sculpture collection. Marie was a distinguished hostess, and we were always likely to meet Alfred Barr or Alexander Calder and his wife if they were in Paris, as well as some French political figures, one or two ambassadors and their wives, and other visitors of note. The conversation was always very animated and the food excellent.

On occasion there were unexpected guests. One day we were rather surprised to meet Father Couturier, who was not a regular visitor. He always looked impressive in his white-and-black Dominican habit, but he seemed more emaciated than ever in this contemporary environment. He seemed to welcome the opportunity to speak to Pablo outside of Matisse's presence, perhaps to make him more receptive to the general intentions of his friend in regard to the decoration of the Chapel of the Rosary, or even to tempt him to do the same somewhere else, regardless of his political convictions.

Picasso was not about to be influenced. He stated clearly that he thought it was all right for Georges Rouault and Maurice Denis, who were devout practicing Catholics, to paint for the church, but he saw no point in a painter's doing so if he was an agnostic or an atheist. He found that a work of art that did not express the deepest belief of the artist was gratuitous and void of meaning.

Stubbornly Father Couturier insisted that *ideally*, the faith of a great artist was the best incentive, as in the case of Rouault, Denis, and Manessier, but in actuality an inspired work of art by a great artist was a more religious act than the routine abeyance of an academic believer.

Pablo would not hear of such accommodations and fuzzy edges in spiritual matters, so he stated, "For me, even with all his neo-Buddhist meditations, Matisse is a van Gogh without God."

There was a silence, after which Father Couturier felt impelled to repeat a remark he had made in Cimiez: "Oh! but of course Picasso always paints with his blood."

But Pablo was not about to be placated, even by a most flattering sentence, and so he quoted something his mother had said when he was younger: "If my son had been drafted as a soldier, he would have become a general; if he had entered the priesthood, he would have become a pope; but since he started as a painter, he ended as Picasso." He added, "If I had been a pope, I would never have allowed inflated rhetoric and sophism as a substitute for faith. But no offense meant—fortunately, I am not a pope, not even in Avignon. I am only Picasso the intractable, and when I don't have red I paint with blue instead."

Father Couturier had the good grace to smile, and the rest of the lunch proceeded without incident.

When the chapel was completed, Pablo and I went to see it, and though we liked the stained glass windows in deep yellow, lemon yellow, royal blue, and emerald green, we did not like the fuchsia light that resulted from the combination of the divided tones. I thought that the sculpted crucifix was the most successful object, along with the door of the confessional. We liked the black-and-white ceramic panels, but not the way they reflected the purple ambient light.

Perhaps it was too ethereal for us; if it was joyous, it was so in such a sublimated manner that it failed to move us. At the time it did not strike a personal chord in me.

Matisse had worked on the chapel from 1948 to 1951. It was dedicated in June 1951.

Gilot holds up her drawing of
Claude riding in his toy car
for the "real" Claude to inspect,
summer 1949.

Her parents cluster around baby Paloma as she sits in the
lap of her nurse, Tati, in the garden at Vallauris, summer
1949. Picasso is on the left and Gilot is in the center.

Webs

ONNECTING the artists to the collectors and to the public at large was the art dealer's function, but in selecting which artists to represent in their galleries they helped manifest certain trends. A team spirit, a comradeship, and a basic understanding was generated among all members of a dealer's group, young or old. An art gallery could become of central importance if the painters and sculptors under contract acquired a sense of loyalty to it and to one another. To an extent the link was a professional, aesthetic one, but it tended to establish emotional bonds between most of the participants and in time it contributed to the specific mood of the gallery. If a dealer failed to give cohesion while maintaining healthy competition within his stable, he did not make a significant mark in the art world. If one observed an art gallery over a period of time, one saw shifts in taste or interest, according to each artist's individual evolution, which in turn influenced the dealer's shifts of interest. Out of this new constellations were formed.

For example, in 1907, when Daniel-Henry Kahnweiler opened a gallery in Paris at 28, rue Vignon, he started with Derain, van Dongen, and Vlaminck, then Braque, then Picasso. Soon he discontinued his business relationship with Vlaminck, van Dongen, and Derain and became interested in Fernand Léger and Juan Gris. Without recording all the successive additions and deletions over the following decades, it is interesting to list the artists represented at the gallery, renamed Galerie Louise Leiris by the time I came to know Kahnweiler. First, he represented the estates of the deceased artists Juan Gris, Paul Klee, and Manolo, the sculptor; then, among the living, Picasso, Léger, André Masson, André Beaudin, Eugène de Kermadec, Suzanne Roger, Elie Lascaux, and the sculptor Henri Laurens were under contract. I was co-opted and added to that list in 1949.

The Galerie Louise Leiris had an array of related galleries, such as the Leicester Gallery in London, the Alex Vömel Gallery in Germany, and the Curt Valentin Gallery in New York (later the Saidenberg Gallery). Each gallery had its own integrity and independence but functioned as part of a network for the artists listed above and for others as well. Artists as important as Picasso and Léger could also establish links of their choice abroad (for example, with Paul Rosenberg or Pierre Matisse), and even in France, with such dealers as Louis Carré, who exhibited Matisse's drawings in 1941 and paintings by Picasso in June 1945 and in 1946.

But at that time an entirely different web was in the making, and it was headed by Aimé Maeght. During World War II he and his wife (then living in Cannes) had befriended Pierre Bonnard and Henri Matisse. Maeght then owned a small gallery in Cannes. But after the liberation he opened in Paris, at 11, rue de Téhéran, and soon had a Matisse show in what was to become an important center for modern art. Soon thereafter Georges Braque, who had been conspicuously absent from the Galerie Louise Leiris, joined the new web, adding to its strength and vitality. In time, with the artistic director Monsieur Clayeux's help, many more outstanding artists were to join the founding group: Miró, Marc Chagall, Alberto Giacometti, Tal Coat, Ubac, and Bram van Velde, to list just a few.

Invasive as always, Pablo wanted to have a say and even a foot in there if possible, but Braque made it clear that this was not to happen or else he would quit. After the intense closeness of Braque and Picasso during the Cubist years of research and exploration, the friendship had cooled down. Braque clearly distrusted Picasso's intrigues and often reported derogatory remarks. Officially they were on good terms, but there were undercurrents. In Picasso's studio one could see a Braque still life with two apples, a lemon, and a teapot appearing and disappearing mysteriously, according to the ups and downs of the relationship.

Because Braque's approach had become more painterly, Pablo used to say, "Oh, my friend has become the Vuillard of Cubism—he is now in a *post* Postimpressionist phase." In fact, to the intransigence of his early work Braque had added in his mature years a chromatic richness of vocabulary, an elegance of brushstrokes, and surprising surface qualities. Far from deterring from the monumental impact, these developments enriched and enhanced his work. After Bonnard's death in 1946, the Galerie Maeght continued to represent his estate, so Braque must have felt that he was in good company. Along with Matisse, he and Bonnard were the strongest champions at the rue de Téhéran.

When we met Braque in Paris, the tie to the Galerie Maeght was not discussed; neither did it come up in Matisse's conversation in Vence or at the Regina. What were Matisse's present feelings toward Braque, the renowned ex-Fauve? We did not know. Silence. And silence on Braque's side as well. The webs could overlap, but not communicate. Also Matisse did not give Maeght exclusive rights. Like Picasso he often exhibited at the Galerie Louis Carré. Out of necessity, on account of Picasso's gossipy habits and unpredictable behavior, a lot of things went unsaid.

In the winter many well-known artists left Paris and the cold gray days to enjoy more clement weather in the South of France. Henri Laurens, the sculptor (under contract to the Galerie Louise Leiris), came to Magagnosc, a small city next to Grasse, and began to do drawings and illustrations, intending not to embark on heavy work for two months. He enjoyed his stay in the small provincial hill town and returned the following winter. When Henri Laurens went somewhere, Georges Braque was never far behind. The two artists and their families had always been very close. So in good time we were advised that Braque, his wife, Marcelle, and Mariette, their secretary, had arrived and would spend some time in St.-Paul-de-Vence. He did not intend to work there, or so it was understood; thus no one could ask to see any work in progress. It was agreed that Braque, his wife, and Mariette would visit Pablo's new studio (an ancient distillery of jasmine and orange blossoms for perfume) in the rue du Fournas in Vallauris. This was an important event, because in Paris Braque never went to the studio in the rue des Grands Augustins, to prevent Pablo from saying that he went there for inspiration.

Braque had always loved cars, and he had a very fast and handsome Jaguar, one of the few luxuries that he really enjoyed. He had a chauffeur, but he also drove it himself. He was more relaxed than in Paris, since all the gossipy people in the art world were far away, but when he visited Vallauris for the first time, instead of coming to see the paintings, he came to look at the ceramics at the Madoura pottery. Since this was far removed from his preoccupations, once there he relaxed even more, and he and Picasso began to enjoy each other's company, as in the good old days. Tall and lean, with a mane of white silky hair and arresting dark eyes, he was dramatically handsome. I was delighted to see a smile on Braque's face; he had such charm when not on the defensive. He even said a few words. Although Marcelle and Mariette were responsible for most of the cheerful atmosphere, I also contributed as much as possible, and Braque was pleased with the way I manifested my regard for him and my genuine admiration for his art.

All this helped, and from then on the relationship between the two great painters eased a lot. They no longer used their encounters as power games, yet they were not entirely open and carefree. They belonged to different webs; Braque was there chiefly to make plans for the future with Aimé Maeght, and Pablo had no part in that. When Kahnweiler came that winter, I believe there was a gathering including Henri Laurens, the Braque family, Kahnweiler, and ourselves, for old times' sake.

During the same period, I was astonished one morning when Kahnweiler offered me a contract with the Galerie Louise Leiris, then at 29, rue d'Astorg. As I wondered what had prompted him to do so, he told me that my way of thinking and the kind of dedication I had to my work reminded him of Juan Gris. After asking Pablo if he agreed that I should accept, I was quite pleased to say yes and to become a member of that prestigious web. I was quite familiar with André Beaudin and his wife, Suzanne Roger; in fact I had met them in 1942, a year before I met Picasso. After 1946 I had also met Fernand Léger several times at the rue d'Astorg. He liked to act tough, but his manner was genial and he did not take part in any intrigues. André Masson and his wife, Rose, spent a lot of time in Aix-en-Provence, where they became close to Tal Coat and Marcuse, the lithographer. Once on the way to the bullfights we stopped in Aix and met Claude Duthuit, Matisse's grandson, who was spending time with the Massons, whose sons he had befriended. So one way or another the webs overlapped, creating elaborate networks of likes and dislikes, of alliances or hidden resentments.

Now, because of my contract with the Galerie Louise Leiris, my status improved in general, especially vis-à-vis Pablo. Although the prices paid for my paintings and drawings were modest, I could and did support myself and the babies, paying for our everyday needs. That was a great improvement, since Pablo always used money, or rather refused money, to control his entourage. From then on I could also purchase canvases and all the necessary supplies without depending on his alternately sweet and sour moods. I could also buy proper clothes for myself and the children.

Since Pablo, a winner himself, always had respect for winners, he started to give me some presents, such as a gold watch in the form of a scorpion. I reciprocated with a gold watch not in the shape of a scorpion and with other presents, always similar to his, because it was very unwise to be in his debt in any way or to allow him to get the upper hand in the power struggle that it was his unfortunate destiny always to seek. For Pablo's own sake I did not want to be bullied, and thus I resembled his friend Braque. Maintaining my dignity was the only way that I could remain a valid interlocutor in front of him. Maybe that's what Picasso enjoyed in his French friends, such as Matisse and Braque; they showed affection but refused to cater to his perverse behavior and general fickleness.

So for a moment I was riding the apex of the wheel of fortune, and on the eighth of March 1950 I received the following letter:

March 8, 1950
Your name day
And the great name day of my life
    Françoise You
      Picasso

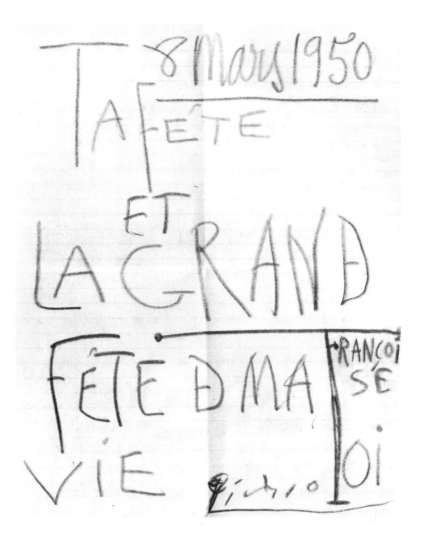

Note from Pablo Picasso to Gilot, March 1950, addressed
"La fête et la grande fête de ma vie."

214

These calligraphic wishes from Pablo on the eve of my saint's day were obviously related to Matisse's similar letters from the previous years. In Spain the greetings for the *verbena* were always presented a day early, which afforded Pablo the advantage of good timing, making sure that he would be the first to reach me, especially since he did not have to mail the epistle and just dropped it on my worktable.

In contrast to Matisse's, the paper was of the most ordinary kind with lines. The handling of the message was clever, though, with the *D* including the *E*, and the capital *F* of *Françoise* used both for my name and as a capital *T* for *Toi*. Furthermore, if I assumed that the capital *F* could also be read as a capital *T* and if I read the letters on each side under the horizontal bar to the *T* on the left, I found *MA*, then *T* in the center, and to the right an *I*, an *S*, and an *E* (not counting the letters belonging only to my name). I found all the letters necessary to write *Matisse*, especially if I indulged in stealing one *S* from Picasso's signature.

That evening, when Pablo came back from Madoura, he was in a very good mood. "Did you find my letter? How did you like it?"

"Very much indeed. It was thoughtful of you to remember my name day."

"Didn't you find it clever?"

"Very clever, very calligraphic, very simplified. Thank you very much."

He looked a bit disappointed, but I was not about to reveal what I thought I had seen and thus be lured into a pitfall of his making. If I said that I saw Matisse's name emerging from the letters as if it had been written with sympathetic ink, he might retort that I was obsessed with our friend, or, worse, that I implied that he himself was obsessed with Matisse. I was not about to provoke my possible downfall for the short-lived pleasure of exhibiting my wits.

With Pablo, as it had been with my father, I had to be very careful to show enough intelligence to hold my own turf but never succumb to the temptation of showing too much. I had to decide ahead of time if I really wanted to make the point and pay the price. I would be given full rein only if I won over someone else and my winning was destined to turn to my elders' advantage. I guess neither my father nor Pablo ever realized how sad it was that in relating to them I had to weigh the balance of forces, and instead of behaving with spontaneity on a ground of mutual trust, I had to be guarded and on the lookout for possible traps. One might think that I had a paranoid disposition, but unfortunately, the necessity for caution was only too true in both cases. First my father during my childhood and then Picasso were always testing my ability not to become ensnared in appearances or overconfident, and I was always on the alert to defend myself, not only against all types of danger but particularly against the ingenious traps they set.

Pablo did not know that from childhood on, I had made a study of how to remain silent in order to have power in reserve, of how not to reveal myself unless I was ready to take a stand (at whatever the cost), if I believed that the issue was worthwhile and clear-cut. So on the eighth of March 1950, the best solution was to be delighted with the obvious content of the message, without referring to Matisse's earlier letters or to the secret inclusion of his name in the text.

Even if other webs provided a support system and a measure of independence, I had no way to extricate myself from Pablo's web, because I was ensnared by my love for him and by the youthful hope that present differences could be smoothed away. Pablo too was ensnared in webs. Unable to clarify his past relationships with women, he lied endlessly (perhaps to avoid hurting them), but in so doing he made them lose all sense of reality; they became confused and unable to function. As I realized more and more what was going on and how he was unable to do anything but add more subplots to the intrigues and melodramas he kept himself involved in, I trusted that the necessary clarity in our lives would come from our relationship through art. Looking at his work in progress was always a stimulating experience, and artistic discussions were not only pertinent and exciting, they were enchanting, because he was not only intelligent but paradoxical and witty. Close to him, no one could dream of being bored.

Another small web was being formed, although I did not see it as such just then. Day after day, I was discovering my children. Almost three years old, Claude was quite independent but very affectionate, and Paloma was a very endearing infant who always seemed to be daydreaming. Because I loved them and felt responsible for their well-being, they became the source of a new confidence, enabling me to measure up to life's demands and increase the complexity of my roles.

Interior at Le Régina, 1952. On the wall are maquettes of the chasubles for the Chapel of the Rosary; Picasso's *A Winter Landscape* is over the fireplace, and Matisse's *Katia in a Yellow Dress* is standing on the floor.

A Winter Landscape

FROM early on, since the time of his friend Casagemas's suicide, Picasso's oeuvre had contained many references to death as a symbol of the futility of all human endeavors. True to his Spanish cultural background, Picasso sculpted and painted human or animal skulls, and many dramatic scenes, which culminated in *Guernica*. These were an intrinsic part of his heroic manner, a nihilistic meditation on *todo es nada*. They were an expression of his revolt against tyranny, a catharsis for his internal as well as external violent, aggressive compulsions.

In the fall of 1950 I was surprised when he undertook a depiction of winter desolation, since when he dealt with landscape he was usually in a happy mood. There in the foreground two tormented trees contorted themselves in a spiraling spasm. Their leafless, skeletal shapes were anthropomorphized; the one on the left looked lithe and feminine, while in the center the second one, masculine, sturdy, and rugged, seemed to lean on a cane. The unseen roots of the feminine tree sank directly into the brown soil; by contrast, the visibly agitated roots of the male tree seemed able to cover seven leagues in one step, like the ogre's boots in the tale of "Hop o' My Thumb." The female tree form appeared to have grown in a dilapidated orchard where meager herbs barely managed to survive. It was confined within the boundaries of a dry stone wall; yet a breach in the wall allowed the possible intrusion of the prowling male tree. The tree trunks were as distant as possible, and the tortuous branches shied away from each other in agony except for two fingerlike twigs that almost touched but did not join, like the image of God and Adam in Michelangelo's Sistine Chapel ceiling or the two hands in Matisse's *The Dance*. Behind the trees, in the middle ground of the painting, a plow had traced deep furrows of worry. Everywhere the lights and the shadows were dramatized and accentuated.

Further back, atop a hill, the horizon line was sinuous. To the right one could recognize a simple cubic house that evoked Matisse's villa, "The Dream," all the more so because the silhouette of a huge palm tree loomed close to it. It stood there impersonating itself and its creator: a symbol of the master who so often had incorporated its image into his works of the 1940s. Here, in Picasso's interpretation, in contrast to the skeletal trees, the palm tree was simple and serene; it stood its ground, occupying the realm of the silver sky, affirming serenity through symmetry. However, its foliage was brown instead of green, and it seemed as if by its very existence the palm tree cast a shadow on the future spring reawakening of the male tree below. Also on the horizon line, but further to the left, a ghost hamlet (which one could interpret as society) seemed to create an unsurmountable obstacle to the possible rebirth of the female tree. The ominous presence of the village was at its most forceful over the two twigs that stretched out and almost met, but didn't. At the extreme left and extreme right of the painting some branches reached the freedom of the sky; they were silhouetted against the light; unlike the palm tree, their shapes were all grotesquely deformed.

The palm tree and the two leafless trees formed a triangle of interest. The palm tree's penetration of the soil just above the most vulnerable breach between two main branches of the male tree was counteracted only by a dead stump, which did not fend off its action, suggesting Picasso's terror of being put in tutelage, or influenced, or dominated. Irrepressible, however, some palm-fronds extended laterally and insinuated themselves in each nook and cranny, and one frond was prolonged by a ray of light that struck a leafless branch of the male tree, while another lightbeam flashed its way to the feminine tree on the left.

From the start, the general tonality of the painting was subdued, made of black, mars brown, various grays, raw sienna, and white, but the strength of the structure was intense. All the different parts, while interacting with each other through the rhythm and the echos in the composition, nevertheless managed to remain isolated and to contribute to the whole a feeling of dejected loneliness. The contrasts of forms, such as the zigzag wall and the meandering trees, rang true. The negative space, whether in the foreground, middle ground or sky, was intriguing, the scale and proportion of each object to the others monumental. Surface tension was considerable, and yet the image was dimensional, it happened in space and time as a true image of desolation.

Entitled *Winter Landscape*, this painting really carried through the sad feeling of nature's temporary demise. It was a strong expressionistic statement, and it was also very moving. Painted on board with industrial enamel colors, it progressed without hindrance; Pablo was driven by a strong motivation, and he successfully completed it on December 22, 1950. Measuring 102 by 125 centimeters, it was not an especially large canvas, but it radiated power.

Pablo, who seldom fully enjoyed his own productions, was for once pleased with the result of his efforts. He was also gratified by my reaction of unqualified admiration. We did not always see eye to eye on artistic matters, but it was fitting for us to experience such unity of spirit on the theme of death. One must remember that the horrors of World War II were not far behind. In spite of my youth, feelings of bereavement were as familiar to me as to him, since many of my best friends had died in the Resistance. During the war Pablo had also suffered cruel losses among his personal friends because they were Jews, such as Max Jacob, and Sonia Mosse—and perhaps, much, much further in the past, the old wound of his little sister Conception's death had never healed.

Yet I knew I was supposed to praise the picture in aesthetic terms, mentioning composition, tone coordination, and contrasts between negative and positive space without referring to the desolation and the meaning it conveyed. Pablo disliked references to feelings, which he condemned as being sentimental rubbish, just good for conventional artists. This was a paradox for someone who could muster the gamut of human emotions with such ease and so convincingly.

In general he recoiled from discussing matters of sensitivity and sensibility with anyone, since that would have allowed another human being to come too close to his innermost core. Also, he avoided broaching the subject of death. In Pablo's entourage no one dared to speak about death unless it had happened in the bullring. The subject was taboo, as if it might bring bad luck to the master.

Illness, that betrayal of the body, was regarded with suspicion. If something got out of whack, it had to be the external proof of some inner and innate weakness. As Picasso enjoyed good health, he thought of himself as the very example of a sound mind within a healthy body and therefore the only model to follow. I was not allowed to be sick (even if I was) under any circumstances. He would shrug his shoulders and say, "I can't have that, it is depressing. Pull yourself together; be more like a Roman." In his mind the ancient Romans stood for stoicism.

Naturally the idea of being like a Roman did not appeal to me in the least, and Pablo was frustrated, since I laughed each time he gave me such advice. Yet this was very much on his mind, and if I overindulged Claude or Paloma he would mark disapproval with the same refrain.

"Can't you be a Roman mother?" he would say, and then he would go on with his diatribe: "No, of course not, no one in my family or among my relatives sets an example of Roman fortitude; even my own mother did not want to be Roman. . . . As to you, your ill-advised culture of subjectivity will only lead to psychosomatic imbalance and to diseases of all kinds for you and our children."

In Pablo's mind the only glorious exception to this sad state of affairs was his friend Matisse. As far as Pablo was concerned, Matisse's illness was the result of surgery and therefore obviously the surgeon's fault. Since the operation, Matisse's exemplary behavior had been 100 percent Roman; he had not relented, and his courage was to be praised. The subject could be approached. Far from being taboo, Matisse's illness was an almost sacred ailment; no ill omen or stigma could be attached to it.

The next time Lydia called to make an appointment for us to come to Cimiez, Matisse was unwell. Pablo decided to take a few of his paintings, among which he selected *Winter Landscape*. He then advised me to bring some of my drawings so we could have an interesting artistic discussion. It is almost certain that the symbolism of Pablo's painting was entirely hidden to him at that time. His creation arose from the deep recesses of his unconscious mind. Otherwise he would not have thought of taking this particular picture to his friend. Even for me the symbolic interpretation was not as clear then as it has become since.

As usual, we had Marcel put everything in the trunk of the car and let him drive us to Cimiez. As one of his idiosyncrasies, Pablo always refused to drive a car for fear of spoiling the suppleness of his hands and wrists. He used to say that a painter should be either too poor to buy a car or rich enough to afford a chauffeur. He always berated Braque, who enjoyed driving fast cars himself.

When we reached Matisse's apartment with the paintings and the portfolios, Lydia helped us along and Pablo put *Winter Landscape* on the mantelpiece of the fireplace so that Matisse could see it well from his bed. Matisse was struck, as if by lightning. He fell in love with that painting. He looked at the other things we had brought along and we discussed them too, but I could not concentrate on what was being said. He also tried to participate, but he could not keep his eyes away from *Winter Landscape*. Matisse surely saw it as a powerful image of winter's desolation, without focusing on the parallelisms and interpretative meanings in it. Since this work of art beguiled him so thoroughly, he asked Pablo to leave it with him for a few weeks so that he could look at it in leisure. Pablo was quite gratified by Matisse's enthusiasm, and he agreed to leave his newborn creation in the hands of his friend.

But as soon as we were on the way back to Vallauris, Matisse's gesture of appreciation no longer appeared pleasant to Pablo. He feared that the absence of the painting might have a negative bearing on his canvases in progress, which was a possibility, since he was in the habit of comparing one painting to another at the end of each workday. He never did paint another landscape as tragic and meaningful, so perhaps he was right.

Yet he did continue to work in the same direction, but in a different

Henri Matisse in 1949.

Pablo Picasso in undated photo.

medium. He agreed to illustrate with original etchings a limited edition of a text by a sixteenth-century writer called Monluc, published by Iliazd and entitled *La Maigre* ("The Skinny One"). The aquatints looked like satirical variations of my own figure, and they were accompanied by comments such as, "Yes, they are drawn from you; you used to be a Venus but now you resemble Christ," to which outburst I retorted sarcastically, "Yes indeed, I suffer like him!" Then he changed the conversation.

Matisse was not feeling very well that winter, and his daughter, Marguerite Duthuit, came to spend some time with him. Either she was already working with him on the archives or she did not especially care for Picasso or both, but when she was around, we were usually not asked to come. However, if his son Pierre and members of Pierre's family came from New York, we would sometimes meet them in Cimiez. We also went to Paris for short trips, or to stay a few months, so we were not always available.

When we went back to Cimiez after an interruption of about two months, *Winter Landscape* still occupied the place of honor on the mantelpiece. Matisse was joyful and effusive, obviously glad to see us; his manner was more open and genial than usual. One could see that he had something in mind and could hardly wait to speak up. After the usual *abrazos* and kisses, the expected small talk of welcome, it did not take him long to come to the point of his request. The benevolent autocrat (whose wishes were orders, if one knew him well) announced to Pablo that he definitely liked *Winter Landscape* and wanted to exchange it for one of his own paintings.

If a lightning bolt had struck at Pablo's feet, he could not have been more petrified. I could imagine what he was thinking. On the one hand, it was a hell of a compliment to find out that the master of Cimiez was intent on acquiring that painting, but on the other hand, Pablo considered this work to be a crucial painting, something that had surged spontaneously from his unconscious, and he had his mind set on being able to study it to see if it would lead to other productions. Nevertheless, he managed to recover fast, knowing full well that Matisse was expecting a positive answer, since he had expressed without any ambiguity how much his heart was set on possessing that stunning picture.

Picasso succeeded in being diplomatic. Yes, he told Matisse, of course he was delighted—a barter, what a marvelous idea! They had done it several times before. After enumerating the previous barters for my benefit, while his friend nodded approvingly, he managed to add that while he wanted nothing more than to have another Matisse in his collection, he would have difficulty parting with *Winter Landscape*, which probably heralded the way to a new vision.

Matisse did not make things easier by agreeing that it was indeed a very intriguing, unique piece; indeed, this was the reason that he wanted it so badly. He was even ready to offer Pablo a painting from the forties, since he had not painted many oils since but had done mostly cutouts.

For once Pablo was ill at ease and did not know where to turn. If he did not accept the deal, it would mean that he did not like his friend's work as much as his own. Matisse realized that things could not be pushed any further, and he suggested that he keep *Winter Landscape* a while longer while looking for an oil of his that might enthuse Picasso. It was a relief to be able to postpone any decisions. Matisse thought that he had carried the day, since the painting remained on his mantelpiece, at least temporarily.

During our next visit Pablo seemed mollified, and in order not to pursue the exchange, he expressed his wish to obtain a Matisse dating from the years 1907 to 1920. His friend replied that in that case, he himself should get a Cubist painting rather than *Winter Landscape*, but that there was no point in doing so. If the bottom line was that Picasso preferred a Matisse from before 1920, and if Matisse preferred a Picasso from the Cubist period, it implied that each of them had been at the apex of their creative powers in those years and that neither had reached such heights since. At times like this, figuratively speaking, they resembled ancient warriors locked in combat (regardless of consequences); they dealt each other deadly blows in a titanesque struggle for dominance.

Soon enough the two masters could see that they were at a stalemate, and, both rather gracefully acknowledging the fact, they went back to some less dangerous topic of conversation. After some more small talk we left, and *Winter Landscape* remained on the mantelpiece.

When we went to Cimiez the next time, we were amazed to see

Winter Landscape still enthroned on the mantelpiece but now surrounded by four models for chasubles to be worn by the priest at the Vence chapel. There were two on each side.

Matisse had had a difficult time reconciling his inspiration with the requirements of the liturgy, which demanded certain colors in specific periods of the year: purple for Lent, white for Easter, red for Pentecost, green after Pentecost, and black and white for funeral services. I think he created twenty-two models, out of which only six were actually executed at the Atelier d'Art Sacré. He got theological advice from Father Couturier, the Dominican priest, but his compositions always broadened the theme. These chasubles were more than religious adornments; they were a quintessence of what Matisse could produce when at his boldest.

These models, made on paper painted with gouache and cutouts, were like murals; they had authority and a sense of eternity. Surprisingly, they were not in the least decorative. In their synthetic simplicity there was something definitive that reached out for the ultimate. Apart from the long Roman cross on three of them or the three crosses on another one, the elements in the design did not refer to a very literal, nor for that matter a symbolic, Catholicism; the feeling was powerful, overwhelming. They spoke of "life divine," but not of any particular religion or cult.

In the cutout model for the rose chasuble, visible on the lower left of the photograph shown on page 218, the intensity of color was almost blinding. The relationship of the mauve-pink to the vibrant light ultramarine evoked the *Still Life With Oranges* (1912) that embellished Picasso's sculpture studio in Paris. Pinned on the wall, it stood its ground in open contradiction to *Winter Landscape*, but higher to the left the preliminary maquette for the black chasuble provided a measure of conciliation between the painters' aesthetic principles. Interestingly, there were palmlike forms in its decor, and an abbreviated Latin text, ESPER LUCAT ("Let hope shine"), which seemed quite related to the light-giving palm tree in Picasso's landscape. To the lower right, on the other side of the chimney, one could see another project for the black-and-white chasuble, also with the palm motif and this time with three crosses radiating light. To the upper right was pinned a final model for the front part of the rose chasuble, so that the two black and the two rose church ornaments echoed each other diagonally. Joy and sorrow, color and light, obscurity and enlightenment were simultaneously present and equated. This was a magisterial *tour de force*.

The pull and push between the four chasubles and *Winter Landscape* was something to behold—it took your breath away. In quality, they all measured up to one another. Seeing these masterpieces together was a great lesson in art, as well as a communion with the essence of life and death. There was a moment of silence in the room where we stood. It was all there, with no need for explanations. The cutouts and the *Winter Landscape* said it all without words, just with shapes and colors.

Again *Winter Landscape* remained in Cimiez for a while longer. There was still talk of an exchange, but Matisse never proposed a specific painting of his as a match for it. The chasubles were the perfect match, and we all had seen them together on the wall. Matisse and Picasso had jousted, and no one had been found wanting.

So when Pablo needed to have his painting returned to Vallauris to be photographed for a new edition of *Verve* dedicated to his recent canvases, sculptures, and ceramics, his friend was no longer reluctant to send it back.

Henri Matisse. *The Painter's Family* (*La Famille du Peintre*), 1911.
Madame Matisse is on the left; Marguerite is standing to the right;
Jean and Pierre are seated playing checkers.

Family Ties

EVEN THOUGH Matisse had the cool appearance of a northern Frenchman and was very private about his emotions, it was easy to see that he had strong feelings of affection for the members of his family.

At the time of his youth, parent-child relationships were quite formal. The intimate *tutoyement* was not customary in the north, and bombastic displays of sentiment were not tolerated. That did not mean that the sentiments did not exist, just that self-control was more prized than spontaneous demonstrations.

The young Henri Matisse felt a great inclination toward his mother, whose sensitive nature was akin to his. His father had established himself as a grain merchant at Bohain-en-Vermandois, in Picardy. His mother, more artistically inclined, painted on china, but she did not limit herself to that achievement. In Picardy and Flanders the weather was gloomy, and houses were kept meticulously clean both inside and outside to render them more cheerful. So Matisse's mother thought of adding the sale of whitewash and ground colored pigments for house painting to her husband's commerce. Soon people started to ask her advice about the mixes and the color coordination they ought to use. She had such a good eye and such good taste that her recommendations were eagerly followed by more and more people. In the small provincial town, she in fact became an interior decorator, long before that term existed; she decided how best to decorate and organize her neighbors' homes. Because her clients asked for it, she painted china sets to match the color of the dining rooms, and even ventured into ceramics for that purpose.

Madame Matisse's creativity exerted a deep influence on her shy but sensitive child. It was she who brought her son a box of watercolors as a distraction when, at the age of twenty, he was suffering from chronic appendicitis in Bohain. At that time he was also suffering from hypochondria and depression. Self-indulgent or not, he was an invalid for a year. After studying law in Paris, in compliance with his father's wishes, Matisse had become a clerk at a solicitor's office in Saint Quentin. After work he took drawing courses at the Quentin-Latour Foundation. But when he recalled his youth, he always linked the revelation of his vocation to his mother's gift of a paintbox. It was as if by her gift she had dismissed the obedience of his rational mind to the necessity of a conventional job and liberated in him the dormant daemon of creativity.

In ancient Europe a profession was usually passed on, either directly or indirectly, from father to son. Even at the time of Matisse's youth, the father's dominance in these matters was seldom questioned. But Emile Matisse's business in grains was coupled with Héloïse Gérard Matisse's sale of housepaint and colors. Becoming an artist, too, usually was due to the influence of the parents' vocation and example. Artemisia Gentileschi was a painter's daughter, as was Louise Moillon. Examples of several geniuses in one family were frequent: the Cranachs, the Brueghels, the Bellinis, the Tiepolos. At other times the transmission occurred by selection; the neophyte entered an older artist's studio, and if he was very gifted, he was soon distinguished from the rest of the apprentices by the master himself, as in the case of Perugino, who trained Raphael; Verrocchio, who taught Leonardo da Vinci; and Tintoretto, who allowed El Greco to paint elongated figures in the background of his own compositions.

Pablo Picasso was tutored by his father from age six on and received his father's tools when he turned fourteen. In the same way I was trained by my mother. The tools had to come from someone who recognized, consciously or not, the presence of the sacred fire in the younger person. They were like a passport issued for that unknown realm of art. Tools especially had to be handed from one generation to the next as a sign of recognition and acceptance. These traditions can be traced back to the customs of the arts and crafts guilds in the Middle Ages. Quite unwittingly, when Héloïse Gérard Matisse gave her son a "magic" paintbox, she blessed his heretofore dormant vocation and fanned an inner fire that would never be extinguished. Matisse himself remembered that his decision to become an artist came not as an act of will but as the acceptance of an irresistible calling.

Another event that he liked to describe was the time when he was waiting at the post office and doodled absent-mindedly, without even looking at what he was doing; then he discovered that he had drawn a quite synthetic portrait of his mother combining a likeness that was not accidental or imitative with a more general evocation of the proud features of women in Picardy. Thus it suggested the way in which his mother's face corresponded to the regional type.

It was not without misgivings and trepidation that the young Matisse gave in to a calling stronger than his conscious will. Maybe an untold number of silent maternal ancestors claimed him to actualize their dream—the conquest of the realm of color, the dream of paradise on earth. His initial relationship and identification with his mother's aspirations must have been of a deeply positive nature, however, because they were reflected later in his open-mindedness to feminine sensibility and acceptance of women in general.

Matisse's father, even if a strict disciplinarian, must have been a good sort, too, because when Matisse abandoned his job in Saint Quentin, he did not hold a grudge; far from withdrawing support, he continued to help his son as much as he could in times of illness, crisis, or financial straits. This positive attitude must have been a source of balance and confidence for the adolescent and later the young man. Matisse's parents' kindness was not the casual financial help given by an affluent family but the generous attention of well-meaning human beings who sacrificed some of their own comfort on their son's behalf.

During a good part of Matisse's life, parental influence lingered:

the maternal side was a source of artistic inspiration, and the paternal side was reflected in the rational aspect of his character and in his generally authoritarian attitude to his family, especially to his sons. His whole household had to revolve around his needs—to sit for him, to be quiet for his sake, to do whatever he decided. Having become a competent violinist, he decided that his son Pierre should study to become a concert violinist, because Pierre once mentioned an interest in music during his adolescence. Matisse seized the occasion, even though it was already too late for Pierre ever to achieve the skill and fluency that must be acquired much earlier in life. Nothing that Pierre said could alter his father's opinion that the skill was just a matter of determination and hard work.

For Jean, Matisse's other son, whose interest was sculpture, it was the same thing. Matisse decided on the course of studies that Jean must undertake and who his teachers must be. Of course his choices were excellent and his letters of advice to his son were well directed, but they were also overwhelming. He prevented Jean from making his own mistakes and developing his own talent in a new and completely original way.

Perhaps Matisse felt guilty for not having followed his own father's admonitions, and perhaps he made up for it by being a strict disciplinarian to his sons. His attitude to his daughter was more intimate. From early in life she shared his concerns, and he confided in her as he had perhaps done with his mother.

During World War I, Belgium and soon after the northern part of France were invaded and became a forbidden zone. No letters could reach their destination, so Matisse could not obtain any information about his mother's circumstances during that period. He did not even know whether she had survived the invasion and what tribulations she and the rest of the family might be going through. (Auguste, Matisse's younger brother, had been seized as a hostage.) At the same time he was unable to let her know of his own tidings or give her news of his family. This probably had some bearing on his comparatively austere style in the paintings of that period. Yet if he was affected, nothing transpired of his anxieties; his paintings did reflect a more ascetic discipline, and their spareness spoke of stoicism, but the themes remained sensuous, even hedonistic. They didn't become tragic by describing the disasters of war and its effects. Matisse did not allow aggression and death to pervade his inner universe. He chose to be the bard of beauty, joy, and peace, and he refused to lend his brush to the depiction of an apocalypse.

Like many artists of his generation, Matisse and his family went through financial straits for many years. When life became easier and even affluent, he maintained frugality and discipline with his children, in the belief that it armed them for life and gave them more acumen for personal achievements. This method worked out well for Pierre, his younger son, who asserted his independence by going to the United States, where he soon became one of the leading art dealers in New York. Pierre continued to have a very positive relationship with his father, but from a distance. He had the temperament of a leader and succeeded in imposing his taste on others, steering collectors toward artists like Alberto Giacometti and Balthus, who were still quite unknown in the States, as well as organizing shows of his father's work in his gallery.

In December 1923 Matisse's daughter, Marguerite, married Georges Duthuit, a well-known art historian specializing in Byzantine art. She continued to keep in touch with her father. Though she sat for him less often, she became very knowledgeable about his oeuvre and began accumulating articles, notes, information, personal snapshots, and photos for the archives. Matisse spent a good part of his time in Nice, and more and more often Jean, his older son, used the Issy-les-Moulineaux studio to work on his own sculptures.

Between 1919 and 1939, in addition to the odalisques and many hedonistic still lifes, Matisse painted serious-minded, penetrating compositions, consistently avoiding dramatic or tragic themes. Ignoring sinister or sordid subject matter, he reached out for beauty. He regarded simplicity, balance, and serenity as the supreme achievement and message of French art. At the onset of World War II, he could have left for the United States, since he had been invited to do so. Instead he secured a visa for Brazil. He had a reservation to go on June 8, 1940, passing through Modane and Genoa to Rio de Janeiro, but when he heard about the collapse of the French military forces, he canceled the trip, writing

Henri Matisse with his granddaughter Jacqueline
at the Chapel at Vence.

to Pierre that he would feel like a deserter: "If all that has value leaves France, what will be left of France?"

The fratricidal wars between Germany and France were especially sorrowful for people who came from places that traditionally were on the roads of invasion. Such families were decimated and scattered at regular intervals, their homes leveled, their possessions destroyed. Yet their ancestors, the Franks or the Celts, were not ethnically different from the Germans on the other side of the Rhine.

Before World War I the Germans had often appreciated avant-garde French artists better than the French did themselves, and the German Expressionist movement was in contact with and ran parallel to French Fauvism. But after the war, with one and a half million dead and the horrors of Verdun fresh in the mind, there was a strong antiwar feeling in France. It was the same in Germany. No one wanted to see a repetition of the nightmare. The socialists on both sides were ardent advocates of pacifism. Romain Rolland, the philosopher and novelist, also advocated putting an end to nationalistic conflicts by adopting a point of view *au-dessus de la Mêlée*, "above the fray."

Yet preoccupied as the French were with the quality of life, the betterment of the human condition, social reforms, and social justice among themselves, they did not look compassionately at what was happening on the other side of the border. They did nothing to alleviate the German political and economic collapse and later did nothing to stop the bizarre little man with the brown shirt and the moustache who had written a very telling book and was now shouting bellicose slogans. The French chose not to see the dark clouds accumulating at the northeastern border; ostrich-fashion, they thought that they were well protected by the Maginot Line.

The result was appalling. Unprepared for war, French democracy soon found itself under the boot of a most vicious totalitarian military ideology. The reasons that led to the French rout were certainly a subject for meditation, and Matisse's reaction at the time was quite befitting his character.

First of all, he decided not to leave. Second, even though in 1941 he was very ill, he managed to continue working in the same direction as usual, not pretending that nothing had happened and thus becoming alienated from reality but staying to maintain what he considered to be the mainstream of French culture: its devotion to the universal, its dedication to the values of civilization against the fall into darkness, fanaticism, and obscurantism. Even more than military action, Hitler's propaganda had corroded the willpower of his intended victims. Defeat came from accepting defeat. Culture had to be upheld; beauty had to triumph; hope had to be sustained. Matisse refused to enter the nightmare; he wanted to project a beacon of light, to represent the values worth living for.

He practiced the asceticism of the joy of life; it was his way to transcend his country's collapse. His illustrations of the poems of Charles d'Orléans, which he started in 1942, were symptomatic of his frame of mind. Charles, duc d'Orléans (1394–1465), was the nephew of Charles VI of France. After the battle of Agincourt, at which he was joint commander-in-chief, he was taken prisoner to England, where he remained for a quarter of a century, since his rank made his ransom very high and his release difficult to arrange. So, while detained in England in the wake of a great disaster in French history, he wrote ballads and rondels that are among the most melodious in French poetry. He felt quite nostalgic about his homeland throughout his exile, even though he was at all times treated in a manner befitting his rank. When he finally came back to France in 1440, he got married for the third time, to Mary of Cleves, and surrounded himself at Blois with the best French writers of the time—François Villon, Olivier de la Marche, Georges Chastellain, and others. In 1462 he fathered a son who later became Louis XII. His motto could have been the same as that of Marguerite de Bourgogne, inscribed at her funerary chapel in Brou: "Fortune, Lack of Fortune, Fortune."

The greatness of a culture always depends on the excellence of some of its individuals. Matisse certainly identified with the poet and with the example provided by his life and creativity. The pen being mightier than the sword, the defeated Frenchman in captivity had given French poetry some of its finest jewels, fleurons on a crown of immortality.

The master worked with lithographic pencils to produce illustrations that were to be printed in color to form a lyrical and sensitive ensemble. Given the wartime and immediate postwar difficulties, the book was not published until 1950 by Tériade, the editor of *Verve*. Fleurs-de-lis were everywhere in the book as a pervading ornament, a leitmotif. Like the rose for the English kings, in France the white lily was the symbol of royalty, blue the color of aristocracy (blue blood). Red, a color representing the people, was added to the flag at the time of the French Revolution. In French, the expression *les lis* stood for the members of the reigning dynasty and by extension came to mean the sovereignty of the state, which accompanied that exalted position. As

Louis Aragon suggested to Matisse, who agreed with the interpretation, Matisse's illustrations of the poems of Charles d'Orléans were an active expression of trust in the survival of French culture at a time when it was threatened in its very essence, in its life and its love of life.

Apart from being exquisite pieces of art, two paintings of 1943, both entitled *Lemons Against a Fleur-de-Lis Background*, were especially moving in that respect. In one of them the frontispiece and title page of the poems that Matisse was in the process of illustrating opened like a window in the upper part of the canvas, showing on one side the profile of Charles d'Orléans and on the other the title in Matisse's handwriting, which reinforced his intent. In the companion piece, now at the Museum of Modern Art in New York, he simplified the background, deleted the portrait of Charles d'Orléans and the title page of the poems, and replaced them with more calligraphic lilies (but traces of the rectangle remain visible in the finished work). The center of both canvases was occupied by a green Chinese vase filled with forget-me-nots resting on the white marble mantelpiece of a pink brick chimney. The background was of the same tone, decorated with a profusion of emblematic fleurs-de-lis. Some acid or bitter lemons surrounded the vase.

In French, forget-me-nots are called *myosotis* but convey the same message: the need to remember. China, the Celestial Empire, is usually called *l'empire du milieu* on account of its philosophy of conciliation of extremes, akin to the Latin proverb *in medio stat virtus*. Green is the color of hope. So in these paintings, as in a riddle, the virtue that stood in the center forced the viewer not to forget hope. It rested above the fireplace, a usual symbol of what brings people together in the household. One painting was explicit, the other more elliptic.*

In order to resist tyranny, at least in their hearts, and restore integrity (the lily being also an emblem of purity), French people had to look up to the opening above, toward the window of spiritual values. If the twin picture belonging to the Museum of Modern Art no longer

---

*Matisse, who liked to say that he used signs but no symbols, did use symbolic allusions in, these two pictures; cryptic allusions were a necessity at that time.

harbored the presence of Charles d'Orléans, it was probably because Matisse, identifying so much with his theme, felt that the painting itself, and the act of painting it in 1943, upheld the values of humanism as wholly as the poems of Charles d'Orléans had done in the fifteenth century.

Through his presence in France at that fateful moment, Matisse was sharing the fate of his compatriots. They were all hostages, they were all in exile within the borders of their own country. He obviously thought that a measure of sovereignty was still within each individual, provided that person did not lose a sense of history, hope, and creativity. At his age and in his condition he could certainly not fight actively, but everybody knew that his sympathies did not lie with the Pétain regime, which would have had people believe that they had deserved the breakdown of their country because of the sins of pacifism, liberalism, socialism, hedonism. In occupied France, Matisse's works were banned from public display in art galleries. The same was true for Picasso, Léger, Max Ernst, and many others. Matisse used to say that France was ruled by people as worthless as academic painters.

During the darkest moments of that period, people of my generation refused to despair. We were sustained by the poems of Louis Aragon and Paul Éluard, the presence of André Malraux in the underground, and the knowledge that neither Matisse nor Picasso had fled. Culture had to be upheld like a flag against Hitler's totalitarian empire, against his cult of superhuman Nietzschean values. He was waging war against civilization as most understood it. Hitler had said, "When I hear the word culture, I draw my pistol." Books had been burned publicly even before people were sent to the gas chambers. While millions were jailed, deported, or dying in concentration camps and on battlefields all the way to Stalingrad, in the center was the calm eye of the cyclone; truth had to supersede the unleashed forces of darkness.

French people at that time expressed their thoughts and feelings in a coded fashion that they alone could understand. As a painter I used similar symbolism myself, and Aragon's poems of revolt were mostly love poems in their obvious content. Paradoxically, in the middle of the disaster France underwent a period of intense creativity. There were never as many lyrical poems as those hastily printed in secrecy and passed from hand to hand or learned by heart and recited during that time. In the moments of their greatest danger, the French were not afraid to appeal to the resources of the feminine aspect of their psyche, and the women were not afraid to show courage and oppose the brute force of a totalitarian regime. Matisse serenely continued to meditate. The fact that he was unperturbed was a beacon of hope for the young. He was a master of freedom; following him, each individual had to decide what freedom was and act accordingly. Remaining faithful to his ideal of pacifism above all was Matisse's choice.

During World War I, German Expressionist painters such as Franz Marc and August Macke had been killed. If they had lived, they might have had power against the rising evil of Nazism. The artist should be a watcher; the artist, like Goya in his *Caprichos*, fights "the slumber of reason that engenders monsters," the falsehoods, the lies, the phony ideologies. The artist, like the sorcerer of old, ought to be a builder of myths but should dispel evil dreams among his countrymen and within humankind. The artist ought to break the chains that prevent humanity from surging forward toward better tomorrows.

During World War II it was not by chance that Matisse's son Jean belonged to the underground; it was not by chance that his wife and daughter also took part in the Resistance within occupied France. After Marguerite's husband, Georges Duthuit, and their son, Claude, left for the United States, Marguerite joined the underground movement. Jean Matisse was also involved and the house at Issy-les-Moulineaux was full of explosives. Both were soon helped in their activities by Amélie Matisse. The two women were captured and imprisoned, Madame Matisse in Paris and Marguerite, who had gone to Brittany to help prepare for the Allies' disembarkment, was caught near Brest and put in jail in Rennes. Marguerite was then tortured and sent on her way to the Ravensbruck deportation camp. Because of Allied bombing of the railways, the convoy had to stop in Belfort before crossing the border into Germany. With many others, Marguerite was parked in a hospital that had been transformed into a jail, where she was fortunately recognized and helped to escape.

Though the family tried to spare Matisse, he learned about his daughter's ordeal, at least partly, and was quite distraught. When reunited with Marguerite, he found her sallow complexion and her skin-niness, telltale signs of what she had been through, too much for him. Unable to express his pent-up emotion, he remained silent for a long while, holding her hand. Then he said, "Let's not talk about any of these events; let's just resume our relationship."

Henri Matisse on the surface always appeared cool and collected, but that did not prove a lack of sensitivity—perhaps the opposite. He did not allow himself to succumb to his own emotions. Because he wanted his passions to suffuse his creations with utmost intensity, it was as if he made himself unavailable for personal feelings. He believed that an artist could give to the world only through the medium of his art.

Under the rough surface of an autocratic attitude, Matisse was hiding a heart of gold. Unfortunately for him, he was quite successful at doing so. Many of his friends complained about his seeming lack of feeling, as did some members of his family, and yet every one of them was deeply devoted to him. They all sensed that in his total dedication to art, he observed the discipline and the sacrifice he required of others. They felt, behind the apparent hedonism and effortlessness of his achievements, the deep-rooted asceticism that was the basic climate of his creation. Also, he had suffered a long period of financial hardship at the beginning of his life, and later on, living in much more affluent circumstances, he could not shed his old habit of thrift. Picasso was the same way; he could write a check for a large amount of money without lifting an eyebrow for something that struck his fancy, and yet he grumbled endlessly about the exorbitant price of cigarettes and matches, because it reminded him of the dire need he experienced during his penniless years.

After Matisse's grandson, Claude Duthuit, was drafted, he came to say goodbye before rejoining his regiment. Matisse delivered a sermon about his future duties and about the dangers he would have to face (by no means physical, since it was peacetime), extolling the desirability of virtuous conduct. In conclusion he handed his grandson an envelope with money inside, which was supposed to be sufficient for his extra needs during the year of his military service. Claude listened patiently to the homily, in the belief that his grandfather would make it worthwhile financially. But when he opened the envelope and saw how meager the sum was, he decided on the spot that the best way to do it justice was to spend it right away, by having a nice dinner with a girlfriend, taking her dancing at a nightclub, and ending the evening at the roulette wheel in a nearby casino, where he lost what was left soon enough.

The next time he saw his grandfather, Claude was asked whether he had behaved properly in the interim and whether he had been thrifty with his money. He was candid and willingly explained what he had done. Matisse was worried about the future implications of such extravagance—a prelude to the ruin of Claude's moral fiber! But he became reconciled to the facts when told that his scale of value for financial expenditure was far from up-to-date. His good nature took over, and he ended up being more generous when he clearly understood that all his fears were pointless and that Claude was perfectly capable of handling himself in a manner suitable to his generation.

Some time later Matisse undertook a series of linear drawings, portraits of Claude Duthuit, who was a tall young man with striking good looks—regular, classical features, blue eyes slightly slanted upward, and Matissian reddish hair. The series was progressing well when Claude went for a motorcycle ride with his cousin, the son of Jean Matisse. Unfortunately, they had an accident and were both badly hurt with contusions and concussions. When Claude was able to resume the sittings, far from commiserating or asking for the gory details, Matisse complained that his face had lost its remarkable regularity and therefore all his schemes for interpretation were ruined.

He told Picasso about this predicament, apparently unaware that he appeared egotistic and unconcerned for his grandson's welfare. Pablo rejoined right away: "Ah, he could have given you a heart attack out of worry! These young people are really insensitive; all they care about is their pleasure, and they love *speed* above all, whatever the risk. Do you know that my son Paulo and Françoise raced, he in front and she behind, on the Grande Corniche from Nice to Monte Carlo, riding a huge motorcycle, a Harley-Davidson, that I had the stupidity to give him? I followed in the car with Marcel, trying not to lose sight of them and sick at the idea of finding them dead at each bend of the road!"

Claude Duthuit well remembered meeting Pablo, our Claude, and me at his grandfather's flat in the Regina in Nice. Being at that time an ebullient young man, he had resented seeing my son, that young brat (who inconveniently had the same first name as he did), being treated like a king—allowed to crawl on the bed, where he was stuffed with the best pastries available in Nice—while he, the grandson, had to sit at attention in a corner of the room; if his posture sagged a bit, he was reminded that not being erect might damage his spine and also indicated a decrease of inner strength and discipline.

Indeed, Matisse had a rather stern mien with the members of his family when they came to see him. He was a man from the north and a man of his generation. He probably felt that it was his duty to act the way he did. He seldom smiled, looking rather stern. He also did not talk about the physical pain he endured as an invalid. He kept his composure, whatever his thoughts or his personal discomfort and anxiety might be. But sometimes, in the absence of his kin, he would reveal this hidden part of himself to Pablo and acknowledge his distress.

Once we found him in a really sad mood, after he had received news that Pierre was getting divorced. "Am I no longer supposed to care for my daughter-in-law?" he complained. "I have grown very fond of her."

"Why not go on?" replied Pablo with equanimity, since it was not his problem. Then he added, "Do you remember when some members of your family gave you a hard time before World War II?" (This was probably at the time of his separation from Madame Matisse.) "I came to see you at Issy-les-Moulineaux and I told them all: 'Listen! Here in your family there is only one person whose given name is Henri, and he carries all the weight.'" That, of course, elicited a good laugh from Pablo's friend.

On the way home, Pablo was curious to know whether I had noticed what he had said. I answered, "Of course, I always listen. But you said so many things. Could you be a little more precise?"

"Oh, it is about that one person named Henri who carried all the weight within the Matisse family. I wish I could deliver that kind of message to you and to my family."

I paused a bit, as if reflecting. "The trouble is that it would be much more difficult. I am exempted, since my family name is Gilot.

Your eldest son's given name is Paul, the French translation of Pablo; our son, Claude, also has your name as one of his given names, and your grandson is called Pablito. So that leaves you just with Maya, who is away at present, and Paloma, who is still in her cradle. You'll be hard pressed to apply the same rule to your own situation!"

Since there was no other way out, Pablo had the good grace to laugh and to concede that he had to find another use for his *bon mot*.

Henri Matisse at work in his studio at Issy-les-Moulineaux.
Matisse's mirror-image painting of himself at work (*Portrait
de l'Artiste*, 1918) is similar in composition to this undated
photograph.

Artistic Affinities

H ENRI MATISSE was endowed with a great capacity for friendship. His first artist friend was Albert Marquet. They met at the atelier of Gustave Moreau at the School of Fine Arts in Paris, where Matisse had been invited by Moreau to come and work without having to take the entrance examinations. Marquet was six years younger than Matisse, but during their student years and later during the lean years when both lived and worked in the apartment building at 19, quai St. Michel, their affection and mutual regard developed steadily. Not only did they often paint the same subjects and go outdoors to sketch together, but they shared tedious bread-and-butter decorative work for the hard taskmaster Monsieur Jambon (Mr. Ham), to adorn the external walls of the Grand Palais.*

When considering Marquet's oeuvre as a whole, one might be inclined to think of him more as a Postimpressionist than as a Fauve, but his major interest lay in light rather than in color, and his great

---

*This was a pavilion built for the 1900 World's Fair that later became a museum.

rapport with and kinship to Matisse as an artist had to do with his uncanny and masterful way of using black as a solid nonreceding local tone—a local tone that holds its plane in space. At the beginning of their friendship there were even times when Marquet dared to explore further than his friend. His expressive shorthand style of sketching displayed a well-assimilated Japanese influence that must have helped Matisse to find his own simplicity, to dwell less heavily on form definition and to orient himself toward an increased dynamism of shapes.

At the Moreau studio Matisse also met Georges Rouault. Rouault's father was a cabinetmaker. At age fourteen the son was put in an apprenticeship with a Monsieur Hirsh, a glazier, where he helped restore Gothic stained glass windows. This agreed with his taste for simplified images in which intensely colored areas were underlined by grisaille engobes and lead partitioning. Later, at the School of Fine Arts, Rouault became Gustave Moreau's most promising student, earning the Chenavard award and, more important, acquiring consummate skill in composition and technique. Moreau was so fond of him that in his will he made him his artistic executor and left him a financial legacy. After completing this period of study and soul-searching, Rouault's first original work was satiric and expressionistic. One of the founders of the Salon d'Automne, he exhibited with the Fauves in 1905. Later his religious mysticism brought him closer to Maurice Denis and the group dedicated to sacred art. Yet he was by temperament a loner, and if Matisse and he acknowledged each other, they were by no means intimate.

In addition to Albert Marquet, Matisse befriended Charles Camoin in the early days at the School of Fine Arts, as well as Henri Manguin. Although these two painters participated in the original Fauvist movement, they soon became rather tame and traditional in their approach. Matisse appreciated their moderation, their very French distaste of all excesses, which was the very opposite of his own radicalism. He also shared their love of Mediterranean landscapes. He was able to keep these artistic friendships going throughout his life because he never assumed a superior or domineering attitude; he remained open to his friends' intellectual and emotional needs, even though they tended to complain about an apparent lack of sensitivity on his part.

At the onset of World War I, Matisse struck up a friendship with Pierre Bonnard. Bonnard was only two years older than Matisse, but he seemed to belong to a different generation because he had earned wide recognition early in his career. From the start a nonconformist, Bonnard had been one of the leaders of the Nabi group. His concern for flat decorative surfaces had earned him the nickname "le Japonard." He had subsequently developed on his own, subtly modulating the light and suffusing the surface of his canvases with heightened color schemes. His pictures were intimate in subject matter yet radical in formal invention and execution. He not only assimilated the lessons of oriental prints and the primitivism of popular imagery, he also learned the secret of unexpected layouts from Gauguin and Toulouse-Lautrec. Bonnard's harmonies were compatible with Matisse's bolder statements. With childlike innocence he revealed the miracles that lie dormant in the simple spectacles of everyday life. His eyes dispelled academic stereotypes; all his life he kept the capacity to wonder and remained a lucid dreamer able to communicate his unique vision. Matisse also strove toward the purity of a primal sensation unadulterated by civilized aesthetic conventions and visual clichés.

A natural curiosity on both sides led Bonnard and Matisse to an affectionate relationship. Both shared an admiration for Renoir and visited him in his later years. After World War I, both artists spent a good part of the time on the French Riviera, one in Le Cannet, the other in Nice. They saw each other whenever possible and carried on a correspondence. Like the early Manet and contrary to the general theory of the Impressionists, they both used black *as color*, and were emulated by Albert Marquet, who was quite inventive and original in this regard. On account of their shared interest in Japanese art, it is tempting to call the three of them the "Black Belt Initiates."

Pablo Picasso was also certainly a "Black Belt Initiate." For him black evoked the drama of primeval matter, out of which worlds of creation could be born. Nevertheless, he hated Bonnard and even Marquet to a lesser degree, and had a fit each time someone mentioned one or the other with admiration. Unexpectedly, he was rather lenient as far as Marc Chagall was concerned and had friendly relations with him, except as far as ceramics were concerned; there he discarded the subject by saying, "It is not for him—this medium does not work to his advantage."*

During our visits, Matisse agreed not to broach the subject of Bonnard as long as he did not have to hear about fiddlers on the roof, fishes embracing clocks in the sky, and lovers playing hide-and-seek with a bunch of flowers in front of a Vence landscape. By tacit agreement, Bonnard and Chagall were hardly ever mentioned during conversations, so as to avoid Pablo's getting tense or Matisse's mumbling something inaudible but disparaging into his beard.

Chagall's second wife, Vava Brodsky, was on very friendly terms with Claude and Ida Bourdet. They owned a beautiful villa, Les Collines, with a large garden on the route de St. Jeannet outside of Vence, very near Matisse's Villa Le Rêve, but they lived mostly in Paris, so they agreed to lease Les Collines to Chagall and Vava. This arrangement worked to everybody's satisfaction, and when the Bourdets acquired an interesting old bastion in the walled city of Antibes, they agreed to sell Les Collines to Chagall. Like everybody else in the upper echelons of the artistic community in Provence, the Bourdets visited Matisse fairly often and probably mentioned the upcoming sale of their house. Shortly thereafter Ida received a note from Matisse advising her that in a few months (June 1951) the Vence chapel would be dedicated and the street renamed boulevard Henri Matisse. If she meant to sell the house to Chagall, she had better do it soon, since he felt that Chagall would hardly enjoy receiving all his mail addressed to him at Les Collines, boulevard Henri Matisse, Vence! Marc and Vava Chagall, because they both loved Les Collines, did not mind dwelling at the new address; on the contrary, they took it quite well and even joked about it.

Apart from artists, Matisse had many friends and admirers among publishers, craftsmen, and poets. Early on he encouraged Pierre Reverdy, the Cubist poet for whom he illustrated *Les Jockeys Camouflés* in 1918 with reproductions of linear drawings. In 1946 the Editions du Chêne published *Visages*, poems by Reverdy, with reproductions of fourteen heads drawn by Matisse in brown crayon and with linocut initials for chapter headings.

---

*This happened in 1947, when Chagall attempted to work at the Madoura pottery.

Matisse was also on very good terms with the poet Tristan Tzara, with whom he had a long-standing relationship. They collaborated many times, including in 1946, when Matisse illustrated *Signe de Vie* for his friend. Tzara came regularly to the South of France, where he found time first for Matisse and then for Picasso. Once we met him at Matisse's bedside at Cimiez. On the way back Pablo mused, "I don't know what those two have in common. I bet you that Matisse understands nothing about Dadaism." I retorted, "Dadaism was a long time ago, and Tristan Tzara is a multifaceted man. By the way, how well do you understand his theories? And yet you like him." And that was that.

Whether Matisse was knowledgeable about Dadaism or not, he was very sensitive to poetry and he knew his authors well. That explained why he was able to illustrate hermetic poets like Mallarmé so successfully. The elliptical echoes and rhythmical qualities of his lines were attuned to the melodious sounds that moved him so. He allowed himself to resonate fully to the music of words. While guided by a powerful poetic emotion, however, he did not forget that the arts of engraving and lithography were an end in themselves, with their own rules, possibilities, and limitations. Artists who did well in both media used them for what they could give, and once they knew how to deal with the technical constraints, they stretched the limits.

Apart from his attraction to illustrating limited editions, Matisse from the beginning of his career was full of curiosity and liked to experiment and try his hand at various things. He showed a great gift for etchings or aquatints, and his interest in graphic arts led him to make his first linear black-on-white lithographs in 1906. They were free and informal studies of his models, figures and faces drawn with a lithographic pencil. Much in the same spirit, he undertook a new series of lithographs, elliptical and spontaneous renderings of nudes, in 1914.

When he came back to the same medium during the late twenties and early thirties, his approach was different. His models, dressed as dancers and odalisques, were observed, described, and rendered with unusual precision and modeling of volumes. Most of these lithographs had a heaviness unusual in Matisse's work. Compared to the previous series, they lacked charm but gained power. Had they been printed in sepia on a gray or buff Rives paper instead of black on a white Arches paper, or on top of a first light tone with patches of white here and there, as Pierre Bonnard would have done, they would have been intrinsically more successful. In Matisse's mind they were akin to his themes, charcoal studies in which he allowed modeling and shadowing, rather than to his elliptical line variations. These lithographs were uncharacteristic, more realistic than most of his paintings and closer to Derain's classical style.

After the liberation of Paris, Fernand Mourlot showed himself to be a great artistic leader.* Not satisfied with printing all the posters for all the French museums, he decided to encourage the great contemporary artists to come to his workshop and experiment freely, as Toulouse-Lautrec and his friends had done fifty years earlier. The first to respond were Matisse and Picasso—once again on a parallel course. Picasso was encouraged by the positive results he got right away, working mostly at the rue de Chabrol on stone. But some of Matisse's lithographs did not come out as well; because of his poor state of health, he often had to work at home on transfer paper with lithographic pencil rather than directly on stone or zinc plates.

This method had one advantage: when drawn or painted directly on stone or zinc plates, the image was a mirror image of the original design, while with a transfer paper the initial design became a mirror image when transposed onto the stone, so that the final proof, obtained by printing the mirror image on Arches paper, was identical to the initial one. In other words, the forms on the left of the drawing on the transfer paper appeared on the right on the stone and on the left again when printed. For many artists this was pleasant, because they obtained an image just like the one they had created. But there were many drawbacks. Stone or zinc plates had a grain that gave a texture to the line, whereas transfer paper afforded less liveliness. Sometimes to compensate for this defect, the artist could place a thick sheet of heavy grain Arches paper under the transfer paper and rub with a lithographic pencil to obtain

---

*By the time the Mourlot brothers inherited their father's workshop, it had quite a reputation. They developed it even further and engineered the second wave of the lithographic renaissance. During the Nazi occupation, the workshop sometimes printed false identity cards with fake official seals, to save the lives of people belonging to the underground movement.

textured lines or interesting effects. Nevertheless, the main flaw of transfer paper was a complete lack of reliability. Often some of the original design got lost in the transfer process, dissolving with the paper glue instead of adhering to the stone. The artist had to be sure to use freshly prepared transfer paper and to have it set on stone as soon as possible to avoid deterioration. Last but not least, even the weather (especially hot weather) could lead to disaster, because the thin sheet of transfer paper expanded in an uneven fashion when slightly humidified and pressed onto the stone, so that the lithographic pencil lines and inkmarks transferred onto the stone and became disengaged from their initial support. The competence of the master printer was usually an essential factor in the success or failure of the endeavor.

Unfortunately, a concatination of adverse circumstances marred Matisse's endeavor to illustrate Baudelaire's *Les Fleurs du Mal*. He worked on the project from 1944 to 1947, first conceptually and then by drawing his final designs on transfer paper. Owing to some financial difficulties of the publisher, the project was put on hold, and the designs were belatedly set on stone during a very hot and dry summer. The expansion and deformation that ensued made the proofs completely distorted and wobbly. Luckily, Matisse had kept photographs of the thirty-three illustrations, so these were used instead of the original designs, printed through a photolithographic technique that was aesthetically satisfactory but not quite as valuable for knowledgeable bibliophiles.

Matisse encountered similar difficulties when he used the same technique for some of his other projects, the poems of Charles d'Orléans and the *Florilège des Amours de Ronsard*, but he was so earnest in his intent and so tenacious in his desire to see the results measure up to his expectations that he found convincing ways to achieve his goal. Both limited-edition books were very successful in combining multicolored flowing lines to create a graphic effect that resembled the use of colored crayons—quite the essence of Matissian personality and style.

In 1941, when Matisse started working on the illustrations of the poems of Charles d'Orléans, it was as if destiny selected that moment to lead another French poet toward his door, someone who had dreamed of meeting him for a long time and who until then had missed the opportunity: Louis Aragon. An important relationship developed between Aragon and Matisse in Nice during World War II. From the early days of Surrealism, Aragon had had a passion for Matisse's art, to the point of giving Matisse's name to a female character in one of his early novels. He had admired the artist from a distance until he came to live in Nice with his wife, the writer Elsa Triolet, in 1941. Nice was not part of the occupied zone, but both Aragon and Triolet were active in the underground movement, and even in that part of France the Vichy police were looking for them. They had to change lodgings several times until they found a small apartment over a restaurant in the area of Les Ponchettes. From the front they had a beautiful view of the Mediterranean Sea, and the back windows overlooked the flower market. Having checked that the police were unaware of their whereabouts, since they might have endangered the artist if they were still being trailed, Aragon wrote Matisse a few letters, then telephoned Lydia for an appointment, and one day took a bus to Cimiez to meet the master, in December 1941. The pretext of the meeting was to ask Matisse for permission to reproduce a few of his drawings in the next issue of a literary journal called *Poésie 42.**

This was only a starting point, since both men showed a real eagerness to talk to each other. Matisse was thinking that Aragon could write a preface for an album about his work that was being prepared, and started to show him many drawings pinned to the walls in what he called his "room of light." Aragon was enchanted, because he was undertaking a book about his favorite artist. Soon Elsa Triolet was introduced to Matisse, and she charmed both the master and Lydia.

Louis and Elsa were a most stunning and charismatic couple. He was very tall and thin, something of a dandy, and even in gray flannels he cut a fine figure. His long, narrow hands were always in motion and quite expressive. In his pale chiseled face his fine aquiline nose and bow-shaped lips were remarkable, yet not as striking as his periwinkle eyes,

---

*Pierre Seghers was the editor and publisher of this review. The numbers 40, 41, 42, and so on marked the year of publication.

whose pupils were always contracted and piercing. Elsa Triolet was small and delicate and had eyes of exactly the same blue. Her oval face was a bit heart-shaped; her complexion pale, with tiny freckles. Her golden Venetian hair with a few threads of gray was wound around her head in a braid, Russian fashion. She affected *les petits bibis*, tiny hats with a veil, often positioned to lean dangerously forward. She always selected the finest kid shoes or pumps and diaphanous silk stockings, which showed the beauty and delicacy of her legs, ankles, and tiny feet to their best advantage. Elegant without ostentation, she wore gray and lavender blue during the day and always black at night. This fragile exterior was in acute contrast to her sharp intellect and domineering disposition.*

As Matisse's relationship with Aragon developed, he started to make a series of theme-and-variation portraits of Aragon, the first one in each series (the theme) a shadowed charcoal study and the others witty line drawings. In each charcoal study he caught a more permanent, slightly thoughtful mood; in the others, all the aspects of the quicksilver conversationalist, from bombastic to melancholic, from argumentative to pensive, from sophistic to paradoxical, from mannered to quizzical, from convincing to convinced, always putting emphasis on the eye in relation to the nose and mouth. How he compelled his mercurial model to sit still was a mystery, since Aragon made people dizzy with his habit of pacing to and fro as he talked, like a hypnosis-inducing pendulum or a caged wild beast at the zoo. Matisse probably took on the role of ringmaster for the occasion and thoroughly tamed the hyperactive poet.

The conquest of Aragon's many facets would not have been complete if the painter had failed to pay due homage to Elsa by portraying the feminine half of the couple in enigmatic yet convincing images. Matisse recovered from the initial faux pas of referring to her as Madame

---

*Elsa Triolet was the sister of Lily Brik, the wife of Mayakovski, with whom Elsa had probably been in love. Her pen name, Triolet, was the name of her first French husband. M. Triolet had a passion for thoroughbred horses and apparently for thoroughbred women too. After her first book, written in Russian, she wrote all her novels in French. She received the Prix Goncourt in 1945 for her book of short stories, *The First Tear Costs Two Hundred Francs*, one of the coded, apparently nonsensical sentences meant for the underground networks that were broadcast by the BBC during the war. She received the award in 1945, but the prize was for 1944, when the award had not been given because of historical events.

Henri Matisse. *Aragon*, March 1942, a drawing of
Louis Aragon.

Henri Matisse. *Elsa Triolet*, 1946.

Aragon instead of Elsa Triolet in one of his first letters by giving her small presents and drawings to ingratiate himself to her. Because Lydia and Elsa could speak Russian together they became friends, and this helped to create a congenial ambiance. So when Matisse proposed to make a series of themes and variations of Elsa, she was pleased to sit for him, though she usually did not care much for "formalist painters," preferring realistic or even naturalistic traditional painters of the Russian school, such as Repin.

In the first charcoal studies Matisse, whether consciously or not, emphasized the general likeness of Louis's and Elsa's features: oval faces, aristocratic noses, almond-shaped mouths rhyming with slightly slanted almond-shaped eyes that looked so lost in total absorption of an inner vision that they stared blindly in front of them, utterly unaware of a viewer out there. Elsa's "mad cap" or hat crowned her supercilious demeanor and accented her Slavic charm, but it came and went in the drawings according to the needs of the artist during the variations.

In the spring of 1942 the Aragons left for Villeneuve-lès-Avignon to see Pierre Seghers, with the intention of coming back for the summer. But the dangers inherent in a life of secrecy did not allow them to return. They were forced to migrate from one hideout to another to escape the police and the Gestapo, who were on the lookout for them especially after 1942, when there was no longer a free zone in France. In the meantime Matisse was hypochondriacal or suffered from diverse ailments, so they did not meet again until 1945, after the end of the hostilities. Because of his previous series of studies, Matisse made new drawings of Elsa very freely, as a tribute to her success as a writer. He had read and liked her novel *The White Horse*. Meanwhile Aragon had completed several texts about his friend, among which was *L'Apologie du Luxe*, published by Skira.

Aragon had become one of the painter's best champions, so later when he approached the artist in earnest about a show at the Maison de la Pensée Française, Matisse thought that it would be callous to refuse. But since that cultural institution was politically left-wing, he accepted with the provision that he could show many of the preparatory works for the Chapel of the Rosary in Vence as well as some other pieces. His handling of the situation was astute: by showing religious images in a left-wing cultural center, he could remain nonpartisan. The choice of the locale proved his immunity to the religious zeal of the Catholics, and no one could accuse him of being a closet Communist because of the thematic orientation of the show. An atheist, Aragon was not antireligious, so he was pleased to agree, and the exhibition took place during the spring and summer of 1950 with great success.

This exchange demonstrated Matisse's independence of mind and the fact that he could drive hard bargains, even with his friends. He was not sentimental but very cool in his dealings with other human beings. People who thought they could cajole him into climbing into their chariots for one reason or another were quite mistaken. Because he was famous, he was careful not to be used and abused by one intellectual faction or another.

When we were residing in the South of France, Louis Aragon and Elsa Triolet often visited us before or after going to Vence or Cimiez. I had already seen Aragon at Pablo's studio, but I met Elsa for the first time in Golfe-Juan in the autumn of 1946. Afterward in Paris we often went to dinner in their small apartment, which evoked Ibsen's doll house, in the rue de la Sourdière, close to the marché St. Honoré. Many times Matisse, though absent, came up in the conversation; he was a presence to reckon with in everybody's thoughts.

While we were tasting smoked sturgeon and caviar on toast, accompanied with a small glass of iced Russian vodka, I wondered what Matisse would have enjoyed if he had been present. Ever since I had met him on the Riviera, Pablo and I had never shared a meal with him. Before his illness he must have been a *bon vivant*; early photographs showed him as a sturdy and stocky man, drinking beer with the painter Hans Purrmann during his first trip to Bavaria in the summer of 1908. At the time I knew him, he must have had to follow a severe diet, but he had the grace to be quiet about his health, never wanting us to feel sorry for him. Maybe he wished to avoid temptation, or perhaps he ate several small snacks throughout the day rather than regular meals.* Whenever we called on him, he was always a delicate host. The feast

---

*Apparently he had a good cook even after the excellent Madame Céline, who served him for ten years, retired.

was his conversation, but occasionally we were offered tea and delicious pastries, even though he never partook of anything in our presence.

So many oysters, shrimps, and prawns were depicted in his pictures that Matisse probably had a taste for seafood. Several kinds of fish were frequently portrayed, as were orange and yellow mussels within their open blue shells, but one did not know if he was expressing culinary tastes or his *joie du coeur et joie des sens*, a purely visual and contemplative sense of bliss. All of the fruits in his masterpieces, from the pineapple to the melon, from the pomegranate to the lemon, could well reveal a kinship to oriental poetry rather than the painter's gustatory inclinations. These objects, once painted, belonged to a different universe; they became metaphors, as in the "Song of Songs":

> *Thy slender waist swings like a palm tree,*
> *And thy breasts evoke a cluster of dates.*

Speaking of trees, Matisse once referred to one of his models not as a palm tree but as "the plane tree." We heard a lot about her, even from Lydia, who used the term in a tongue-in-cheek manner with a hint of sarcasm in her voice. She obviously did not appreciate the shadow this model cast.

Pablo commented that he would like such plane trees to grow in his garden.

"Yes," said I, "but in your garden they would not remain a merely visual delight for long." Everybody laughed.

"So nobody trusts me around here—you all think I am the slave of an unquenchable lust! But you are all wrong. I could be an ascetic if I wanted to."

I retorted, "Yes, you are the ascetic of the plethora!"

Pablo insisted that asceticism was a fundamental trait of the Spanish character, as was a pronounced idealism that we did not understand at all.

Matisse added, "That makes me think: we prepared some especially delicious dates. Can you bring them now, Lydia?"

She went, came back with a porcelain dish full of dates stuffed with marzipan dyed in all kinds of bright colors, and put them in front of Pablo. This was more than Pablo's Andalusian relish for sweetmeats could endure, and he succumbed wholeheartedly, even though he usually exercised restraint and asceticism as far as food was concerned.

"Between Françoise, who divines when to bring me candied fruits, and you with this, what a conspiracy," said Pablo jokingly to Matisse. "Both of you know some of my weak points and how to use them. Is there anything that you want today? I am ready; just name it." And he opened his arms as if ready to be crucified.

"No, my friend—only the pleasure of frequent visits, and if you wish, you can see some of my cutouts in progress." Matisse was working on a very geometric set of three quite arresting large cutouts.

Pablo abandoned himself to the flavor of the moment, looking absolutely at peace and relaxed. These precious afternoons reached a perfection out of time. Close to Matisse, trivial worries and cares became obsolete, anxieties were banished, harmony prevailed, and its afterglow lingered for a while. The feeling was perhaps captured in a one-line poem by Paul Eluard: "The white illumination to believe all the good possible." This climate of serenity had a soothing effect on Pablo, and Pablo's vitality, wit, and alertness had an energizing effect on Matisse.

Pablo was more active than ever at the Madoura pottery, but he was also using all kinds of debris from the nearby garbage dump as building blocks for his sculptures. The handle of a broken teacup became the ear of a she-ape, an earthen pot its belly, a forlorn piece of iron its tail, two of Claude's toy cars its head. He expanded the conceptual method of collages to the realm of sculpture.

Meanwhile, at home in the garden Paloma, still ensconced in the ecstasy of babyhood, cooed like a most beatific and peaceful dove. Matisse's "curly ones," his white pigeons, still shared their pen with the tortoise, and Claude, almost four years old, was having a marvelous time. All the people who idolized Picasso brought Claude lots of presents to remain in his father's good graces. Once someone had the unfortunate idea of giving him a play set of carpenter's tools. He went to work right away, knocking down his own toys and attempting to saw the legs off one or two chairs.

It was imperative that we develop Claude's more peaceful interests. I showed him some art books, which he immediately divided into three categories: the "nice ones," his favorites, from antiquity to just before the Renaissance; the one he called "the movies," encompassing the Renaissance: Tintoretto, Veronese, Michelangelo; and last "the moderns," his father's friends. To these he soon added a liking for "Grandfather's pictures," a reference to the *douanier* Rousseau, whom he believed to be his grandfather because Tati, the Provençal maid, said he was. Claude called his father's paintings "Cranachides," since he overheard us speaking about Cranach, whom Pablo much admired. For a child of his age, Claude's discernment was unusual.

But that was just the beginning; soon Claude experienced his first artistic passion. One morning he rushed in from the garden carrying the mail and brandishing a magazine called *Roman* ("Novel"). He shouted excitedly that the cover had been designed by Matisse. Asked how he knew, he answered that he had already noticed the same yellow-orange, white, and purple together in Matisse's pictures and at his apartment. He concluded triumphantly, "He is a real artist, he does not use my broken toys to make a monkey sculpture like Papa.* He works in luxury. His rooms are just like his paintings."

We were delighted to be the parents of a child prodigy art critic. Pablo laughed until he had tears in his eyes. He telephoned Matisse right away to tell the anecdote. Afterward "the young Hercules" was often invited to go to the Regina with us. When he accompanied us, there was an abundance of petits fours, cookies, éclairs, pralines, macaroons, tartlets, and the like. I am sure that no other art critic in the whole history of art was ever treated in a more regal fashion or showered with more delicacies. For Claude, each time was an ecstatic experience. At home he was on a more spartan diet, since we preferred his health to his pleasure, so for him the visits to Matisse, with the beautiful paintings in the beautiful rooms and the delicate offerings from the benevolent patriarch, were a foretaste of paradise. Without recriminations he accepted being dressed up for each occasion and was very well-

---

*This was a reference to a sculpture of a she-monkey whose head was made of two toy cars belonging to Claude.

behaved during the whole visit. He looked steadily into the great artist's all-knowing blue gaze with the innocence and intensity of his large dark eyes. A soft kind of authority emanated from Matisse which had a soothing effect on Claude—one more proof that the great artist could tame all wild beasts, large and small.

The Idol from the Pacific

AS MATISSE spent so much time indoors, he migrated from one room to another within his large apartment, asking Lydia to redecorate periodically under his direction and thus alleviating the monotony of his routine and also refreshing his eyes with new or unexpected assemblages of familiar objects.

Usually when we arrived at the Regina, we were shown into a medium-size sitting room to the right of the hallway. Two small Picasso paintings, a still life and a portrait of Dora Maar, both of the early 1940s, were the only stable fixtures, along with a large philodendron. The two oils were there as a result of an exchange between the two artists. Picasso, who constantly kept in view at his Paris studio at least four or five works by Matisse (most of which he had bought, a few of which he had bartered for), wondered if his two pictures were on the wall all the time or only when we came. In any case, the philodendron and the two paintings were always present when we entered. These three familiar items greeted us as we sat to wait and looked around.

Each time we discovered a new arrangement of different canvases: large horizontal pieces, one with fishes and the other with birds stenciled in white on beige linen, entitled *Oceania*, or very large cutouts made in tapestry, such as the one entitled *The Sky* from the series about Polynesia, or a simple yet daring female form. A modern reclining chair upholstered in zebra skin appeared and disappeared, and the sofa and cushions, chosen to match the paintings on the wall, exhibited unexpected color combinations. Apart from these few items and the splendor of the art, the sitting room was rather austere. The window opened toward the hills, and did not quite succeed in illuminating the walls, which were tinted a rather unpleasant shade of raw sienna. A neutral gray would have provided a much softer background for the pictures, but we did not have time to dwell on the why and the how of the burlaplike tone, since we were given just enough time to take a good look at the most recent productions before we were led directly to the place where Matisse was nesting on that specific afternoon.

I remember one room in the back of the apartment. It was full of light and seemed to be used mostly when Matisse was unwell and in need of a nurse, for it was close to the living quarters of the staff. There he enjoyed talking about his models. Some were students earning a bit of money. One, Jacqueline Duhème, made illustrations in a naïve, childlike style to enliven children's books. We knew her well, since she was also a friend of Jacques Prévert and shared her time between Nice and St.-Paul-de-Vence, with a few excursions to Vallauris. She spoke with a well-rehearsed *titi parisien* accent and must have been a ray of sunshine with her vivacity and her anecdotes, mimicking the people she knew and rolling her eyes in the most comic manner. Some other young women were professional models at the School of Fine Arts in Nice. They all liked to sit for Matisse, who enjoyed conversing with them. He was preoccupied with their well-being, with their progress in life.

In this room the mohair plaid on the bed matched the artist's sweater or cardigan. He wore a turban that matched or contrasted with a purple piece of satin embroidered with silver-thread Chinese ideograms, which hung on the wall opposite another large Chinese calligraphy, a wood-carving in black and gold. Vases, often depicted in Matisse's canvases, overflowed with flowers and were reflected in the mirror. The green leaves found an echo in the emerald irises of the cat, which was

Matisse's studio at Le Régina around 1953. On the left-hand wall is *Large Decoration with Masks* (1953); on the right-hand wall, *Acrobats* (1952) and portrait heads. On the chair is a mask from the New Hebrides often referred to as the "Idol from the Pacific."

allowed to lounge close to its master. This room gave me the odd feeling of having absentmindedly stepped inside one of Matisse's paintings; even Matisse's presence, or Lydia's, did not shatter the illusion, since both often appeared within the painter's universe.

Even though the windows were numerous and faced south, the other side of the huge room remained dark, protected by drapes and embroidered see-through oriental curtains from Morocco. At times we were escorted to another bedroom, where Matisse would be resting in the subdued light of partly closed shutters. For some reason it was the place where he spoke most willingly about the artists of the past or about his family. He liked to reminisce with Pablo about the days when each of them had gone separately to Ambroise Vollard's gallery to look at the Cézannes, and the impact those pictures had had on their work. Since both already very well knew all there was to know about Cézanne, it seemed that some of these recollections were exchanged mostly for my benefit. They wanted to impress upon me, almost to brand me with, the importance or rather the necessity of the master of Aix as the initiator of their deepest development.

Matisse once described how he had bought his first Cézanne, instead of a Vincent van Gogh that he also coveted, and what a lesson it had been. I acquiesced without conviction. My mother, a great art lover and in a way my first teacher, had already failed to persuade me of the relevance of Cézanne's theories to my generation's preoccupations. For me, Cézanne was a sacred cow whose milk had been entirely sucked into Cubism and who was therefore barren as far as I was concerned. I could appreciate his impeccable logic, and the intelligent use he made of cold and warm tones in order to create a third dimension with little or no recourse to linear perspective. He had wanted to emulate Poussin's abstractions but with nature in front of his eyes, but I preferred Poussin and his baroque rhetoric to Cézanne's methodic rationality. Though I objectively admired many of Cézanne's paintings and knew how the whiteness of the paper in his watercolors began to glow with just a few of his famous directional brushstrokes, he was never a favorite of mine. Shame on me, but I was prepared to carry this blemish to the end of my days rather than be insincere!

My two mentors knew that I acquiesced because they were my elders and because I respected the importance of Cézanne's influence on the artists of their generation, but they were well aware that they had failed to convince me, so in one way or another they would come back to the subject and try again, hoping to discover a sign of approbation on my face, which remained sphinxlike on each occasion. Of course, their consensus was genuine, but certainly it was less dangerous to burn incense at the foot of an altar at which they thoroughly knew what to expect of each other than to risk a sharp difference of opinion in front of a witness. Sometimes I would try to direct the conversation toward Gauguin or van Gogh, without much success; the subjects were too loaded for both of them, too sensitive and touchy. It was easier emotionally to vow allegiance to a strict disciplinarian of perception than to either of the accursed reprobates, who had been singled out and excommunicated by Cézanne. (About Gauguin, Cézanne had said, "He stole my little sensation and cruised with it on all the great liners of the world." He accused van Gogh of insanity, to which accusation van Gogh retorted, "And yet my curves are not demented"—a sentence that Matisse later incorporated into *Jazz*.)

Gauguin's search for the archaic and the primeval, which had led him first to Brittany and later to the Pacific islands, was of utmost importance to me. He had possessed the courage to discover and express the savage within himself. I could not believe that his achievements had not been central to Matisse's meditations, but Matisse probably did not want to face the parallelism of Matisse and Gauguin's primitivism on one side and van Gogh and Picasso's expressionism on the other.

In the same way, references to African art did not seem to stir any interest in Pablo. At least in front of Matisse, he did not welcome discussions on that topic, and he dropped the subject if by any chance it was brought into the conversation. Right away Pablo would declare his present enthusiasm for the early idols of the Cycladic islands or for the *kouros* and *korai* of the archaic period; he added that his taste had evolved and followed his current interests in ceramics and clay statuary. He had become intrigued by the red clay funerary sculptures found in the Etruscan tombs of Cervetri and Tarquinii. Did his reluctance to discuss African art have a special meaning vis-à-vis Matisse? I did not see how, but of course there was a lot I did not know about their past interactions.

Anyway, after noticing this reticence, Matisse took little time to present Picasso with a gaudy four-foot-tall idol from the southern part of Malekula, one of the New Hebrides islands in the Pacific. It was a human effigy made of interwoven fibers and arboreal ferns, rather grotesque in proportions, wildly painted in red, white, and blue, and having nothing to do with the abstract, organic, rhythmical sculptures that we usually associate with tribal art from that region. Pablo smiled and thanked him, but from his tight jaws I could tell right away that he did not like it.

Matisse did not forget to inform us at length of how it had been given to him by a French captain in the merchant marine. He insisted that it was especially interesting because it was in fact a ceremonial headdress from the Nevinbumbaau Vanuatu tribe—a woman's effigy (the dancer had to put his head and torso inside the creature's body; powerful magic indeed). Pablo's eyes darkened by the minute, and when we left he apologized for not taking it with us, saying that it was too large for our car and that Marcel would come back another day to pick it up with an appropriate vehicle. We then left hastily, rushed to the car, and told Marcel to drive away. At last Pablo was free to explode.

"Ah, naturally, Matisse thinks I have no taste. He believes I am a barbarian and that for me any piece of third-rate tribal art will do! This caricature is not good enough for him in his *grand bourgeois* surroundings, but it is good enough for me, the poor chap from Málaga!"

"Don't worry," I consoled him. "You make yourself unhappy on account of an altogether unimportant incident. If you don't like this piece from the New Hebrides, you have plenty of rooms upstairs at the studio in Vallauris. Nobody will even see it there, and you will satisfy your friend at the same time. His intentions may be excellent."

"Certainly not! His intentions are not excellent, and I will not accept this awful object."

"But you keep repeating that you don't give a damn about aesthetics," I ventured. "You even enjoy such ugly places as Monsieur Fort's house or our place in Vallauris, and nobody thinks the less of you for it."

"Don't you see the difference? The absurdity of our dwellings is a part of our eccentricity, but if I accept the hideous gift from my so-called friend, I will have to put it in a place of honor. If I don't, the relationship is in jeopardy. I am in a bind; what am I to do?" And he cursed abundantly.

I kissed him to soothe his vexation and agreed that this particular tribal object was far from being the most desirable ceremonial mask in the world, especially when one thought of some splendid pieces from New Guinea that we had seen in Paris together. So far Pablo's tactics had been very good, and the best strategy would be conveniently to forget the idol each time we visited Matisse in the future. After a while he would get the message and no longer push such a cumbersome object on us.

We were fooling ourselves if we thought the matter could be solved so easily. Matisse was stubborn about his gift. During our visits the idol sat there reproachfully, and now and then Lydia would call to remind us to send Marcel to pick it up. By then I suspected that the whole affair might be a revenge on Matisse's part. He had been told that one evening at a restaurant Pablo, finding a hair in his soup, had exclaimed that it looked like a line drawing by Matisse. Whether the rumor was true or false, Matisse felt that it was not becoming to ask for explanations or apologies, so perhaps the ugly gift with all its implications was the small vengeance that he allowed himself to exact.

There was no way out. Nothing was ever said about the hair in the soup, but Picasso successfully procrastinated, and the already decaying red, white, and blue idol made of arboreal ferns remained where it was. Even in friendship, an eye for an eye and a tooth for a tooth ensures proper respect and mutual esteem on both sides.

It was indeed a surprise when in 1985, on the opening day of the Picasso Museum in Paris, I discovered the gaudy idol from the Pacific enshrined in a glass showcase. Even after life, there was indeed no way to escape a present from Henri Matisse.*

---

*I used to believe that the fern mask had been brought to Picasso in the summer of 1953, shortly before I left for Paris with my two children. But apparently it was only later, in 1957, that Picasso, by then in a different mood, at last claimed Matisse's gift and received it from Pierre Matisse. The huge head telescoped between the small limbs was to have a definite impact on his later work, in which one often found large heads ensconced between embryonic limbs; having eaten up all the available space on the canvas, their archaic savagery was very impressive. So Matisse had foreseen his friend's further evolution, or even after life provoked it.

The Sadness of the Kings

BY THE END of 1951 there was much dissension between Pablo and me, but our link through our professional activities was stronger than ever. Creativity was at the center of our lives together. We worked long hours every day until late in the evening, and afterward we still had enough stamina to debate aesthetic preferences and discuss the relative merits of past or contemporary painters. We were tied by an ardent passion for art rather than for one another, or rather our passion for each other had become a passion of the mind, in which each was enthralled by the other as a thinker and an artist rather than as a human being. It appeared essential to communicate that way, and because that kind of exchange was satisfying, we neglected to wonder why we had begun to drift apart emotionally.

My grandmother died in August of 1951, and I kept silent about my grief. I met my father at her funeral, and after many years of estrangement, we set aside mutual grievances and resumed a positive relationship. I did not talk about that either. On his side, Pablo was having an affair, which I had to learn about through the very unwelcome good offices of Madame Ramié of the Madoura factory. I thought that it was vulgar of her to deliver information that I had not asked for. I armed myself with resilience, in the belief that art was stronger than life's unwelcome anecdotal intrigues.

That year, apart from ceramics and sculptures, Pablo started some drawings and paintings of knights in armor, damsels in distress atop impregnable towers, and cats prowling around lobsters. Knights in armor and lobsters in their carapaces were of course all one to him, a sign of defensive hardening. He subconsciously knew that I had set a protective shell around myself. With his sharp sense of humor, he once asked me if there was a can opener in the house, adding that it could come in handy. I didn't take the hint that I should appear less stern, and I kept working all the more, in the belief that instead of drifting further apart we could be reunited through painting.

In the nineteenth century Fantin-Latour had painted an *Homage to Manet* in which the master stands beside one of his pictures on an easel, surrounded by the artists of the Impressionist group. Later Maurice Denis had gathered the Nabis around a painting by Cézanne. Beside Denis and his wife, one could identify Pierre Bonnard, Odilon Redon, Paul Sérusier, Édouard Vuillard, Félix Vallotton, and even Ambroise Vollard. So, in the spirit of the homage tradition, I wanted to create a large composition in which three generations of artists would be present, with Picasso in the center, showing one of the drawings of the *Face of Peace* series. Around him I put Édouard Pignon, a well-known French painter deeply influenced by the Spanish master, about twenty years Pablo's junior; myself, forty years younger than Pablo; and another painter, Pierre Gastaud, also my age.

I did not need studies of Pablo and myself—I had already done many—nor did I need any for Gastaud, because his face was easy to memorize (it had the regular features and classical proportions that I like to draw from imagination). In 1951 and 1952 I made sketches and paintings of Pignon, who came to spend summer holidays at Pablo's studio in Vallauris with his wife, Hélène Parmelin. (Pignon had a strongly built and expressionistic face, like a van Gogh, but I had to study it because it was alien to me.) I based the composition on a crisscrossing of horizontal and vertical sections, which obliged the eye to travel up, down, and sideways. The ground was of an earthy ocher tone on which the feet of the painters were strongly rooted and simply delineated. That same tone traveled all the way up to Pablo's face and to the easel at the left. I wanted Picasso's eyes to be like beacons of light, the dark pupils directed toward his portrait of me, and the drawing of the dove-face treated like a collage but painted in oil, the lines furrowed into the fresh paint with a graphite pencil.

There were complementary contrasts between the red of Gastaud's sweater and the green of my dress. The upper part of the painting was separated into square areas of different sizes: sky blue for the window, to emphasize the hope expressed in Picasso's drawing, with its verse by Éluard "L'Homme en proie à la paix se couronne d'espoir." ("By surrendering to peace, man crowns himself with hope"); a neutral gray behind Gastaud; black behind Picasso's face, to offset the sunburned shade of his skin; and white behind my head, an echo of the drawing to the left. The main problem was to find enough space for Pignon, who was a tall and sturdy man. I wound up having him simultaneously bending over and crouching forward, inscribed in a square below Pablo's arm, turning his neck in the other direction, toward the collage. This twisted position gave importance to the verticality of Pablo and myself.

At first the painting looked crowded, but as the work advanced I found that since the faces were the most expressive parts anyway, Gastaud and I could be on a second plane without losing the intensity of our presences, and thus the bodily presence of Pablo became more powerful and the rest more integrated. The relations between the figures at the front and the receding ones achieved the purpose of showing how artists of different generations proceed from one another.

The painting was finished in 1952. At first I was pleased with the result, and Pablo liked it too. I had not forgotten his ever-present sailor's T-shirt, nor his favorite slippers, a detail he found priceless. (Painters work most of the time standing up, and for ten hours in front of a canvas, comfortable slippers instead of leather shoes can make a lot of difference.) Pablo also enjoyed the way in which I had introduced his drawing within my oil as a collage.

But soon I thought that the general handling of the composition was stiffer and heavier than in my other canvases of the same period. It was willful and contrived, yet it was valid as a testimony to my state of mind at the time. I had been concerned with mathematics in structure as a way to make the composition itself organic to the theme (as Poussin and Vouet had done in the seventeenth century). Not only in that painting but throughout that year, color was a secondary concern, because I knew I was a born colorist and could always come back to it later.

In 1952 I was bent on penetrating the whys and the hows of Picasso's architectonic and plastic ideas in order to understand the evolution of his thinking. During Cubism and afterward, one of his main interests was the reduction of the dimensionality of space to the plane of the painting. Another important concern was the analysis of the anatomy of different components in a complex form (be it an object or a figure) within the pictorial field, and the similar reduction of volume to a two-dimensional articulated shape integrated in the two-dimensional space. This reduction was by no means a decorative flattening of field and figure; it was more akin to a geometric descriptive report on canvas of the planes as they stood and intersected in space. It was a multivision brought about with dynamic torsions to give the image a sense of completion. Once on the surface, these shapes twisted by movement often appeared to the viewer as distorted; hence the word "deformation," which was completely inappropriate.

Studying Picasso's work and inner motivation was also a form of love, and it was very rewarding and important to my evolution. In doing so I could have quoted Matisse: "I never avoided the influence of others. I would have considered that a cowardice and a lack of sincerity toward myself. I believe that the personality of the artist develops and asserts itself through the struggles he has to go through when pitted against other personalities. If the fight is fatal and the personality succumbs, it means that this was bound to be its fate."

In March and April 1952, the Galerie Louise Leiris gave me an exhibition, mostly of my works of 1950 and 1951. It was quite well received by collectors and critics alike, but the *Homage to Picasso* was not included, since it was not yet finished. People raved about my "white period" just when I was in the process of turning my back on it, but this encouragement goaded me forward, unleashing an irresistible surge of creative power. Pablo appeared pleased with this display of masculine strength and its accompanying lack of regard for refinement, but in fact he felt threatened by my independence. Still, between time spent in Paris and time spent in Vallauris, nothing changed on the surface. When we returned to the Riviera that summer, our visits to Matisse proceeded as usual.

The blue-and-white cutouts on the walls were becoming larger and larger. In the first room to the right, *The Pool* was displayed: on a background of burlap canvas, a bold array of blue and white forms surged, unifying the swimmers and vegetation of the lagoon. Alternately light ultramarine on white and white on light ultramarine, Matisse's nude bathers and swimmers of 1952 held a special glow beyond their structural and dynamic qualities. Was the cause of such radiance the contrast of the intense electric blue with the absolute white?

From early on, since the time of *The Blue Nude* of 1907, subtitled *A Souvenir of Biskra*, Matisse had dreamed of painting bodies in celestial tones. When we had met him in February 1946 he was working on a pale blue nude, and Pablo had remarked that such a color transposition demanded a similar nonimitative treatment of form. Now, in 1952, he had achieved his goal. His dream had come true. The shapes were nonimitative and the relationship between form and background permitted the interaction of swimmers, seaweeds, and starfish swaying in a dazzling whiteness, while immaculately pale divers splashed into an azure sea.

Matisse's nudes had reached the timeless intangibility of celestial bodies. No longer submitting to the laws of gravity, they floated freely in harmony with the universe. Having transcended the laws that set limits to the human condition, they became the glorified bodies of resurrected beings. Embraced in an ever-ascending arabesque, Matisse's creatures were released to swim in ethereal space and to dance in the Milky Way.

In addition to unfolding his anima in this song of beatific joy, that year Matisse also meditated on the world he had to renounce, as he was trapped in the body of an aging invalid. To this end he poured his soul into violent sets of contrasting colors in a vast composition entitled *The Sadness of the King*. In this work, black competes with white, royal blue with yellow-orange, magenta-purple with lemon yellow, several

The dining room in Matisse's apartment at Le Régina, 1952. Around the walls is *The Swimming Pool* (1952) and in the corridor, *Acrobats* (1952).

greens with a dash of red. The horizontal and vertical sections in the background and the foreground do not attempt to stabilize a general leaning of the composition toward the left, where the black window of death lurks in the upper corner. Elements of vegetation seem to fly in the air or to creep along the throne; a musician strums away on the guitar; a dancer whirls in the foreground; but these do not prevent an element of pathos from prevailing, because of the melancholy posture of the king himself.

Never before or after did Matisse allow one of his compositions to reflect a subjective feeling so far from exultation and joy. For once, the aging genius confided. For once, he shared his sentiment about the impermanence of all things, giving voice to a deep and pathetic melancholy. For once, his pride melted and he disclosed a measure of sadness about leaving a world to which he had added so much beauty. There was no regret, no fear, simply sorrow in the knowledge that given more years, he could have reached out even more fervently toward the wholeness that was uniquely his to reveal.

At the age of eighty, Hokusai, the Japanese artist, said that he was beginning to know how to draw but that he would need four hundred more years to match the naturalness of a bird's song. Birds sing well in Matisse's paintings, but he also would have needed four hundred years more to attune his soul to other mysteries, to the silent marvels blown in all directions like golden leaves in the autumn wind.

Picasso and I were not shown *The Sadness of the King* when it was in progress. Perhaps we were in Paris. The picture derived its monumentality not from its large size but primarily from the richness of its content, obtained with a great economy of means. It beguiled the senses, it mesmerized the soul, while at the same time it revealed the disenchantment of the magician himself. It was evocative of Guillaume Apollinaire's "L'Enchanteur pourissant" ("The Rotting Magician").

One afternoon as we sat by his bed, Matisse surprised us by showing us a large black-and-white photographic reproduction of an equestrian portrait of the victorious general Guidoriccio da Fogliano by Simone Martini. Though concise in composition, it exuded the determination of the sturdy warrior in full regalia on his way from his home town to the fortified city he wanted to attack. Matisse had seen the original in

Siena years before and began to rave about it, without mentioning Pablo's own *Knights in Armor* series, which he had seen and heard about. He extolled the dynamic progression in Simone Martini's painting as being quite close to his own intent in *The Pool*: a lateral movement proceeding from one end of the painting to the other, as in a Japanese scroll, never retarding the motion by an appeal to any sense of depth.

Pablo was nonplussed by his friend's unexpected enthusiasm for the depiction of a warrior, even if space in the picture was flattened into an ornamental surface. He could not counterattack by being Paolo Uccello's champion, since perspective, a new sense of dimensional space, had been the Florentine's primary concern in his huge triptych *The Battle of San Romano*. So Pablo punctuated Matisse's monologue with affirmative exclamations while Matisse kept pointing at the reproduction, expressing with apostolic zeal all the reasons that he liked it. Matisse's enthusiasm became contagious, and soon I joined the chorus, adding my "ah's" and "yeses" to Pablo's.

It was a masterful discourse, a coherent demonstration of principles. No wonder Pablo was exhausted when we left. He had just enough energy left to protest that if both Matisse and I were going to his macho territory of violent affirmation, he wondered what his next step would be. Yet it did not take him long after that moment of verbal paralysis to imagine and to launch an important project of his own that was not unrelated to the conversation with Matisse about Simone Martini. Along with a series of pencil and india-ink studies and sketches, he planned twin monumental compositions of *War* and *Peace*, intended to be set in the concave narthex of a disused Gothic chapel in Vallauris. Once decorated, the chapel was to become part of a future museum in the adjacent castle of Vallauris.

First he began the panel about war, eager to be more successful than he had been the previous year with a painting entitled *Massacre in Korea*.* A man stands alone against the fierce attack of a sickly pink monster that is dealing disease and death from a hearselike war chariot,

---

Massacre in Korea was painted on a wood panel. In the spirit of the *Tres de Mayo* of Goya and the *Execution of Emperor Maximilian* of Manet, it depicts a group of naked women and children about to be shot by equally naked but helmeted men.

Pablo Picasso. *War* (*La Guerre*), 1952.

with the help of ghostly henchmen. Structurally there is a powerful contrast between the pitched immobility of the white figure to the left, armed with a spear and protected by a shield, and the dynamic onslaught of the warmongers coming from the right. The painting is strong, full of lyricism and expressionistic invention, but beyond the obvious pathos, the general feeling is one more of sadness than of drama. This is no longer the spontaneous outcry of *Guernica*, but a more allegorical and more intellectualized depiction of the horrors of war.

Apart from black and white, there is an abundance of morbid greens, red, yellow, and pink—almost the same combination as in *The Sadness of the King* (by pure coincidence), but of course so very different, because instead of evoking a nostalgia for the refinements of oriental culture, the painting evokes the crude menace of the mindless violence still latent in the reptilian, limbic layers of the human brain. Much in the vein of Goya's pronouncement that "the sleep of reason engenders monsters," *War* delivers a message: entropy threatens to take over and heralds an apocalyptic return to chaos.

After that paroxysm of emotion, Pablo felt that *Peace* might be

Pablo Picasso. *Peace* (*La Paix*), 1952.

an anticlimax. He was a bit disheartened about what symbols to use: "I wonder what people can do during peacetime—go to the office from nine to five, make love on Saturday night, and go for a picnic on Sunday? It is really trivial!"

Willing to help, I proposed a logo of my own making: "In peacetime all is possible. A child could plow the sea."

He liked the idea and translated it into an exciting visual element on the panel. A boy leading a winged horse in harness is plowing the

expanse of a vast blue sea, while a child standing on a rod stemming from a woman's hand is balancing a cage full of fish and an aquarium full of birds at either end of a perch. To the left women and adolescents disport themselves while to the right a group of women are gathered, cooking, drawing, or reading. All the figures are mostly whitish on blue, with the exception of the sun and some leaf green in the background. These figures can be paralleled with Matisse's swimmers and divers in *The Pool.* Both compositions are successful. But Picasso's whole design, though comparable to Matisse's in thematic aspiration, is geared in a different direction. It does not condense a contemporary simplified vision of form, light, and color, but rather, though in a modern idiom: it speaks of a nostalgia for the ancient cultures that once flourished around the Mediterranean. The *Peace* panel does not quite carry the intensity of the *War* panel, its counterpart, but both were quite impressive as they stood on opposite walls in Picasso's large studio at Vallauris, just when they were completed.*

If one tries to relate these major works of Matisse and Picasso in 1952, one finds that they coincide superficially but could not be further apart spiritually. Matisse reached a sublime simplification of his major themes and style, which revolved around the truth of what was for him "the way." Picasso, in contrast, dug deep down in the abyss of the archaic, chaotic part of the human psyche, attempting to exorcise its aggressive impulses by using the archetypal images of past Mediterranean civilizations and thus to achieve his goal through the simultaneous use of his protean abilities, which he liked to call "the ways."

The Pool and *Peace* reflect hope, the feminine side of human character, the life instinct. *The Sadness of the King* and *War* both deal with death, one in melancholic meditation on the twilight of a heroic individual existence, the other in the throes of terror over the possible annihilation of mankind through apocalyptic warfare. All four works were characteristic of their respective artists: Matisse the Apollonian, the poet of clarity, and Picasso the Plutonian, the apocalyptic prophet of doom. One had traveled to ethereal regions and the other to the realm of Hades. And yet their endeavors were symmetrical; they mirrored each other. As Hermes Trismegistus said, "All that is above is reflected below."

The two painters were not conscious of this incredible symmetry, but it was astonishing to become fully aware of it in 1952, the year that could be entitled "The Sadness of the Kings." This year was the apex of Matisse and Picasso's artistic dialogue, in the same way that 1910 had been the apex of Picasso and Braque's dialogue. Matisse's unity of

---

*Both paintings traveled and were successfully exhibited in Milan and Rome before they were placed in the chapel. Because of the curvature of the walls, they were never seen to full effect there.

spirit was matched by Picasso's existential anxiety, and the modernity of the former was matched by the allegorical electism of the latter, but above all hope counterbalanced despair, and there was hope and despair in both men.

Animus and Anima

IN ORDER to become universal, artists should be able to perceive, feel, and express both the masculine and feminine polarities; artists need to be androgynous beings, regardless of their own male or female gender. Although easy to conceive, this state, where intuition is tempered by discursive intelligence and reason enhanced by emotion and sensitivity, is not easy to achieve. To reach androgynous equilibrium one needs the early assimilation of characteristics of both genders; unconscious and subconscious impulses must not be repressed. Androgynous equilibrium often depends on the ready acceptance or rejection of the parent of the other sex during infancy and childhood.

The bonding between Henri Matisse and his mother must have been strong from the start. She was caring, especially attentive to him because his health was fragile. The child identified with his mother and idealized her on account of her own artistic aspirations. Later still she symbolically played the part of benevolent fairy when she gave him his first paintbox, a spontaneous and loving gesture, a blessing that unleashed his heretofore unconscious desire to become an artist. She was the guardian figure pointing the way toward the future.

A perhaps excessive idealization of his mother caused a timidity of expression in his early work; his relationship with Amélie, his wife, brought him to a crucial realization. She was very much her own person, not just an object of contemplation. Characteristically the Fauvist explosion opened with the famous portrait of Madame Matisse, *The Woman in the Hat*, shown at the Salon d'Automne of 1905. The hat was Madame Matisse's own creation; it was an exultation of felt, frills, feathers, flowers, and fruits, revealing a bold and sensuous temperament, a lushness of taste certainly unknown at Bohain in Picardy. In subsequent works of the period, other hats of her making crown their daughter Marguerite, who also seems to possess poise at an early age as she carries in one painting a flying-saucer-like edifice on her head.

Thus the authoritative but not authoritarian figures next to Matisse were probably the amicable "wild beasts" whom Matisse did not need to tame, but with whom he learned to live in harmony because he liberated these forces within himself. These first privileged relationships were followed by other positive and reinforcing relationships with his models, muses, and female friends. No wonder that Matisse felt he could give free rein to the feminine polarity through color, and through the arabesque. From then on his work was always suffused with the joyous acceptance of the feminine aspect of his psyche.

All the same, women like Gertrude Stein and Claribel and Etta Cone always insisted that in their eyes Henri Matisse was the very image of virility, and given their avowed or cryptic taste for the fair sex, their testimony, unbiased by passion, was quite reliable. It seems that far from being an arena for inner conflict, Matisse's psyche hosted the masculine and the feminine poliarities with ease and had achieved balance probably during the summer of 1905 along with the explosion of Fauvism, as is visible in his work.

Matisse's mastery grew out of positive identification with both his parents in their archetypal roles. With such a solid foundation his career was one of a dynamic progression. Even when he encountered hardship in his life or when during world wars I and II he became anxious for his loved ones, his heroic determination and singlemindedness were only strengthened.

In comparison, Picasso's own birth and early years were full of traumatic events. On October 25, 1881, the midwife who delivered him thought him to be stillborn, so she just laid him on a table and went back to take care of his mother. He uttered his first shout only because an uncle who was an M.D. grabbed him, shook him, and blew the smoke of his cigar into his mouth and lungs. Three years later while his mother was heavily pregnant, there was a severe earthquake in Málaga. The first shock was felt around 9 P.M. on December 25, 1884. Wrapping Pablo in his cape, Don José led his young wife and child across town toward the more secure shelter of a friend's house on the western slope of the rocky hill of Gibralfaro. While they were fleeing along the Calle de la Victoria, the young child must have heard shouts of pain and been terror-stricken by the destruction and chaos he witnessed while being carried in his father's arms. There were six seismic shocks that night, followed by other shocks and aftershocks during the next two days. Still, this was not the end of the ordeal for young Pablo, since as soon as the family returned home his mother entered labor and he most probably overheard her cries and moans before he was presented on December 28 with his newborn sister Dolores (Lola).

Panic-stricken as he already was, he must have felt dethroned by the arrival of a baby with whom he had no hope of competing since she belonged to the female sex. Three years later the birth of another sister, Conception, again threatened his dearly acquired central position; he had become a child prodigy in painting. Moreover his second sister had the advantage of being fair and resembling Don José, the beloved father. The event, coinciding with his having to go to school for the first time, triggered the irrational fear of being abandoned in an "alien" house, as he imagined might have happened earlier during the earthquake. He was frozen with fright, unable to learn anything, and each day he brought with him to school either his father's cane, his paintbrush, or one of his pigeons to insure that they would not forget to come to take him home after class.

The idealized image, the parent he could identify with and emulate, was his father, an artist of note but a man subject to withdrawal, melancholy, and depression. In the household there were five domineering women—four spinster aunts and his mother—who treasured him but stifled him and preyed on him. His mother was a small, compact woman; he said that when she was sitting her feet did not touch the floor. Though much younger than her husband, she was willful and stubborn, the more so because her horizons were more limited intellectually. She insisted on a ritualistic discipline based on a code of behavior that was altogether conventional; she was constricted and constricting, fearful of poverty, of change, of social intercourse. Pablo was her firstborn; she had high ambitions for him and soon proclaimed him to be a future genius, but behind the lofty words there was no understanding of what that entailed. She could have tried to understand the reason for his intellectual paralysis at school, for example. When her son went through puberty she pitted him against his father and the father against the son to chastise his precocious sexual awakening. She loved him, of course, and he loved her, but their love was accompanied by hatred and suppressed violence.

Early on Picasso began to use her family name in addition to his father's name when signing his pictures, but finally he dropped "Ruiz" altogether and began using only "Picasso."* But when he did so he had already firmly established residence in Paris, well out of reach of his mother's influence.

The father's image, though idealized, remained veiled by anxiety and fear, since his father had to abandon painting because he was becoming blind. He was a role model, but one with which it seemed dangerous to identify; and thus Picasso's animus remained fragile.

The mother-image and the proliferation of women in his home— aunts, sisters, mother, all needing attention or even salvation—was an unbearable burden. In addition to the almost cannibalistic affection of his female relatives, he was tormented with unwarranted guilt feelings after the early death of his sister Conception. Thus, his anima became divided against itself, establishing a pattern of retrogression.

Progression and retrogression should not be understood as judgmental terms, but simply as patterns that once established early on tend

---

*Adding the mother's family name to the father's family name is a frequent custom in Spain. So he started by signing Pablo Ruiz-Picasso until he reached his majority.

to determine different paths. For Matisse it was an arrow aiming toward modernity. For Picasso, elements of terror, like the earthquake at the time of his first sister's birth, the fear that he would be abandoned or forgotten at school, or the threat of his father losing his eyesight, compounded with his mother's domineering personality and limited outlook, all contributed to a desire to return to earlier phases of his own development, as well as a growing interest in primeval cultures. The early experience of mayhem and tragedy also enabled Picasso to imagine (remember) convincing images of destruction and death—as in *Guernica*, a remarkable composition assembling in a coherent whole many of the symbols of his inner drama. The pathetic mother holding her dead child in her arms wails her loss in the shadow of a protective totemic bull. From above, a woman is shedding light on a fallen warrior, a fatally wounded horse, a scene of desolation, while another woman is running aimlessly and a man is falling from a building on fire: all are the recurring images of an initial catastrophe, a night of chaos—not a new experience, since Picasso did not witness the bombing of the small Basque city which *Guernica* represents.

Life being an interweaving of many threads, there are certainly other patterns to examine, other events to analyze.

For Matisse, his illnesses at critical moments in his life were of crucial importance to his developing animus-anima. During such periods, the temporary weakening of his rational mind allowed him to become attentive to his own creative urges rather than remaining within the bounds of his father's admonitions, his taste for established order and decorum, and his bourgeois values.

Sometimes a forced period of inactivity results in a complete *retour sur soi*, a time of introspection, a reflection on one's attitudes and motivations. If not for the long period of forced inactivity during a period of chronic appendicitis when he was twenty, Matisse might not have left his job as a clerk to consecrate himself fully to painting.

A well-known epiphany similar to Matisse's own comes to mind.

It happened four centuries before and it was the conversion of Ignatius of Loyola. Born in 1491, he was sent as a page to the court of Ferdinand and Isabella, then he took service in the army with the Duke of Najera until his twenty-sixth year. The turning point occurred in 1521 when he was wounded during the French attack on Pampeluna, then the capital of Navarre. On account of his accident, Ignatius, who until then had been a man of action, was forced to meditate, to speculate, to undergo a kind of self-analysis, for at that time the process of recovery from a broken leg was a lengthy one. In his despondency, he had leisure to reexamine the principles that heretofore had guided his life. Moreover, he allowed the feminine aspect of his psyche to surface symbolically under the guise of two different images. When his daydreams went in the direction of a worldly conquest he conjured ways to win the love and subjugate the lady of his thoughts. When keen on metaphysical pursuit he devised spritual exercises that led him to experience the presence of the Virgin Mary and her Divine Child. In more contemporary terms, both the desire for courtly love and the vision of the Madonna might be interpreted as the two sides of the same coin, announcing the release of the profane and sacred aspect of his anima, his feminine self that until then had remained dormant, eclipsed by the efficacy of the animus or masculine part of his being.

Similarly, during Matisse's first long period of inactivity, thanks to his mother's paintbox, he indulged in an avocation that might not have surfaced otherwise because it would have been successfully repressed by the value system of his rational personality. The illness, accompanied by a temporary weakening of conscious control, allowed the explosion of vital forces never to be thwarted again, since they brought along such an enhanced sense of self, such fulfillment of his human potential. In time, this first surge of a victorious anima led to a sensuous celebration of womanhood that equaled Ignatius's courtly love of an aristocratic beauty. When Matisse went through his second ordeal in 1941, he almost experienced death and resurrection. Again the inner locks sprung open and the divine aspect of his psyche emerged. He opened himself even more than before to the feminine side of his nature, whether in an idealized sense as in the effigy he made of the Madonna and Child in the Chapel of the Rosary, perhaps as a tribute to his mother, or in a spiritual sense as when designing the immortal beings that swam or dived in *The Pool*.

Even though these major events occurred over a longer period of time for Matisse than for Ignatius of Loyola, the parallelism in their symbolic vision of anima as the profane and sacred aspects of the psyche is striking. From the time of his first inner realization, Matisse made a sacrament of his dedication to art and did so with as much zeal, passion, and perseverance as a man entering the priesthood.

Picasso's experiences and feelings regarding his own anima, far from achieving clarity, were quite ambivalent. The feminine for him was either wounded, and therefore had to be salvaged, or danger-laden, and thus to be avoided or better still destroyed, at least metaphorically. His major epiphanies were connected to death. When his younger sister Conception became ill with diphtheria, the young Pablo vowed to sacrifice painting if she recovered. His sacrifice somehow was not accepted (in the bargain that children strike on such occasions with supernatural forces) and she died. Later, his friend Casagemas committed suicide on account of Germaine Pichot, someone Picasso called "a dangerous woman" perhaps on account of guilt feelings since he himself had had sexual relations with her and therefore he thought he was partly responsible for the tragedy. Later still these patterns were reiterated symbolically and existentially. While his anima remained negatively afflicted, his animus, though fragile to start with, grew stronger with time through the positive reinforcement of friendly figures. Max Jacob, Guillaume Apollinaire, and later Paul Éluard gave him idealized images of himself in their writings. Picasso often quoted full sentences that one of them had written about him. Even his left-wing political allegiances could be traced back to his father's very liberal political opinions. Don José Ruiz Blasco was a friend of someone who had been president of a very short-lived first Spanish Republic. This acted as a very strong positive identification and it was always a dynamic force in Picasso's life and work. So Picasso's lucid consciousness prompted him forward while early psychological traumas made him look in the other direction, toward the original terror of his beginnings. Thus, he became interested in the archaic ways and means used by primeval sorcerers to thwart or placate these hostile forces.

Pablo's magical incantations in art resembled Gertrude Stein's prose in the field of writing—like this sentence in her portrait of the Cone sisters, "Two Women":

"They were large women, both of them, anybody could see them. They were large women either of them. Very many saw them. Very many saw each one of them. Some saw them. Really not very many saw them, saw both of them." Gertrude Stein was spinning a vortex, a silk cocoon of words to ensnare reality. In Picasso's later "stream of consciousness" texts, a whirling dance of chaotic images allowed automatic associations of verbal patterns to surge in the mind, helping him to reach a state of auto-hypnosis conducive to the creative act.

In contrast to Picasso's torrential outpour of obsessive images, "with their wings open to madness," Matisse's writings were Apollonian and logical. Often very formal, they remained under the control of the "animus." Yet this Apollonian clarity helped him to describe the ecstatic state he attained while at work:

> In art, truth and reality begin when you no longer understand anything you do or know and there remains in you an energy, that much stronger for being balanced by opposition, compressed, condensed. Then you must present it with the greatest humility, completely white, pure, candid, your brain seeming empty in the spiritual state of a communicant approaching the Lord's table. You clearly must leave all your accomplishments behind you and know how to keep your instinct fresh.
>
> Love . . . sustains the artist. Love is an important thing, the greatest good which alone lightens that which weighs heavy and enables to bear with an equal spirit that which is unequal. For it carries weights which without it would be a burden, and makes sweet and pleasant all that is bitter.

Matisse's writings about his art are lucid, concise, and essential to the full understanding of his quest. When thinking about Matisse, the French writer Colette also comes to mind, in the same way as Gertrude Stein does in Picasso's case, not simply because they belonged to the same generation but because there were so many similarities between them as artists. The cause of this association of ideas in me may go way back to a memory of my own childhood. While traveling with my parents in the South of France we stopped in St.-Tropez. My father, who was a great admirer of Colette's novels, took my mother and me to a small café nestled in the harbor in the crook of the jetty* where local people, artists, sailors, and foreigners danced to the shrill sounds of a mechanical piano. Indeed, Colette was there; my father pointed her out to me. Her short mane of curly hair, her big beautiful bare arms frightened me; she looked like a "wild beast." She wore a sleeveless striped cotton jersey befitting the great feline image she conveyed. Sturdy, compact yet supple, she could have pounced at anyone that she did not like; yet she was relaxed and carefree. I already knew about her because I had been given *Dialogues of Beasts* to read. She looked larger than life in that tiny, crowded cafe. My thoughts, my perceptions, were confused. I tugged at my father's sleeve and we left. I never forgot that vision of a "sacred monster" at play. Later I read all her writings and she became one of my role models as an artist.

Strangely enough, though aware of each other, Matisse and Colette didn't become close friends. There were sporadic attempts, however. Once it was agreed that she would write a text on some of his drawings, but she found that she was unable to do so and the project was abandoned. Much later toward the end of both their lives, Matisse finally managed to illustrate one of her texts with a masklike Eskimo kind of face. They shared mutual friends such as the painter Camoin and some others among the lesser Fauvists. It was as if the lion and the tigress each had to pace on its own territory, allowing only lesser "wild beasts" in their retinue.

Yet in their driving force they mirrored each other almost exactly. Brought up in the provinces, they loved their mothers with passion and took interest in the rhythmical pattern of everyday life, in nature, in the teachings they received at grammar school at a time when children were encouraged to enrich their minds through the activation of all sensory perceptions.

The sensory richness of their early observations and their slow rhythm of development as artists made them intelligent but not overly intellectual. The sensuousness that permeated their work was an apt

---

*The café and the jetty were destroyed with explosives during World War II. Later the jetty was rebuilt, but not the café.

Henri Matisse. *The Hair* (*La Chevelure*), 1952.

expression of their love of life and not a form of hedonism. Both were skillful in the presentation and interweaving of sensory images, in the evocation of the physical world and its effect on the nonphysical, the feelings, the emotions, the understanding. It was through this external world about which their curiosity was relentless that they reached the intangible.

For them both, the doors of the senses were gates through which passed seemingly inconsequential pieces of information. Fragmented like the tiny pieces of an intricate puzzle, they appeared meaningless at first but they acquired significance in time by being assembled and concentrated in a coherent vision. Then, as if effortlessly, came the perfect sentence, the perfect painting.

A perfect sentence by Colette, "A feeling of an indescribable blue, a mental blue," could be the perfect legend for Matisse's cutout *La Chevelure.*

And, it is difficult to resist quoting Colette once more:

"A little wing of sunshine is beating between two shutters touching with irregular pulsations the wall or the long heavy table . . . sometimes the wing of sunshine is pink on the pink-washed wall and sometimes blue on the blue cotton Moroccan rug." It echoes so well what we feel in front of one of Matisse's *Windows.*

This game of parallelism could go on and on and I could throw into the jumble the love of animals, especially cats, the taste for untidy gardens, cozy armchairs, well-corseted teapots, even the love of Algeria and Morocco.

The parallel lines and the arabesques they drew in words and pictures met in an endless dream where Matisse could aptly answer Colette:

"The effort needed to see things without distortion takes something very like courage and this courage is essential to the artist, who has to look at everything as though he saw it for the first time: he has to look at life as he did when he was a child. If he loses that faculty, he cannot express himself in an original, that is, a personal way."

The Quest for the Ultimate

THE ULTIMATE represents a limit beyond which further progress or investigation is impossible. It also represents an achievement in its highest form. For both Matisse and Picasso, the quest was to reach out, to stretch the limits assigned to that highest potential accomplishment far ahead into the future.

In 1941, after his almost fatal brush with illness, Matisse had a miraculous reprieve; he felt as if he had been reborn. He thought, "In this respite, oh life! let me resume the quest for the ultimate." Because he had been physically crushed, he reacted, characteristically, by intensifying his thought processes. In relation to this work, he might have been inspired by a Chinese aphorism: "The less matter there is, the more substance there will be." Since he could no longer spend long hours painting at his easel, he remembered experiments he had done in the early 1930s, at the time of his decoration *The Dance*, undertaken for the Barnes Foundation in Merion, Pennsylvania. He had used pieces of paper to test the effect of some blacks and other tones he intended to use in the mural without spoiling the work in progress.

So in 1941 he asked Lydia or Monique (the future Soeur Jacques-Marie) to paint sheets of paper of different sizes with bright colors. Under his direction, the women became his hands. Then he took his large scissors and started to cut into pure color. He thus unified researches heretofore undertaken separately in sculpture and in painting. Out of his meditations came the decision to take another drastic step —to simplify his style even further. Color created a third dimension all its own; it existed directly on top of another, equally strong color, and their mutual interaction was defined by the outline made by the scissors. Colors fought for supremacy; they could still try to eat each other up like wild beasts, but the contours and edges glowed in closer encounters than ever before. Once carved, the colors defined form and in addition gave form to the negative space around them.

Not allowing any afterthought, the process was entirely sincere, in the same way that a marble statue was sincere ("sine cera") when no unfortunate action of the chisel had to be hidden by inserting some wax into the place that had been inadvertently chipped away. When Matisse the magician was at work, his creative thrust originated in his emotion. He always went boldly forward, yet he also tried to see the *reason* underlying his thunderbolts of intuition.

Between 1949 and 1951 he realized one of his most memorable cutouts, *Mimosa*, intended as a model for a carpet. It measures 148 by 96.5 centimeters and is one of the most complex compositions he ever undertook in that medium. The intricate vegetable and floral color-forms intersect, penetrate, and eventually supersede one another in shades of black on royal blue, royal blue on black, and gray interlocking with black and yellow. These are placed on a background made of square or rectangular pieces of vivid red paper of different sizes, from very small to large, in closely related hues. In that way the background, while keeping its unity, appears modulated, as in a painting. The scale of each positive or negative cutout is attuned to the whole and adds dimensionality to the parts. Now in a museum in Japan, the original model for the *Mimosa* composition evokes the exquisite fragrance of this most fragile of flowers.

In 1952 Matisse's creative powers again reached an apex of lyricism, summarized in two major works: *The Pool*, a pure expression of bliss, symmetrically matched by *The Sadness of the King*, with its meditative melancholy. What more could there be after such a culmination? In 1953 came a stunning explosion of flower-shaped fireworks. (Matisse once said: "Find joy in the sky, in the trees, in the flowers. There are flowers everywhere for those who want to see them.") These were the ultimate masterpieces, creations that were beyond joy and sorrow, not surreal but rather suprahuman. In 1953 color dispelled darkness once and for all; the alchemical wild beasts were exalted, they were transformed into the glorious mysteries of their gemlike contours.

These were mural works. Embedded in the blinding effervescence of white chalk walls, many carved and colored enameled tiles (reproducing original cutouts) were placed at some distance from each other to allow each color-form the maximum power of expansion. Some elements of linear drawings were often introduced to stabilize the composition, as in *Large Decoration with Masks*, where the columns at both ends and the two graphic, masklike faces give order to what might otherwise have been only regularity. In *Apollo*, the rectangular shapes, the face, and the fanlike shell above it steady the whimsical qualities of overflowing spring vegetation that seems to ascend with the blue curvilinear rhythms of almost symmetrical branches. *Apollo* was a particularly successful composition.

Flowers, fruits, vegetation—all were ethereal, they floated in whiteness. They were a meditation on the pure essence of things. The artist was there to make that offering and to open the viewer's eyes to a realm where flowers never wither, where balance is achieved without sacrificing vitality. Once more Matisse was throwing flowers at the world, a thing he had seen done in Nice so many times during the carnival season. He was tirelessly giving, giving, giving his therapeutic vision of youthful beauty to a very aged and sick world full of dissension, hatred, fear, envy, and egotism.

At the same time, as if to show that he could outdistance all the nonfigurative painters if he wanted to, he produced *The Snail* and *Memory of Oceania*. These two very large, bold cutouts reveal the radicalism of his insight and demonstrate it in an exemplary way, as if he were saying, with or without flowers, "It is not this, it is not that. My way is not beholden to any specific action. Give me a few simple pieces of colored

The ceramic pieces for *Apollo* laid out
on a chalk background, 1952.

paper; I'll consider them, and by the way in which I distribute them, I'll give sight. You will no longer be blind."

After Matisse, Nicolas de Staël was the only artist who ventured in the same direction and who dared to take the same risks using the wild path of pure color, the language of instinct. Though Picasso handled color very well, it was for him a secondary preoccupation. His primary concern was form, and he was constantly breaking new ground in that direction. While ascribing an individual shape to each part of a given figure, he wanted at the same time to assemble the parts and unite them into a compact whole. When depicting the human body, he insisted on the dissymmetry of the limbs, which are almost never seen in parallel postures, and on the asymmetry of the face (when separated vertically, the halves are distinctly different in size and expression). In order to maintain the unity of the whole, he had to make sure that each identifiable shape interlocked exactly with others and became a fitting subunit of the final synthesis. This necessity led him to further and further modifications of the initial shapes. As he worked, forms interacted with each other and changed to match each other more closely. Toward the end, the fitting together was impeccable—that is, as well ordained as a compact car on the assembly line. Picasso liked to say that his paintings were so well ordained that he could cable their formulas to New York and have them reproduced exactly. This was only a witty remark, but it was consistent with Picasso's frame of mind.

In the same way that Matisse played freely with color interaction, Picasso gained complete freedom of the proportions of the parts to one another and of any part to the whole. For instance, in one canvas the head was huge in relation to the body, while in another the head was no larger than a pin. With such changes of scale he obtained dramatic effects.

While Picasso was breaking through the boundaries of Western tradition, he was also preoccupied with the masters of the past. He reinterpreted works by Lucas Cranach and others in several lithographies or etchings, not to learn from them—that was not necessary—but rather to check whether they had been somewhat wrong in their conceptions or their formulations. Perhaps he was wondering whether abandoning Western tradition did not at times work to his detriment. Picasso would then draw with a purity equal to that of Ingres or Raphael and promptly reassure himself. At other times (and these were the most fascinating), he analyzed a specific masterpiece of the past, brush in hand, as if to ascertain that his predecessor had reached the ultimate conclusions possible; that he, Picasso, had fully understood the intentions and actual achievements of his predecessor; and above all, if he, Picasso, could not improve on the result.

In February of 1950 Picasso decided to study the famous piece by Gustave Courbet entitled *Les Demoiselles des Bords de la Seine*, not by looking at the painting itself, which he knew well, but by working from a reproduction in a book about the nineteenth-century realistic master. It was awesome to see how fast and with what ease he was able to recapture the sensibility of the original artist. Once he was satisfied with the outcome, it was even more fascinating to follow the evolution of his thinking as he began to systematize *Les Demoiselles des Bords de la Seine*, using the method of linear patterns initiated first for the illustrations of *Le Temps des Morts* and then in November 1948 with the two abstract compositions entitled *Kitchen I* and *Kitchen II* and the series of portraits of me that followed. It resulted in an intricacy of interlocked designs that opened brand-new possibilities.

Picasso always emerged rejuvenated and enriched from his forays into the past. They were an important aspect of his work, as it was incumbent on him to scrutinize famous masterpieces and translate them into his own idiom. But above all Picasso challenged his predecessors' intentions and the intended effect and meaning of their work.

During these years Picasso's output was of an incredible variety. Apart from painting, sculpture, etchings, and lithographs, he managed to break ground in ceramics. Not only did he decorate plates, but he created three-dimensional pieces, either by assembling several "thrown" pieces together or by actually folding and bending pots just as they emerged from the potter's wheel. His imagination seemed inexhaustible and his skill uncanny. The grace of these figurines is unique. Some can still be seen at the Picasso Museum in the Grimaldi Castle at Antibes.

As the Lines
Converge . . .

THE DISSENSION between Picasso and me had never degenerated into quarrels, and most of our close friends did not understand why I wanted to leave him. I admired and understood his work, but the burden of his often cruel behavior had become unbearable. I also wanted to educate my children in Paris and would have preferred an amiable separation, but given Picasso's overbearing attitude, a break was unavoidable, so at the end of September 1953 my children and I left for Paris.

During the last months of 1953 and in 1954 I spent most of my time there, painting and drawing. Claude and Paloma, respectively six and four years old, went to L'École-Alsacienne, a coeducational school well known for its use of modern methods derived from the Montessori system. During the Easter holidays and again in July 1954, I accompanied them to Vallauris to spend time with their father. Since Picasso and I were no longer partners in art or in life, it would have been awkward to visit Matisse, a friend who had liked us as a couple and who might have tried to reunite us. Even though his own health was declining rapidly, Pablo proposed that we go together, but I was adamant about not going, since the great magician in Cimiez might have found a way to bring me back into the fold, or attempted to, with only the result of increased sadness on all sides.

The Vallauris fiesta took place in July. A wooden arena was erected for the occasion on the mall, as in a Spanish village. There was a lot of excitement, with music in the streets. When the *corrida* was about to start, I (rather than the traditional *alguacils*) rode ceremoniously into the arena on a horse that I had trained to do the Spanish step. Then Paul, Pablo's eldest son, made a few passes with a cape before the matador and his *quadrilla* took over.

Toward the end of July I went back to Paris. In late September I met Picasso and the children in Collioure; a few days later we all went to Perpignan, and after a disagreeable farewell scene, Claude, Paloma, and I took a night train to Paris. During the day the children went back to their school and I to my routine as a painter. Soon we moved into a new apartment that I acquired with the proceeds of the sale of my grandmother's home. There at last we settled down in a rather pleasant environment.

Even though I had never been particularly intimate with Alberto Giacometti during the "Picasso years," he behaved with integrity afterward. Far from giving me the cold shoulder when I came back to live in Paris with my children, he remained quite friendly, or rather became friendlier than before. I noticed it by the way in which he greeted me if we met casually at La Coupole or at the Brasserie Lipp for a late dinner. He often insisted that I join his group of friends. Also he sometimes came to dinner at my home with the poet Oliver Larronde, Diane Deriaz, and Jean-Pierre Lacloche, who were mutual friends.

During 1954 I had a great explosion of creativity. It was as if a window had burst open, liberating vivid color schemes from the strict rules of formal composition into more atmospheric, light-suffused, dynamic arabesques. I shed my ties to Neocubism that year, and rekindled my interest in creating "color-space" directly with different sets of complementary hues. More than ever Matisse's lessons remained present, advocating the alliance of unconscious and conscious forces to ignite and refine the creative fire. Little did I know that 1954 was to be the last year of Matisse's life.

Henri Matisse around 1952.

Whenever I met Giacometti, we eagerly discussed the Fauvist master. Of course our opinions diverged, but our interest was equal. In addition to being a sculptor, Giacometti, whose father was a well-known painter in Switzerland (and whose paintings can now be seen at the museum in Basel), devoted a lot of his time to painting, more and more as years went by. Perhaps because his father's work was color-oriented, Alberto devoted his undivided attention to the effect of light and distance on form. He was on very friendly terms with Pierre Matisse, who acted as his art dealer in New York and the rest of the United States.

It so happened that the Department of Medals at the Hôtel des Monnaies, in the impressive ancient Mint Building in the rue Guénégaud, wanted to coin a medal in honor of Matisse. In France, such publicly owned monopolies, which had been in existence for centuries, were usually headed by a very conservative director assisted by even more conservative curators and their sheepish assistants, who mostly had recourse to the conventional skills of ancient recipients of the Prix de Rome and other official academic artists. It came as a surprise when someone from this august institution, probably wanting to shed the dust accumulated through centuries of unimaginative workmanship, took a bold step forward and pursued Giacometti. He was commissioned to make a bas-relief portrait that could serve as a model for the future medal. The request rang pleasantly in Giacometti's ears, because he had always had a great regard for Matisse's art.

Though his father was unwell, Pierre Matisse interceded on his friend's behalf, asking his father to allow the sculptor to visit him in Nice and make a number of sketches, from which he would later extract the concept of the medal. Giacometti's method was to start with a number of studies from nature in similar postures and from different viewpoints, always seeing the model in both space and time and from a distance. His mind then would slowly integrate the notations that best corroborated his intuition of the being in front of him, and later the work in clay slowly emerged from these meditations. Giacometti's drawings resembled spider webs of observation and feeling, woven around the model to form a cocoon where shapes underwent a metamorphosis. A deep assessment of the give-and-take between the sitter and his environment emerged in due time, through a relentless quest for characteristic traits that conveyed more than the different planes of the face. Giacometti worked by retracing the causes and effects of the concave or convex planes in relation to the inner truth of a human being.

Giacometti was enthused. He looked forward to making studies of Matisse in Cimiez and then working on the project according to his own views at his studio in the rue Hippolyte Maindron in Paris.

Alberto was a man of strong convictions. First and foremost, he had to be true to himself and to his own conception of how any work coming out of his hands should look. What he did not know was that the head team at the medal department was not only conservative in its tastes but formalist to the extreme in terms of the technical rules to be followed in making a model for the intended medal. For instance, the team wanted the artist's model to be four or five times larger than the future medal so that their expert craftsmen could reduce it to the appropriate size for the mint. Another dogma concerned the consistency of the relief to the parts that were destined to be at a lower level. Then, even if the uniformity of the raised parts was achieved successfully, the relief itself had to be in a certain mathematical relation to the future size of the medal. In other words, the relief had to be extremely flat. No one, or at least no sensitive creative artist who had not been specially trained to achieve these effects, could produce a valid model to the satisfaction of such an antiquated assembly of perfectionists. Last but not least, the medal had two sides, so both sides had to be acceptable.

For Giacometti, it was essential to work in the exact scale of the future medal. The actual size of a sculpture determined a mental perspective. In other words, if the size was, say, one quarter life size, the model was, say, ten yards away from the artist (or the viewer, for that matter); therefore the portrait would be of the person seen from that distance. Consequently, each line or relief related to what was visible of the model as seen from a certain distance and was perfectly in proportion to the size of the sculpture. If the sculpture was made in a different size (larger), it became the portrait of someone seen at closer range and the indications, lines, or reliefs were those appropriate for a distance of, say, four yards. Furthermore, in a bas-relief, as far as Giacometti was concerned, the consistency of the ratio of raised surfaces to background intaglio had to be in terms of sensitivity and creativity and not a technical, mechanical, and purely mathematical flatness and regularity.

Giacometti pursued his project with all his energy according to his own lights, and when it was completed it was incompatible with the formal standards in use at the mint. He refused to redo the model in a larger scale just to see it reduced again, which would cause it to lose its most important qualities. So ultimately the project was abandoned.

Alberto Giacometti. Drawing III, Nice, June 6, 1954, from
Six Studies of Henri Matisse.

Alberto Giacometti. Drawing V, July 5, 1954, from
Six Studies of Henri Matisse.

Later, Matisse's portrait was cast in bronze as a bas-relief, but the other side of the medal, thoughtlessly discarded, was never cast, and therefore the medal as conceived by Giacometti never saw the light of day.

In pencil on paper, Alberto had familiarized himself with his subject; he had made in all about sixteen portraits of the Fauvist master during three trips to Nice. Knowing of my regard for Matisse, he telephoned me soon after returning from his third visit to Cimiez and told me to come to his studio if I wanted to see the series while he still had it in his possession and before the drawings were shown anywhere. So of course I responded positively to the invitation. The sketches were not very large, but what intensity!

I remember a profile drawn on May 20 in which Matisse appeared very introverted and thoughtful. Alberto had perceived the massive skull as if all its planes were defining radiuses going to the ear. The gaze was hidden by the spectacles, and the sinuous mouth appeared sad or in pain. The bulk of the torso was just indicated as diverging lines starting from the neck, and yet it filled the lower half of the sheet of paper.

In another sketch, dated June 5, only the head was present. Though bent forward by the weight of age, Matisse's eye, well framed between the brow ridge and the glasses, still emanated blue light. On June 6 Alberto had drawn a three-quarter view of the head, sleepy or self-absorbed, while the body was presented full face, hands resting on the thighs. The feeling was concentrated in the proportion of the domed cranium in relation to the sensibility of the mouth and the vastness of the abdomen.

On June 30 the pyramidal volume of the body seemed to ascend while the massive head, leaning forward, seemed to descend. The two contrasting forces were still in a precarious balance, as if the sketch were a depiction of Doctor Faustus before his rejuvenation by Mephistopheles. Behind the head, the back of a tall armchair gave an illusion of enthronement.

On July 5 the paper remained mostly untouched—there were no features; the face was reduced to a mask. Dome of the skull, eyebrow, eyes, nose, mouth . . . an enigma. One last time, Matisse the sphinx . . .

Looking at another sketch made the same day, I thought I could understand the reason for the concentration, the oneness of purpose in the first one: Matisse was still drawing, and seemed absorbed in his own dreamworld. The next day, however, fatigue and exhaustion had set in. The overall feeling was peaceful, because there was a total acceptance of the laws of nature, a silence that created its own music. Most of the vectors of the lines tended to rush diagonally downward. Still, there was presence in the oceanic bulk of the torso and abdomen, as if life flowing away from the higher regions was now engaged in finding the path of least resistance, like water rushing down mountain slopes.

Giacometti had been very moved by his encounters with Matisse, seeing a great artist still so absorbed in trying to create when death was at his doorstep, when his body had become a prey of gravity, when all the forces that had converged in him had begun to disengage and diverge, when there was no longer time. He told me that one day, coming out of a moment of prostration, Matisse had regained enough bite to tell him: "Artists nowadays no longer know how to draw." That would have been a bizarre statement if it was meant to disparage Giacometti. Since Matisse was never unkind, and since Giacometti was always deprecatory about himself and subject to self-doubt, I could not believe that Matisse meant anything of the kind. More probably, if he vented his spleen, he did not mean to include Alberto in this negative pronouncement.

Giacometti went back to Nice a third time, and then in September of 1954 drew the great man as he was approaching the end of his life's pilgrimage. Instead of concentration there was mostly exhaustion; instead of awareness there was abandonment; instead of clear-mindedness there was sleepiness; instead of strength there was weakness. Death had passed the threshold of the apartment and was now in the room, waiting for the moment to strike. Matisse's flesh had to go the way of all flesh. As in the past, all the lines converged . . . and became whole. Now everything was undone. Mind and matter had to go their own separate ways; as the lines had converged, in the same way they started to diverge. The end was near.

Thanks to Giacometti's thoughtfulness, I saw these drawings at his studio just a few days after Matisse's death on November 3, 1954. These images remained in my memory like a last adieu, a wave of the

313

hand to the next generations of artists. Shedding some tears, I thought, "Thank you, Matisse; thank you, Giacometti. Thanks to you, the dance will go on. The hands will almost meet, uniting a long chain of artists, but will not touch. Each painter, though related to all others, remains a loner and will have to define his own universe in his own unique way. In art there are as many truths as there are great dreamers to reveal such possibilities in ways as yet unseen."

Funeral Cortege

Ⓘ N ANCIENT tragedies a signifi-
cant death was always announced and followed by other deaths. A hero
did not leave this world without being heralded and accompanied to the
Elysian fields.

The first event was Colette's death. Since July 1954, Colette's life
had been ebbing softly away. She slept for long hours, then would say
a word or two, look at lithographic reproductions of some cherished
exotic butterflies, and sink back into daydreaming. Her literary genius
was akin to Matisse's artistic genius. She had given voice to the pulsing
of the senses, to the instinctual forces governing nature, beasts, and
humans, as he had redeemed condensed sensations in the visual arts.

At dusk on August 3, Colette regained consciousness for a moment.
Her hands uplifted, her lips silently moving, she was probably back in
the garden of her childhood, addressing Sido, her mother: "To attempt
achievement is to come back to one's starting point. . . . My natural
inclination tends toward the curve, the sphere, the circle."

The circle was complete; no more amorously selected words would
align themselves on the pale blue paper under the light of the blue lamp.

The eyes were closed; the hands fell back and were still. It was all over. Colette had expired, in her apartment overlooking the gardens of the Palais-Royal. The blue beacon that accompanied her laborious, sleepless vigils would no longer shine over Paris as a tutelary sign of life.

By order of Cardinal Feltin, the Catholic Church refused Colette a last benediction, because she had been married three times and also because she had been known for her lesbian affairs. Nonetheless, she was given the honor of a state funeral and was escorted to the place of her last rest at the cemetery of Père-Lachaise by everyone who counted in the intelligentsia and, more important, by all the simple people who loved her in the city where she had chosen to spend her adult life.

The second event, a month later, was the death of André Derain. Hit by a car not far from his home in Chambourcy, he did not recover, and died at the age of seventy-four on September 8, 1954. It is true that after 1910 he turned his back on the color revolution of Fauvism and felt safer with more traditional means of expression, yet his early London and Collioure landscapes forever stand as testimony to his first beliefs. Thus brutally ended the life of Matisse's good companion, an ally during the decisive years between 1900 and 1908.

Was Matisse told about that accident? Did the sad news accelerate his own demise? It is always hard to say goodbye to one's own youth.

Often Picasso had said, "There are a number of things I shall no longer be able to talk about with anyone after Matisse's death," and "All things considered, there is only Matisse." Matisse's death, though not unexpected, was quite a shock for his old friend and rival. Picasso had to attempt a last pictorial tribute before too much time elapsed and before the positive momentum he had acquired during the dialogues of the past ten years was lost. He undertook this tribute obliquely. He selected Delacroix as the most suitable reference point to his past impassioned arguments with Matisse. Delacroix's works had always been central to many of their conversations about art.

On December 13, 1954, Picasso started a series of paintings of all sizes on the theme of *The Women of Algiers*, by Delacroix, a masterpiece that had been a well-loved favorite of Matisse as well as himself. What had been a miracle of balance, serenity, and sensuousness under Delacroix's lyrical touch became under Picasso's brushes a rather syncopated exercise of style. The original composition was altered. The woman to the left became a nude on the right, with interlocked legs going upward. The black servant moved from the extreme right backward, toward the center. The woman in profile increased in stature and sat upright on the left, while the odalisque in the center, if present at all, figured as a nude in the background. The bodies looked like broken puppets. None of Delacroix's coordinated color scheme remained; neither did the nonchalant charm of an oriental scene. Strident lines and patches of yellow, red, and blue battled for dominance, accentuating the utter devastation of structures. In terms of linear virtuosity, Picasso displayed his mastery, but he also displayed his usual ferocity toward women as well as a nihilistic despair over his friend's demise. Between December 13, 1954, and February 14, 1955, Picasso finished fifteen oil paintings and two lithographs, all free interpretations of *The Women of Algiers*.

Such was Picasso's participation in Matisse's funeral cortege. Irrationally, he experienced his friend's death as a kind of betrayal. As he felt abandoned, he somehow had to exact a revenge for his own sadness, selecting Delacroix's masterpiece as scapegoat.

Matisse's passing was a loss deeply felt by the artistic community, but it may have struck one artist at a deeper level. Over the years, Nicolas de Staël had clarified his vision. Instead of using mostly earthy tones, he had made his palette more vibrant. He began to position each shape frontally, rather than having it participate in sweeping motions or meandering circuits, and he simplified. Geometric patterns emerged. Forms were still pure forms, but he started to relate them to strong sensations from the outside world. Slowly he resumed figurative work as an evocation of his passionate feelings, consonant with actions in the outside world, as in his series of canvases on the theme of football players, but of course he did not resume a link to descriptive reality. This evolution was surprising, since de Staël so adamantly believed that representation had to be left behind once and for all.

In 1954 this artist, who was born close to the shores of the Baltic Sea, went to reside and work close to the Mediterranean, within the walls of Antibes, a city founded by the ancient Greeks. There he surpassed himself, getting always closer to what had been Matisse's sun.

His paintings, extremely simplified, acquired even more power, clarity, and feeling. Fireworks of color were superseded by limpid tonal harmonies akin to the hues of his earlier achievements.

Perhaps when he was at the apex of his glory, having apparently conquered the darker forces of noise and fury, de Staël did not possess Matisse's ultimate power of *retour sur soi*, to hold in balance the opposite pulsations of explosive passion and lacerating anxiety. Unable to sleep, unable to exorcise the ancient, tragic memories of his youth and to solve deep inner contradictions, in March 1955 he threw himself from his home's upper terrace onto the rocks below. His flight was broken, like that of Icarus, but his trajectory was magnificently accomplished. Not only had he followed the chariot of the sun from its dawn in the east to its fall into a starless night, but he had dared to fix his gaze on the sun and to spread on his palette the colors of the spectrum.

Since de Staël and I had mutual friends in Antibes, I regretted not having made an effort to meet him again and to renew our discussions about art before his tragic end. Perhaps the memory of his bad temper kept me at bay; I had withstood all the storms one could crave for a lifetime. Now was the time to tackle my own difficulties in life and my own dilemmas in art. I no longer wanted any admonitions, good or bad; I had to find my own path toward artistic freedom. This did not mean having less regard for the gods and demigods atop Mount Olympus, but simply recognizing that, each human experience being unique, each artist has the burden and the privilege to bear witness, thus adding something to the wealth of human culture. Since for generations women have been notoriously silent, it was incumbent upon me and my female contemporaries to reveal an as-yet-unfathomed side of the planet—the emergence of a sunken continent of thoughts, emotions, and wisdom. In this I still trusted Matisse and Colette; their blue light was always a beacon during a lifelong quest for the green paradise of innocent love.

A last sign came in the form of a telephone call from Marguerite Duthuit. She and her mother wanted to donate a Matisse piece to an exhibition auction for children of deported parents. They thought Matisse would have liked to participate. They invited me to the apartment at 132, boulevard du Montparnasse to have tea and to collect the painting for the organization called Art and Solidarity, for which they knew I campaigned.

It was moving to find myself again within those walls so charged with history, and even more to meet Amélie Matisse for the first time. Right away I felt very much the same vital presence that had emanated from all the portraits her husband had made of her so many years earlier. Although her hair, combed into a chignon, was now gray, her figure was firm and well muscled, her movements supple and precise; there was a no-nonsense energy about her, and yet she was gentle and peaceful, like a great cat at rest.

I had brought some violets, which luckily matched the black-and-silver harmony of her dress. Both she and Marguerite were eager to know how I was progressing with my painting, about which Matisse must have spoken. I was struck by their insistence on encouraging me, almost as if I did not know enough about my own vocation or did not trust myself. Madame Matisse said that it was a sacred duty to develop my talent and that I should never allow anyone or anything to sidetrack me. The conversation went on amiably but forcefully, as if to temper my will of iron into a will of steel.

Mother and daughter spoke alternately, as in a piano and violin duet; the love and harmony between them was palpable. I stayed there transfixed, for a while looking at their intense features and seeing the two parallel columns at the entrance of Matisse's temple. I don't remember how long this went on, for it was an experience out of time.

I had seen the true inspirers, the caryatids who, by supporting the weight of the temple, enabled the artist to become fully himself and to create.

Henri Matisse reused objects and images in different paintings. He quotes visually from *The Dance* in this work entitled *Nasturtiums and The Dance* (1st Version) (*Les Capucines avec un Fragment de sa Peinture la Danse*), 1911.

Farewell

THE SUN set on Matisse's life, but not on his oeuvre; on the contrary. Since the paintings of the heroic period (originally collected by Shchukin and Morosov and augmented by more recent donations due in large part to Lydia Delectorskaya's generosity), now belonging to the Pushkin Museum in Moscow and to the Hermitage Museum in Leningrad, have been put on view and have been lent for comprehensive exhibitions in the West, the real impact of Matisse's work has begun to be felt by the public. Of course the artistic community has recognized it for a long time.

Shows have multiplied, and books exploring one aspect or another have accumulated, but Matisse's fame will endure beyond all the well-deserved homages and tributes. By refusing to imitate even light, by liberating color, Matisse unleashed the positive actions of the unconscious and brought them not under the control but under the scrutiny of his intelligence, to be selected, intensified, and harmonized. He set free the eye and the mind. This great ascent toward innocence, toward the rediscovery of childish wonder—undertaken first by Paul Gauguin, the savage, and by Vincent van Gogh, the mystic, then developed during the Fauvist movement in France and the Expressionist movement in Germany—was brought by him to its ultimate consequence. Matisse restored through his art the belief in the possibility of an earthly paradise.

The philosopher Emmanuel Berl once mischievously said that Picasso and I had joined our destinies because we were both in love with Matisse's art and that we separated as Matisse's death became imminent. Matisse's dream had become Picasso's hope, had become my own dream. To be with Matisse was to dance, to experience generosity of spirit and truth. All his life he pursued the evanescent vision of a golden age. Was it an intuition of a return to Edenic bliss, or an accession to unity within the diversity of a multifaceted world? Without him, it was just a farewell to paradise, and the lonely and painful undertaking of finding one's truth alone. Picasso went his way and I went mine, inventing my own dream as I went.

As he bade farewell to the world, Matisse left his oeuvre behind to enlighten "the way." Each man, each woman, can reinvent the golden age, can rediscover innocence. And remember what Matisse said to Dina Vierny in 1941: "*Et surtout, il ne faut jamais mourir*"—And above all, one must never die.

Appendix

When I started writing this book, in 1978, I obtained Lydia Delector-skaya's address and telephone number. In the belief that she still owned the portrait *Claude in Flight*, I asked her whether she could have it photographed for my project. She told me that *Claude in Flight* had indeed flown very far, since the gouache was now somewhere in the USSR and it would be next to impossible to receive a photograph in time. In fact there was plenty of time, since my own work as a painter kept me very busy and therefore unable to concentrate on my book project on a regular basis.

During my next stay in Paris, Lydia helped me select a number of photographs of Matisse made by Madame Adan, her cousin. So all seemed very straightforward, and I returned to California, where an author and editor of many books about art who always laid out his books himself proposed to make a model for mine. At that time, I envisioned my book as full of reproductions and photographs. My friend then flew to Paris, and along with business of his own, he went to see Lydia and Madame Adan. I had indicated to him that if it was not possible to get a photograph of *Claude in Flight*, given its location, I could replace that illustration with a reproduction of another piece from the same series. I intended to inform readers that the gouache reproduced was *not* the one selected by Lydia. I also intended to include a self-portrait, a profile that was *not* the one I had originally sent to Matisse, for the same reason and with the same acknowledgment.

To my amazement, this led to a misunderstanding. Lydia seemed to believe that I intended to release inaccurate information, a thing that would not have made sense. Nonetheless, she sent me a photograph of *Claude in Flight*—the original—and an interpretation of *Claude in Flight* by Matisse, dedicated to Lydia. Since I didn't know this existed, I was very pleased to add it to the other documents.

Notes

p. xii Introduction: Henri Matisse sent me a certain number of letters, eight
of which are reproduced here and accompanied with comments. All the letters
had been left in "La Galloise," a small home I shared with Pablo Picasso
until the end of 1953. Soon after my marriage to Luc Simon in 1955, the
house was emptied of its contents on Picasso's order and my belongings and
personal property remained confiscated until his death in 1973. Even after-
wards, all my books, collections and private papers that had been taken away
remained lost for me, and it is only much later through the efforts of my son,
Claude, and my daughter, Paloma, that two cut-outs and eight letters were
found and given back to me. Perhaps other letters will surface that may have
been destroyed or left in the archives, perhaps they were lost, the future will
tell. Fortunately, no one could reach what I kept intact inside my mind and
what makes me a unique witness.

p. 6 "After the student demonstrations": The Wehrmacht declared that each
time a German soldier was murdered in a given area, reprisals would involve
the execution of as many as fifty students whose names appeared on the lists
of hostages in that area.

p. 35 "Emmanuel Tériade": A Greek from the island of Lesbos, Tériade first assisted his countryman Zervos as editor of the avant-garde magazine *Cahiers d'Art*. Later, in the thirties, he was instrumental in the creation of another famous review, *Le Minotaure*, with the Surrealists. He was a great admirer of the French poet Pierre Reverdy (a contemporary of Georges Braque and Picasso). The empathy being mutual, it was a deep friendship. A mystic who had left Paris to reside near the Benedictine abbey of Solesmes in order to meditate on the human predicament, Reverdy also cultivated a good relationship with Coco Chanel, who liked to surround herself with intellectuals. Tériade's dream was to found his own art magazine and to be able to publish limited-edition illustrated books. By coincidence, an American financial group came to see Coco Chanel in Paris to ask her whom she would recommend for just that purpose. Pierre Reverdy became the eager go-between. The negotiations were positive; an agreement was reached, and the most luxurious art quarterly ever was successfully launched. Tériade was naturally thankful to the poet who had made his goal attainable. After the war, when he was able to resume publication, he became mostly interested in the illustrated limited editions.

p. 51 "After all, no one could understand": Important honors were bestowed on them. Matisse received the Carnegie Prize in 1927, and he sat on the jury that gave Picasso the Carnegie Prize in 1929. One can assume that, generous as always, he campaigned for his friend.

p. 52 "It could also be": Vlaminck wrote an infamous article about Picasso that could have cost the latter his life, only to be rebuked by André Lothe in a courageous article that could also have meant death for *him*. Out of weakness, other artists, including André Derain and the sculptor Charles Despiau, became traitors by accepting a trip to Germany in wartime. It is true that they were told that their acceptance would help liberate some French prisoners.

p. 52 "Perhaps they wrote": Paris was in the occupied zone, and the South of France was for a while in the nonoccupied zone. To begin with, correspondence was allowed only through special postcards on which most of the text was printed; one could only fill in *yes* or *no* in the blanks, write the address, and sign. Matisse's friends Camoin and Rouveyre then resided in the nonoccupied zone, as he did. Paradoxically, the situation improved after the complete occupation of France, as did telephone communications.

p. 57 "It was not by chance": It was as if special telluric forces were at play in that region. Many, many years later, in 1942 and 1943, I underwent a complete transformation in that part of France, both spiritually and artistically.

p. 73 "A fragile masterpiece": During the following summer, Gjon Mili, the distinguished American photographer originally from Albania, came to see us and used special devices to capture Picasso's movements while he drew with light in a dark room. Mili also photographed me using the same technique. Afterward he asked to make a portrait of me outdoors. It is remarkable to see how his intuition converged in color and composition with Matisse's definition, since he had not seen Matisse's cutout of me.

p. 89 "They were talking to me": Later, in 1965, what I found so appalling about Picasso's attacks on my book about him was that they contradicted his own wishes. Ever since he had met me, he had wanted me to read Gertrude Stein's and Fernande Olivier's memoirs, and he kept encouraging me to develop my writing talent and become his hagiographer, as Jean Racine had become the biographer of the Sun King, Louis XIV. Actually, he had been far from delighted when Gertrude Stein's book had come out, and he had done everything possible to prevent Fernande Olivier's very nice memoir, entitled *Picasso and His Friends*, from being published. Characteristically, he had conveniently forgotten his fury by the time he knew me, and he was eager for me to read these books.

In 1945 Pablo saw a series of my prose poems, a manuscript that impressed him. Afterward he asked me to compose a piece about his work. In 1951, Tériade asked me to write the text for a book about Picasso's paintings in the *Verve* collection. All this was very flattering, but I did not see how it could be possible to keep my freedom of expression in such a venture, and rather than becoming a sycophant, I preferred to decline the offer. Everybody was displeased with me. So it appears that I could never do anything according to other people's wishes. I did not write when asked to do so, and when I did it on my own terms later, Pablo filed a lawsuit against my French publisher. He lost, both at the magistrates' court and again at the court of appeals.

p. 96 "He started learning": Madame Matisse reported to Raymond Escholier that he started to study the violin very seriously in Nice in 1918. When asked the reason, he answered, "It is a fact that I am afraid to lose my eyesight and not be able to paint. When blind, one must renounce painting but not music." In an interview with Léon Degand, he said, "I love music. . . . I used to play the violin. . . . I had a certain amount of feeling, but as I strove to acquire too rich a technique, I killed my feeling. Now I prefer to listen to others."

p. 114 "My tendency": While very bright, my father was domineering, par-adoxical, and short-tempered. I resembled him and was never a weakling; that's why I was never afraid of Pablo. Yet my father's goals were altruistic, and it was at times possible to challenge him, to discuss things with him, and to come to an agreement that was mutually binding, whereas with Pablo no resolution could be reached; he thrived on conflict.

p. 116 "Most of the gouaches": In 1978, after Paloma returned to me some of Matisse's letters that had remained until then in her father's estate, I began to think about writing a book about the visits and the conversations that I treasured as an artistic legacy. Unfortunately, I had not kept a photograph of the original gouache of *Claude in Flight*, since I had had no interest in documenting all my work at the time, thinking that it would be pompous to be so earnest and that by keeping records of everything, I might impede my future evolution. So, in 1979, while wondering about the possibility of locating some remaining photographic documents that I could not find, I reviewed other gouaches of the same period that I still possessed. To my amazement, I saw that my flying figures were all drawn in 1948, three years before the series that Picasso did in 1951 of my face stylized as a dove. These were published with haiku-like poems by Paul Éluard entitled *The Face of Peace*.

p. 121 "From his first dwelling": According to the legend, Montmarte, the highest hill in Paris, got its name from the first Christian martyrs, among whom were Saint Denis, the patron saint of Paris, who was able to walk all the way to the plain *after* being beheaded—quite a feat indeed! Montmarte was well liked by the Romantics, the Impressionists, and the Cubists. Mont-parnasse, named after the home of Apollo and the muses, attracted radicals like Lenin and artists like Fernand Léger and became the preferred artistic quarter after World War I.

p. 139 "With his serious legal background": Vollard had well-known idio-syncrasies. He would offer a painting at a certain price; if the collector did not purchase it on the spot, he would raise the price the next time around, or, pretending that the painting had been misplaced, he would never show it again. At other times he conveniently fell asleep during a discussion, and when he woke up he would not remember a thing he had said or promised. All the conversation would thus come to naught and the visitor would have to start from zero during the next visit to the gallery.

With the help of his gourmet chef, Vollard held famous dinners in his vaulted basement, inviting his buddies Pierre Bonnard and Alfred Jarry, the pataphysician, along with various well-to-do members of the upper classes whom he knew to hate each other. (Alfred Jarry, the author of *Ubu Roi, Ubu Cocu, Le Surmale*, and so on, had coined the concept and the word *pataphysics*. When asked what it was about, he answered superbly: "Pataphysics is science; it is the science of imaginary solutions." He was the first pataphysician. After World War II, a College of Pataphysics was formed, of which I happen to be a member.) Vollard sat them together, his buddies and himself leading the conversation toward controversial subjects until even the best-behaved guests could bear it no longer and vented their spleen in bitter arguments. Jarry then produced his pistol to end the din, and everyone rushed outside, sometimes coming to blows or even challenging one another to a duel. Vollard considered such an evening highly successful.

Jarry had given his pistol to Picasso, who had used it in 1908 to chase the German art critic Wilhelm Uhde around Montmarte and for other pranks; of course, he shot in the air. The serious Matisse had no patience for that side of Picasso's character or for Vollard eccentricities, so the matter was dropped and we left.

p. 169 "He learned that in 1832": Because many philosophies originated there and also because the sun rises in the east, it is a cliché to say that "all light comes from the Orient." From before the Crusades, the French always had an interest in Eastern cultures, be they Arabic, Indian, or Chinese. Precious objects were traded, and later several books were translated, including *The Thousand and One Nights* by Galland, which increased everyone's curiosity and triggered a romantic passion for customs and mores that were different from the generally accepted Christian values. Of course the Magreb was geographically to the south of France, but because of its Muslim culture it was considered part of the Orient.

p. 182 "Without doubt, his haptic sense": "When the artist is using the heptic sense, the painting or drawing is not based on any visual perception of the object. It is the representation of tactile and other nonvisual images derived from internal physical sensation" (*Education Through Art* by Herbert Read, 1956; *The Nature of Creative Activity* by Lowenfeld, 1939).

p. 184 "In the photographs": Marcello and Hortensia de Anchorena did not collect paintings, they collected only doors for their apartment in the avenue Foch. They sent a door to each artist of their choice and placed the completed doors in their apartment. Matisse did the door to Hortensia's bathroom. It was superb. The bronze doorknobs were from Diego Giacometti; the piano was decorated by Jean Cocteau. Picasso designed an abstract silhouette of my figure, but never sent it back. It is now used as a door to the library in my son Claude's Parisian apartment.

p. 195 "Then Father Couturier": I had been educated in a Dominican school where he preached retreats, and I had had interviews with him on theological matters when the nuns no longer knew how to discipline my rebellious spirit. We had marvelous discussions. I studied there for eight years, until graduating from high school.

p. 197 "The size of the chapel": One wonders what solution Le Corbusier would have devised. It was strange that he was not consulted, given the fact that he worked with the Dominican order for the church at La Sainte Baume, close to Saint Maximin in Provence. Perhaps Matisse did not like him. If one visits the church that Le Corbusier designed on the hill at Ronchamp in the east of France, which is admirable both as an edifice and for the indefinable spiritual quality that suffuses it, one regrets that these two men did not have the opportunity to work together. Perhaps Matisse did not want to give pre-eminence to the architecture.

p. 210 "Without recording": Because Kahnweiler was German, his paintings were confiscated and sold in 1918 as the property of an enemy alien. The gallery was renamed Gallerie Simon after World War I. Then during World War II, because Jews were not legally allowed to own businesses in the occupied zone, it was purchased by Louise and Michel Leiris. Louise, Kahnweiler's sister-in-law, and her husband, a writer and anthropologist, were French and not Jewish, so Louise became the director and succeeded in saving the gallery. In 1945 Kahnweiler resumed his activities in association with her.

p. 215 "I found all the letters": The reader might think that I exaggerate this interpretation, but it is well known that Picasso enjoyed sending ciphered or cryptic messages to his secretary and friend Sabartés, who many times could not make head nor tail of them. Sometimes Picasso himself forgot the hidden meaning.

p. 231 "That did not mean": Still, even strictly disciplinarian parents became very solicitous when a child became ill. Dreading an early death in the absence of many remedies discovered since, they indulged a child's every whim as long as he showed an elevated temperature. Unconsciously the parents encouraged the child to remain ill as long as possible. Fever was a welcome ally, obviating the obligation to attend school and learn tedious lessons.

p. 251 "Artists who did well in both": During the nineteenth century's last decade, Thadée and Misia Nathanson, publishers of *The White Review*, and a group of young writers and painters around them promoted a new and more direct approach to graphic art. All believed in the power of simplified images, brought about through the originality of the artist's conceptions, not by an absence of skill or by naïveté. They advertised their publications with posters by Pierre Bonnard and Toulouse-Lautrec and pioneered editions of lithographs by all the painters of the Nabi group, drawing the attention of the public to their unexpected color schemes and intriguing layouts.

Some artists favored woodcuts or other types of etchings and engravings, but on the whole, most favored lithographs as a more spontaneous medium. As the technique was relatively less demanding and less time-consuming, they could concentrate on the vivacity of the image itself. The cost of printing was less prohibitive, and polychrome editions could be produced.

The artist worked on several stones or zinc plates that were etched and prepared; each was then inked in a different hue and printed in turn, with a good registration superimposing one tone on top of the other on the same paper to produce the final print. The quality of the result depended on the combined skill of the artist and the master printer. Much was contingent on their unity of purpose, on mutual understanding of the aesthetic drive and the requirements specific to the craft. If the master printers in a given workshop were willing to experiment, then a thorough renewal could occur. At the turn of the century in Paris, the two best workshops were Clot and Ancourt; the second one later became the Mourlot workshop on the rue de Chabrol.

p. 253 "Matisse encountered similar difficulties": Master printers rightfully proud of their skill could at times be single-minded and stubborn, but Matisse managed to seduce everybody at the workshop. For them all he became and remained "the great old man." At Mourlot there were some designers who could assist the artists, especially with color lithography. Charles Sorlier especially assisted Marc Chagall. They were not to be confused with the master printers; their mission was to help the artist in the analytical process of the number of stones and zinc plates necessary. They could also do by hand the colors that the painter did not want to figure out himself. Many years after he had worked there, Sorlier, one of the best designers then active at Mourlot, would show the artists in residence the contents of a box left there by the master, with exactly harmonized samples of colors as bright and vivid as birds' feathers. These samples from Matisse's own palette were so well selected that now and then one artist or another would come to Sorlier when they were about to indicate the exact blend they wanted the printer to mix when inking a stone. Looking at these small rectangles and lozenges acted as a tuning fork. Far from diminishing, this practice grew as the years went by. It had become an in joke that when a painter got exhausted from working on a difficult color lithograph, or when he felt out of sorts, he would go to see Charles Sorlier and ask for Matisse's box. Thoughtfully, he would finger the samples and soon enough start to feel better, able to go back to the stone or zinc plate and work with renewed impetus.

As in Pandora's box, what remained in Matisse's box of color samples was hope.

p. 294 "Thus, he became interested": Around 1909, at the time of his friendship with Henri Rousseau, Picasso reported that "Le Douanier" had told him: "What I do is modern, but you are working your magic in the ancient Egyptian style." He was referring to Cubism. Little did he know that Picasso, while breaking ground relentlessly, would also reincorporate and rehash the whole history of painting, in an effort to achieve temporal and spatial ubiquity as a means of beating death at her own game by negating the three dimensions of space and the three dimensions of time to reach iconic truth.

p. 295 "In contrast to Picasso's torrential outpour": The quotation is from Picasso's poem published in *Cahiers d'Art*.

p. 295 "Yet this Apollonian clarity": The quotation is from *Jazz* (1947), pages 112 and 113.

p. 316 "By order of Cardinal Feltin": Apropos of Colette's and Matisse's passing, Father Couturier said to Marie Cuttoli, "Beyond the shadow of a doubt both of them will go to heaven," thus showing himself to be more liberal than Cardinal Feltin, as could be expected.

Photo Credits

334

128: Courtesy of Ida Bourdet/© 1990 Succession H. Matisse-ARS N.Y. **131**: Courtesy of Françoise Gilot/© 1990 Succession H. Matisse-ARS N.Y. **133**: Courtesy of Françoise Gilot/© 1990 Succession H. Matisse-ARS N.Y. **135**: Photo Hélène Adant/Rapho **140**: Photo Hélène Adant/Rapho **154**: Private Collection/© 1990 Succession H. Matisse-ARS N.Y. **155**: Photo Marc Vaux/© 1990 ARS N.Y.-SPADEM **163**: © 1990 ARS N.Y.-SPADEM **166**: (top) The Baltimore Museum of Art: The Cone Collection, formed by Dr. Claribel Cone & Miss Etta Cone of Baltimore, Maryland. BMA 1956.253/© 1990 Succession H. Matisse-ARS N.Y., (bottom) Musée d'Art Moderne de la Ville de Paris/© 1990 Succession H. Matisse-ARS N.Y. **173**: The Hermitage, Leningrad, Courtesy of Scala/Art Resource/© 1990 Succession H. Matisse-ARS N.Y. **179**: The Baltimore Museum of Art: The Cone Collection, formed by Dr. Claribel Cone & Miss Etta Cone of Baltimore, Maryland/© 1990 Succession H. Matisse-ARS N.Y. **197**: Photo Hélène Adant/Rapho **198**: Courtesy of Françoise Gilot/© 1990 Succession H. Matisse-ARS N.Y. **201**: Courtesy of Françoise Gilot/© 1990 Succession H. Matisse-ARS N.Y. **204–5**: (all) Photo Hélène Adant/Rapho **208** (both): Robert Capa/Magnum Photos, Inc. **214**: Courtesy of Françoise Gilot/© 1990 ARS N.Y.-SPADEM **218**: Photo Hélène Adant/Rapho **224**: Gisele Freund/Photo Researchers, Inc. **225**: Robert Capa/Magnum Photos, Inc. **230**: The Hermitage, Leningrad, Courtesy of Scala/Art Resource/© 1990 Succession H. Matisse-ARS N.Y. **236**: Photo Hélène Adant/Rapho **246**: Collection: Estate of Pierre Matisse **256**: © 1990 Succession H. Matisse-ARS N.Y. **257**: © 1990 Succession H. Matisse-ARS N.Y. **266–7**: Photo Hélène Adant/Rapho **278–9**: Photo Hélène Adant/Rapho **282–3 + 284–5** (both): Musée National de Vallauris/© 1990 ARS N.Y.-SPADEM **297**: © 1990 Succession H. Matisse/ARS N.Y. **302**: Photo Hélène Adant/Rapho **307**: Photo Hélène Adant/Rapho **310**: Courtesy of Mme. Alberto Giacometti **311**: Courtesy of Mme. Alberto Giacometti **320**: The Pushkin Museum, Moscow, Courtesy of Scala/Art Resource/© 1990 Succession H. Matisse-ARS N.Y.

COLOR INSERT:

1. Musée National d'Art Moderne, Centre Georges Pompidou, Paris/© 1990 Succession H. Matisse-ARS N.Y. 2. Private Collection, Courtesy of Thomas Ammann Fine Art, Zurich/© 1990 ARS N.Y.-SPADEM 3. Private Collection/© 1990 Succession H. Matisse-ARS N.Y. 4. Colin Collection, New York City/© 1990 Succession H. Matisse-ARS N.Y. 5. The Hermitage, Leningrad, Courtesy of Roos/Art Resource/© 1990 Succession H. Matisse-ARS N.Y. 6. Statens Museum for Kunst, J. Rump Collection, Copenhagen/© 1990 Succession H. Matisse-ARS N.Y. 7. The Pushkin Museum, Moscow, Courtesy of Scala/Art Resource © 1990 Succession H. Matisse-ARS N.Y. 8. Musée National d'Art Moderne, Centre Georges Pompidou, Paris, Courtesy of Giraudon/Art Resource/© 1990 Succession H. Matisse-ARS N.Y. 9. Private Collection/© 1990 Succession H. Matisse-ARS N.Y.

Index

About the Author

Françoise Gilot is an artist and writer who was born and raised in France, and now divides her time between New York, California, and Paris. The years she spent with Pablo Picasso are wonderfully captured in her first book, *Life with Picasso*. Gilot is also the author of *Interface: The Painter and the Mask, An Artist's Journey,* and two books of poems, *Paloma Sphynx* and *The Fugitive Eye.*